PIONEERING ECONOMIC REFORM IN CHINA'S SPECIAL ECONOMIC ZONES

For my parents

Pioneering Economic Reform in China's Special Economic Zones

The promotion of foreign investment and technology transfer in Shenzhen

WEIPING WU
Virginia Commonwealth University, USA

LONDON AND NEW YORK

First published 1999 by Ashgate Publishing

Reissued 2018 by Routledge
2 Park Square, Milton Park, Abingdon, Oxon, OX14 4RN
711 Third Avenue, New York, NY 10017

Routledge is an imprint of the Taylor & Francis Group, an informa business

Copyright © Weiping Wu 1999

All rights reserved. No part of this book may be reprinted or reproduced or utilised in any form or by any electronic, mechanical, or other means, now known or hereafter invented, including photocopying and recording, or in any information storage or retrieval system, without permission in writing from the publishers.

Notice:
Product or corporate names may be trademarks or registered trademarks, and are used only for identification and explanation without intent to infringe.

Publisher's Note
The publisher has gone to great lengths to ensure the quality of this reprint but points out that some imperfections in the original copies may be apparent.

Disclaimer
The publisher has made every effort to trace copyright holders and welcomes correspondence from those they have been unable to contact.

A Library of Congress record exists under LC control number: 98045772

ISBN 13: 978-1-138-33010-8 (hbk)
ISBN 13: 978-1-138-33017-7 (pbk)
ISBN 13: 978-0-429-44804-1 (ebk)

Contents

List of Tables	*vi*
List of Figures	*viii*
Acknowledgments	*ix*
List of Abbreviations	*xi*
Glossary	*xii*
Introduction	1
1 Conceptual and Policy Context	6
2 Foreign Investment in Shenzhen: Proximity to and Complementarity with Hong Kong	26
3 Local Policy Environment and Labor Costs	51
4 Technological Content of Foreign Investment	76
5 Export Performance and Domestic Linkages	105
6 Conclusions and Policy Implications	122
Notes	*137*
Bibliography	*148*
Index	*163*

List of Tables

1.1 Selected Indicators for China's Four Special Economic Zones, 1994 — 11
2.1 Actually Utilized Foreign Investment in Shenzhen, 1979-1994 — 28
2.2 Shares of Shenzhen's Foreign Investment in Guangdong Province and in China, Selected Years, 1979-1994 — 30
2.3 Utilized Foreign Direct Investment in Selected Coastal Open Cities and Special Economic Zones (SEZs), 1985-1991 and 1994 — 32
2.4 Main Sources of Contracted Foreign Investment in Shenzhen, 1986-1994 — 33
2.5 Industrial Distribution of Hong Kong, Japanese and U.S. Direct Investment in Shenzhen, 1979-1990 (Cumulative) — 36
2.6 Factors in Hong Kong Pushing Local Investors to Invest in the Pearl River Delta Area — 42
2.7 Imports from China Related to Outward Processing, by Processing Areas in China, 1989-1994 — 43
3.1 Promotion of Foreign Investment in Shenzhen and Guangzhou, 1979-1991 and 1994 — 55
3.2 Investment in Shenzhen's Capital Construction and Infrastructure Development, 1979-1991 — 62
3.3 Municipal Infrastructure Investment as Percentage of Expenditure, Selected Cities, 1979-1989 — 64
3.4 Macro Indicators for China and Selected Developing Countries, 1979 and 1990 — 70
4.1 Sectoral Distribution of Actually Utilized Foreign Investment in Shenzhen, 1979-1991 — 78
4.2 Shenzhen's Top Ten Manufacturing Industries Receiving Foreign Direct Investment, 1979-1990 (Cumulative) — 80
4.3 Net/Gross Output Value of Shenzhen's Selected Manufacturing Industries Receiving Foreign Investment, 1991 — 82
4.4 Structure of Hong Kong's Manufacturing Sector, Selected Years, 1970-1995 — 87
4.5 Exports from Hong Kong to China for Outward

	Processing, by Commodity Group, 1989-1994	90
4.6	Hong Kong's Manufacturing Establishments by Employment Size, Selected Years, 1975-1995	91
5.1	Shenzhen's Export Performance, 1986-1994	108
5.2	Export Performance of Shenzhen's Industrial Enterprises, 1986-1991	109
5.3	Composition of Net Output Value of Shenzhen's Industrial Enterprises, 1986-1991	114
6.1	Factors in China's Pearl River Delta Area Pulling Hong Kong Firms to Invest	123
6.2	Gross Output Value of Shenzhen's Industrial Enterprises, 1979-1991	124
6.3	Industrial Labor Productivity in Shenzhen, 1979-1991	125

List of Figures

2.1	Actually Utilized Foreign Investment in Shenzhen, 1979-1994	29
2.2	Dominance of Contracted Hong Kong Investment in Shenzhen, 1986-1994	34
3.1	Government Infrastructure Investment and Actually Utilized Foreign Investment in Shenzhen, 1979-1991	63
4.1	Sectoral Distribution of Actually Utilized Foreign Investment in Shenzhen, 1979-1991	79
4.2	Size Distribution of Shenzhen's Foreign-Invested Enterprises, 1979-1990 (Cumulative)	83
4.3	Hong Kong's Impact on Foreign Direct Investment (FDI) in Shenzhen's Manufacturing Industries, 1979-1990 (Cumulative)	86

Acknowledgments

I am grateful to the University of California Press for granting permission to reprint portions of two articles in this book. A portion of chapter 2 was published under the title "Proximity and Complementarity in Hong Kong—Shenzhen Industrialization." It appeared in the August 1997 issue of *Asian Survey*. Portions of chapters 1 and 6 were published under the title "Export Processing Zones in Asia" (co-author Hooshang Amirahmadi), which appeared in the September 1995 issue of *Asian Survey*.

This book is based on the doctoral dissertation I wrote while at Rutgers University. Its completion would not have been possible without the advice and support of many individuals and institutions. My sincere thanks go first to the Department of Urban Planning and Policy Development at Rutgers University, for offering me an excellent opportunity and environment to pursue an advanced degree in a field that I had learned to love.

I want to extend my gratitude to members of my dissertation committee for their guidance, support and patience. To Professor Hooshang Amirahmadi, thank you for spending countless hours with me to hammer out structural problems and for teaching me how to write coherently through three collaborative efforts. To Professor Susan Fainstein, thank you for offering me invaluable moral support when my confidence ran short and for lending me a helping hand when I was desperate to learn about field research methods. To Professor Ann Markusen, thank you for prodding me to improve my arguments through the generosity of your constructive criticism and for guiding me to a wider, richer literature of scholarly work. To Professor Chester Rapkin of Princeton University, thank you for providing me with precious opportunities to indulge in discussions about China and for showing me how rigorous research should be done.

I am deeply indebted to the Brookings Institution not only for offering me a research fellowship to complete the dissertation, but, more than anything else, for giving me a wonderful working environment. Whether they were directly or indirectly related to my work, I benefited tremendously from the monthly brown bag lunch discussions, research fellow luncheons, foreign policy Thursday seminars, and a seminar to present findings from my dissertation. My gratitude goes in particular to Dr. Harry Harding, then a senior fellow at Brookings and currently the Dean of the Elliott School of International Affairs at George Washington

University. Thank you for offering me your constructive comments and engaging me in an enlightened discourse with you about China.

My sincere thanks go to those who have assisted me in my field research, for taking the time to talk with me and give me invaluable insights. They include the senior managers in charge of international investment in fifteen U.S. firms that established joint ventures in Shenzhen, the Chinese staffs of eleven of them, the managers of nine joint ventures with investment from Hong Kong, Singapore and Japan, and seven Chinese officials in Shenzhen and the central government. For the purpose of confidentiality, I cannot acknowledge them individually. My gratitude also goes to my dear friend Yao Bo, who led me through the bureaucracy during my field trip in Shenzhen.

I want to thank other individuals who offered suggestions and guidance: Dr. Shahid Yusuf at the World Bank, Drs. John Steinbruner and Lincoln Gordon at the Brookings Institution, Professor Karen Polenske at MIT, the circle of research fellows at the Brookings Institution, my fellow doctoral students at Rutgers, participants in a seminar at George Mason University, and faculty members in the Department of Urban Studies and Planning at Virginia Commonwealth University. My utmost gratitude goes to my husband, Michael, who has offered me invaluable moral and emotional support throughout the preparation of the book manuscript and has spent countless hours helping me polish the writing.

Also, I would like to extend my gratitude to Dorothy Silvers, whose editorial expertise has made the writing of this book much more consistent. I am grateful to Anne Keirby, Peter Nielsen, Sonia Hubbard, Valerie Polding, and Claire Annals at Ashgate, who have assisted the production and publication of this book.

This book is dedicated most of all to my parents, Yanzhi Wu and Huijuan Li, as a meager expression of my gratitude to them for having taught me that hard work and discipline are what counts.

List of Abbreviations

ACFTU	All China Federation of Trade Unions
CCP	Chinese Communist Party
CND	*China News Digest*
EPZ	export processing zone
FBIS	Foreign Broadcast Information Services
FDI	foreign direct investment
FEER	*Far Eastern Economic Review*
FIE	foreign-invested enterprise
GNP	gross national product
GVIO	gross value of industrial output
NICs	newly industrializing countries
NYT	*New York Times*
R&D	research and development
RCA	revealed comparative advantage
SCN	*Shenzhen Commercial News* (Shenzhen Shang Bao)
SEZ	special economic zone
SSZD	*Shenzhen Special Zone Daily* (Shenzhen Tequ Bao)
TNC	transnational corporation
WSJ	*Wall Street Journal*
WTO	World Trade Organization

Glossary

Assembly/processing—The foreign partner supplies raw materials or intermediate goods to the Chinese partner for assembly or manufacture. The Chinese are paid for their services and the foreign partner markets the product abroad.

Compensation trade—The foreign partner provides technology and equipment. The Chinese partner repays with goods produced using the technology and equipment. The foreign partner markets the goods internationally.

Contracted foreign investment—The amount of investment from the foreign partner(s) as specified in a contract.

Contractual joint venture—Also called a co-production or co-operative project. It can involve the foreign partner providing the technology, and a capital share. The foreign investor is paid on a schedule of return negotiated beforehand. The Chinese partner usually provides land, materials, workers, buildings, services, etc.

Equity joint venture—A limited liability corporation in which Chinese and foreign partners invest jointly in and operate a corporation, and share the profits, losses and risks.

Foreign direct investment—Includes equity joint ventures, contractual joint ventures, and wholly foreign-owned enterprises.

Foreign investment—Includes foreign loans, foreign direct investment, and other foreign investments.

Foreign-invested enterprises—Enterprises receiving any form of foreign investment.

Gross output value—Monetary measure of the total output.

Net output value—An approximate indicator of value added. Major components include profits and taxes, wages, employee welfare payments, interests, and other payments.

Other foreign investment—Includes international leasing, compensation trade, and assembly/processing.

Registered investment—The amount of investment registered with the Shenzhen Administration for Industry and Commerce, including contributions from all partners of an enterprise.

Utilized foreign investment—The amount of investment actually provided by the foreign partner(s).

Wholly foreign-owned enterprise—The foreign partner covers all production, labor, and utility costs.

Introduction

China first designated four Special Economic Zones (SEZs)—Shenzhen, Zhuhai, Shantou, and Xiamen—as part of the domestic economic reform initiated in 1979. The SEZs are geographically insulated but economically open areas, where special and flexible economic policies are carried out primarily to promote foreign investment, technology transfer, and exports. At the outset of the economic reform and open door policy, the central government realized that China should take advantage of the global trend of industrial relocation to attract foreign investment to its capital-starving economy. Such investment would allow China to make full use of its large reserve of inexpensive rural surplus labor to produce labor-intensive goods for export and, ultimately, foreign exchange earnings. The government also recognized the importance of advanced foreign technology for stimulating growth and the channel through which technology transfer often happens—foreign direct investment (FDI). Thus the government promoted foreign investment, not merely as an end in itself, but as a means of bringing foreign technology to China. The role of the SEZs was to experiment with and to digest western technology and management techniques so that inland enterprises could learn from their experience.

Moreover, the SEZs had secondary objectives: to function as a buffer between China and certain external territories, and to experiment with new reform policies and a market system. The locations of the SEZs were carefully chosen in proximity to Hong Kong, Macao and Taiwan. It was hoped that the integration with these external economies would eventually facilitate or lead to political reunification. Moreover, the experimental nature of the SEZs implied that they would implement unprecedented economic policies and that, undoubtedly, some policies would succeed and some would fail. The role of the SEZs in the national economy would thus evolve as the country progressed towards further reform. The introduction of a market system into the zones would confront socialist planning with problems in both economic policy and ideological orthodoxy. For instance, one major feature of the SEZs was that they fell outside the State Plan, which affected their sources of investment and supplies. They were to rely primarily on foreign and non-state sources for capital and technology to develop export production (Reardon, 1991).

There were also certain political considerations, and these overrode the economic ones because of strategic locations of the SEZs and uncertainties related to new reform policies. As a result, the zones were not selected on the basis of whether there was a strong industrial base, an adequate urban infrastructure, or a technologically innovative capacity. First, the zones needed to be easily separated from the vast inland areas, since drastically different policies were to be experimented in the zones. All four SEZs were located along the coast, which made physical separation from the inland areas easier. Fences were built around them and check points were stationed to inspect traffic. Administrative procedures also were used to control population inflows to the zones. Non-SEZ residents have to apply through local police departments for entry permits, usually valid for a month for a legitimate visit. Second, the SEZs were not to be built into major industrial centers at first, so as to avoid significant losses if the experiment should fail. Third, the central government intended to use these zones as intermediary or 'buffer' zones for future reunification, especially in the case of Taiwan. Last, the central government's recognition that the overseas Chinese community was a potential source for productive capital promoted attention to towns along the southeast coast in Guangdong and Fujian, which have been homes to many overseas Chinese. It was thought that historical links would lure them back. The SEZs are close to the setting-off points for three of the most important dialect groups among overseas Chinese: the Cantonese (spoken in Shenzhen and Zhuhai), which predominates in Hong Kong; the Fujianese (spoken in Xiamen), which is used by 85 percent of Taiwan's population and much of Singapore's; and the Teochews from around Shantou.[1]

Promoting foreign investment has always been the center of attention in SEZs' development, whose objectives can be summarized symbolically as "*waiyin, neilian*"—attracting from the outside and linking with the inside. Although the scholarly and policy circles worldwide have been attentive to the evolution of China's SEZs, little attention has been paid to analyzing the composition of foreign investment inflows by sector and industry, particularly those from the dominant source—Hong Kong. Neither the effects of foreign investment on the local industrial structure nor, more importantly, the extent of technology transfer has received significant attention.

The purpose of this book is to examine SEZs' promotion of foreign investment during the recent fifteen-year period—1979 to 1994—and, in particular, the magnitude and composition of foreign investment inflows, their technological content, and export performance and the creation of domestic linkages by foreign-invested enterprises (FIEs). The focus of the inquiry is Shenzhen SEZ, the largest zone and the one that has garnered the largest volume of foreign investment and the most attention.

The book pursues four goals. The first goal is primarily descriptive: to measure Shenzhen's performance in promoting foreign investment against the explicit targets of the central government. This account of both the magnitude and the composition of foreign investment inflows examines its major sources, and assesses Shenzhen's importance to China in attracting foreign investment. Given the fact that investment from Hong Kong has accounted for between one-half and two-thirds of all foreign investment, for China as a whole, it is plausible that Hong Kong also has been a principle source of investment for Shenzhen.

The second goal is to understand why Shenzhen has been able to attract large foreign investment inflows, and particularly those from Hong Kong. Traditional investment theory identifies labor costs, investment incentives, and domestic market potential as the main factors in investment decisions. A chief argument of this book, however, is that the growth of foreign investment in Shenzhen has been a positive function of its proximity to a major source—Hong Kong. It will be shown that, in addition to geographical proximity, a powerful impetus is provided by the strong economic complementarity across the border, manifested in factor endowment, production, trade and services. Cultural and historical affiliations, too, have significantly facilitated economic integration and contributed to mutual development. These economic and cultural ties have been reinforced by a historic political change: the return of Hong Kong to Chinese sovereignty in July 1997.

In demonstrating this proximity and complementarity, this book also answers these relevant questions: (1) Has the proximity to a neighboring source with an advanced economy and higher factor costs favored Shenzhen's development above that of cities less well situated? and (2) Has Shenzhen's success in attracting foreign investment, particularly that from Hong Kong, been a zero-sum game for China (i.e. occurred at the expense of other cities)? Or has it captured investment inflows that otherwise might have bypassed China altogether?

The third goal of the book is to show why more investment from other sources has gone to Shenzhen rather than to non-SEZ areas in China. An underlying, broad question here is whether favorable treatment with special investment policies and government infrastructure investment, has led Shenzhen to fare better than other cities have as recipients of foreign investment. To answer this, I use a comparison with Guangzhou—the more industrialized city that is the capital of Guangdong Province and has similar proximity to Hong Kong and distance from other sources. I have found the difference to have been the local policy environment, specifically reflected in policy autonomy and openness, liberal investment policies, and large government investment in infrastructure. The analysis also shows labor costs to have been only a residual factor, despite the fact that most foreign investment related to industrial relocation has been labor intensive. In fact, labor costs in the SEZs have been higher than those in other cities in China and may not be as competitive as those in some Southeast Asian countries. Nonetheless, in Shenzhen the pull of a large, relatively inexpensive, disciplined labor reserve has been stronger than that of the domestic market potential. The fact is that market access has been extremely limited for FIEs; they have had to export between 70 and 80 percent of their output value. Moreover, the actual size and purchasing power of the Chinese market have been overestimated.

The last goal of the book is to examine whether the proximity to a major source of investment has biased the composition of these inflows to Shenzhen and limited meaningful technology transfer. The book's analysis of the sectoral distribution and technological content shows that foreign investment has, indeed, been low-tech in nature, and that technology transfer has been limited. Such a result can be accounted for largely by the dominance of Hong Kong investment. Another factor constraining technology transfer has been Shenzhen's lack of a strong industrial base and modernized infrastructure. The only intrinsic advantages Shenzhen could offer investors have been cheap land and unskilled labor. Even when some foreign investors have considered transferring advanced technology, serious roadblocks to doing so have been the lack of a proper framework for intellectual property rights and Shenzhen's underdeveloped industrial capabilities. Designed to function as pivots between the Chinese and international economies, the SEZs also have been expected to lead the country in exports and create domestic linkages. The analysis here of gross exports and net exports finds that Shenzhen has performed poorly in increasing net exports and, ultimately, foreign exchange earnings. The explanation lies in the high import propensity of FIEs. Their import activities and the limited domestic supply capabilities, together, have seriously undermined the possibility of FIEs establishing production and supply linkages with inland Chinese enterprises.

The scope of the book is confined to Shenzhen's foreign-invested sector and leaves aside the domestic sector, comprising mostly of state and collective enterprises. The evaluation focuses on economic performance; such areas as income distribution and social consequences of foreign investment are not addressed but may be appropriate topics for further research. The analysis concludes with suggestions of methods to attract more foreign investment and technology transfer to a non-market economy and to enhance their positive effects. Specifically, the book demonstrates the importance of spatial placement and government planning in designing foreign investment policies and special zones. Some feasible measures that can enhance the effectiveness of a special zone policy also are presented.

This book couples statistical analysis with a chiefly qualitative analysis that aims to tell a story about Shenzhen, as a single embedded case study. What is tested with this case is the extent to which each of the primary and secondary objectives have been met, and why. To answer such "how" and "why" questions, a case study is appropriate. The empirical work relies on several methods, including secondary information collection, in-person and telephone interviews, and case studies of enterprises. Specifically, a time series on foreign investment inflows has been constructed, using data from official publications, statistical yearbooks, and other scholarly research. As a supplement to the time series, a sample of 1,621 FIEs in Shenzhen has been drawn from an official directory, to demonstrate the industrial distribution of overall foreign investment and of investment from different sources, and the size distribution of investment projects. In addition, through telephone and in-person interviews, I have investigated the perspectives of all the agents involved in foreign enterprises in Shenzhen, including Chinese officials at various levels, agents of foreign firms, and Chinese management staffs of joint ventures. I also have conducted enterprise case studies that demonstrate the various means of technology transfer employed in joint ventures.

There are six chapters in the book. Chapter 1 is an overview of the policies, concepts and research that form the context for evaluating China's SEZs. Chapter 2 examines the magnitude of foreign investment in Shenzhen and the primary contributing factor—proximity to and complementarity with Hong Kong. Chapter 3 then explores the secondary and residual factors—the local policy environment, labor costs, and domestic market potential. Chapter 4 focuses on the technological content of foreign investment inflows and the underlying factors, and assesses how well technology transfer has proceeded. Chapter 5 studies the export performance and creation of domestic linkages by FIEs. Chapter 6 concludes with a discussion of the consequences of promoting foreign investment, points out policy lessons that other developing countries can draw from China's experience, and suggests the prospects for China's SEZs.

1 Conceptual and Policy Context

The creation of the SEZ policy and the subsequent establishment of four zones in Guangdong and Fujian Provinces were a direct response to the changes in China's economic policies around 1979. After breaking up with the former Soviet Union in the late 1950s and being closed economically and politically for over two decades, China for the first time opened its door to the outside world. This drastic reorientation, coinciding with local enthusiasm from Guangdong Province, paved the way for the development of the SEZ policy aimed at using special zones to promote foreign investment, technology transfer, and exports. China's SEZ policy borrowed heavily from the experience of Export Processing Zones (EPZs) in Asia, but embraced a wider array of economic activities such as services, agriculture, real estate and tourism. In order to attract foreign investment, China needed to create a legal framework compatible to international norms and to reduce official red tape often associated with a planned economy. This chapter gives an account of the conceptual and policy context for the SEZs and reviews the pertinent research in order to devise a framework for evaluating SEZs' performance in promoting foreign investment and technology transfer. It also outlines the political changes leading to the creation of the SEZs, the legal and administrative framework established to promote foreign investment, and a chronology of investment guidelines developed for the SEZs.

Assessing Shenzhen's Performance

There is a fairly rich body of literature in English on China's SEZs. Scholars have examined the various aspects of SEZs' economic performance: infrastructure building, industrial development, promotion of foreign investment and technology transfer, foreign trade, and financing systems (see Chai, 1986; Chen, 1988; Chu, 1987; Kleinberg, 1990; Oborne, 1986; Sit, 1988; Wong, 1985). In general, their evaluations of the actual economic accomplishments of the SEZs reveal a rather unsatisfactory performance in the early period, but a much improved one towards the late

1980s. Among these studies, two volumes are particularly comprehensive in scope, although different in approach. Kleinberg (1990) offers an analysis of the performance of the zones, in particular that of Shenzhen. He argues that by market standards, Shenzhen has been a success. Created out of a backward rural community within a decade, it is now China's most modern city and has become a model of efficiency. However, this local success story, when measured by its intended contribution to national development, is a failure. It has failed to introduce high technology and has drained capital investment as well as hard currency from the rest of China. Kleinberg puts forward three major underlying causes of this failure: the inadequacy of the investment environment, the inefficient management structure of Chinese enterprises, and the unwillingness of foreign investors to transfer high technology.

Crane (1990) tries to link the experience of China's SEZs to a more general discussion of political economy. He asserts that political instability and erratic performance are not simply questions of individual administrative failings or poor economic planning. The causes are deeply embedded in the nature of the Chinese state and society. Two aspects of China's "politicized bureaucracy"—the SEZ bureaucracy and the State bureaucracy—are the sources of "bad" policies and poor economic performance. But Crane does not adequately account for the international forces affecting China's zone policy. For instance, the general trend of a declining share of developing countries in the worldwide stock of international investment may very well undermine SEZs' goal of attracting foreign investment and promoting technology transfer.

Many authors agree that the SEZs have been fairly successful in attracting a large quantity of foreign investment (Chen, 1993; Falkenheim, 1986; Hsueh and Woo, 1988). There are some reservations, however, about such an optimistic conclusion (Crane, 1990; Kleinberg, 1990; Phillips and Yeh, 1989; Sklair, 1985). First, the zones have attracted most of foreign investment from Hong Kong. Second, the nature of the activities attracted has been criticized. For example, it was envisaged that the SEZs would develop thriving, innovative enterprises and attract high-tech projects from which the rest of China could learn and develop skills. But many of the initial projects involved tourism, recreation, retail, and luxury housing development. Even as the situation gradually changed in the second half of the 1980s, most industrial joint ventures were still of a low-tech nature. Third, several authors have pointed out the large discrepancy between the magnitude of foreign investment contracts and the actual amount of foreign investment in the zones.

The majority of the authors attribute such a mixed performance in attracting foreign investment to economic factors. They point out that the SEZs and China in general have two special advantages in attracting overseas investment: the size of the potential Chinese market and the continuity of the clan system that connects overseas Chinese. These two factors help to explain why, in some cases, foreign investors have overcome their reluctance to commit capital to invest in the SEZs (see Sklair, 1985). Several authors single out the Hong Kong connection, specifically, to explain SEZs' performance. The relocation of Hong Kong's labor-intensive industries across the border has been a major factor for the zones' rapid development. This connection is further strengthened by long-established trading links, geographical proximity and cultural similarity (Chan and Kwok, 1991; Smart and Smart, 1991; Sklair, 1985). Access to China's cheap labor, land, and raw materials is another draw, since the SEZs have enjoyed a privileged status in recruiting labor and sourcing materials.

The discussion of such factors in relation to China's SEZs draws upon the "neoclassical" theory of foreign investment. The variety of possible factors determining foreign investment inflows to developing countries includes both macro and micro ones, and their effects differ from country to country. The major macroeconomic determinants are believed to be natural resource endowments, level of economic development as indicated by per capita gross national product (GNP), rate of economic growth, domestic market potential (aggregate GNP and purchasing power), and labor costs and skills (see Dunning, 1988; Grub and Lin, 1991; Schneider and Frey, 1985; Westendorf, 1989). Micro factors normally include siting, infrastructure, industrial capabilities, administrative procedures, and incentive packages (Amirahmadi and Wu, 1994; Sit, 1988).

The calculus of foreign investment decision-making differs by industry with respect to selecting a host country. For instance, the natural endowments of a host country and also their accessibility are major considerations for primary industries. Such industries can be characterized as weight-losing and resource-oriented (Root, 1990). Domestic market potential, on the other hand, is most important for weight-gaining or market-oriented industries, such as automobile, construction, food stuffs, and beverage manufacturing. In addition to the size of the host country's population, the growth of per capita GNP and income contributes to domestic market potential (Schneider and Frey, 1985). For those industries producing luxuries in a developing country, the maintenance of a certain market segment, namely the high-income proportion of the population, is crucial. For industries undertaking rationalization and restructuring, minimizing the comprehensive transaction costs, particularly labor costs, is the main goal in overseas investment. In that case, the existence of a pool of disciplined, low-skilled or semi-skilled labor (depending on the level of product standardization) can be an important attraction for investors.

Some authors point to a series of obstacles in SEZs' investment environment, and their consensus is that these zones are not yet ready to absorb the kind of industrial investment Chinese leaders have hoped to attract (Chu, 1987; Crane, 1990; Pepper, 1988; Phillips and Yeh, 1989; Stoltenberg, 1984; Yuan, 1993). The resulting foreign investment is largely low-tech and technology transfer has not been very successful (Chan and Kwok, 1991; Chen, 1993; Chu, 1987; Crane, 1990; Yuan, 1993). The low technological orientation of foreign investment is first and foremost the result of the fact that the majority of investors are small and mid-sized Hong Kong firms that only want to take advantage of the cheap labor. Moreover, hidden costs are created by an unskilled labor force unaccustomed to industrial production. Further dampening the interests of foreign investors is their inability to convert local profits in Chinese currency into foreign currency, because of the rigid foreign exchange system. The SEZs, it also is alleged, lack an export orientation, and their products are uncompetitive in export markets (Chan and Kwok, 1991; Crane, 1990; Pepper, 1988; Phillips and Yeh, 1989).

A number of authors, on the other hand, focus on politics, exploring the factors that have brought about inconsistent policies for China's SEZs from the beginning (Chan and others, 1986; Crane, 1990; Pepper, 1988). The experimental nature of the SEZs leads to policy inconsistency, and changing administrative rules and political controversies in turn affect the zones' performance. The scenario is presented as a "two-line struggle," with zone supporters drawn from the ranks of the reformist leaders managing changes in post-Mao China versus SEZ detractors found among the conservatives. These authors conclude that political factionalism has rendered the SEZ policy less effective, despite the strong political and financial commitment from the central government.

As an illustration of how political struggles have driven economic policies, the question of why the Chinese embarked on a set of ambitious market reforms around 1979 cannot be answered simply by pointing to the poor performance of China's previous economic system or to the post-Cultural-Revolution crisis. The proximate cause can be found in the succession contest between Deng Xiaoping and Hua Guofeng, the successor hand-picked by Mao. From its very origins, the Chinese economic reform has borne the mark of political competition among ambitious politicians (see Shirk, 1993). In consequence, the political basis of the SEZ policy has been unstable at times. Certainly, the SEZs have constantly drawn ideological and economic criticism. Without accounting for economic factors, however, such political analysis has limited utility in explaining SEZs' economic performance.

The scholarly literature reveals a mixed performance of the SEZs in attracting of foreign investment. Largely following the "neoclassical" theory, the general emphasis of the literature has been on low-cost labor, domestic market potential and incentives as major determinants of SEZs' performance. This book is an effort to fill in the gaps in the literature and to show why and how well the SEZs have performed in promoting foreign investment, technology transfer and exports. The major theme is that spatial placement and unique planning activities are more important in explaining the performance of the SEZs than is acknowledged in the literature. Spatial placement here refers to active state initiatives in site selection, with an additional political dimension beyond the concept of location in traditional economic theories.

The focus of this book is Shenzhen, the largest and most successful zone among the four (see Table 1.1). The assessment of Shenzhen's performance in the period of 1979 to 1994 is largely based on its primary objectives, namely the promotion of foreign investment, technology transfer, and exports. The contributing factors underlying its performance are investigated. Shenzhen's fulfillment of the secondary goals—integrating with particular external economies and experimenting with a market system—are examined as I emphasize the importance of spatial placement and unique planning activities. The book assesses five major propositions:

- The growth of foreign investment in Shenzhen is a positive function of proximity to major sources of investment, in physical, economic, cultural and political terms.
- The growth of foreign investment is positively related to a favorable local policy environment, operationalized in terms of policy autonomy and openness, liberal investment policies, and sizable government investment.
- The growth of foreign investment is only weakly responsive to labor cost differentials between Shenzhen and other potential sites, and to domestic market potential.
- The growth of foreign investment has not led to meaningful technology transfer, primarily because of the low-tech nature of investment, but also because of the lack of an effective regulatory framework and because of Shenzhen's low industrial capabilities.
- The growth of foreign investment in Shenzhen is not accompanied by substantial net exports and domestic linkages, largely because of the

high import propensity of FIEs and the limited domestic supply capabilities.

Table 1.1 Selected Indicators for China's Four Special Economic Zones, 1994

Indicator	Shenzhen[a]	Zhuhai	Shantou	Xiamen[b]
Area (square kilometers)	2,021	1,583	2,064	1,516
Population (millions)	3.4	0.6	3.9	1.2
Employment (millions)	2.2	0.5	2.1	0.9
Fixed asset investment (current prices, US$ billion)[c]	1.86	1.14	0.87	0.60
Gross domestic product (current prices, US$ billion)[c]	6.71	1.96	2.33	2.24
Gross value of industrial output (current prices, US$ billion)[c]	11.27	2.85	3.49	3.38
Contracted foreign investment (US$ billion)	2.99	1.27	1.33	1.87
Utilized foreign investment (US$ billion)	1.73	0.76	0.77	1.24
Exports (US$ billion)	18.31	1.49	2.20	3.39

Note: All data are for city proper.
a. The original Shenzhen SEZ was 327.5 square kilometers, and this was expanded in 1993 to include Baoan County. The population figure for Shenzhen includes both registered permanent residents and temporary migrants.
b. Foreign investment data for Xiamen only include foreign direct investment, not foreign loans and other foreign investment.
c. These figures are converted from the Chinese currency (RMB), based on the 1994 exchange rate of RMB 8.45 yuan = US$1.

Source: Ministry of Foreign Economic Relations and Trade, *Almanac*, 1995; *Business China*, 27 November 1995, p.9; Shenzhen Statistical Bureau, *Statistical Collection*, 1991; and State Statistical Bureau, *China Statistical Yearbook*, 1995, and *China Urban Statistical Yearbook*, 1995.

The Political Economy of China's SEZ Policy

Domestic Political Changes and SEZs' Creation

The formation of the new open door policy around 1979 led to the creation of the SEZ policy. That particular domestic policy shift, however, was not accidental. In the mid-1970s there was an economic policy debate in the central government that presaged such a change. Deng Xiaoping had taken the lead in criticizing China's old economic policies, pointing to widespread and fundamental problems such as stagnant grain production, declining industrial productivity, obsolete production technology, and inadequate use of international resources. Although at the time Deng had no real power, he nevertheless proposed to emphasize agricultural development, the acquisition of advanced technology, greater enterprise autonomy, and integration into the world economy. He also recognized that the successful exploitation of international opportunities could be achieved only if it were accompanied by domestic economic reform (Crane, 1990). By late 1978 Deng and the liberal reformist line finally had gained power, and the Four-Modernization Program (industry, agriculture, defense, science & technology) was launched shortly afterwards, to steer China toward a large-scale restructuring of its economic systems.

The domestic policy shift in China in the late 1970s was reinforced by changes in the international arena at that time, particularly in the global economic and production systems. In the 1960s and 1970s, profit rates declined in many industries in western developed countries, and particularly in manufacturing industries. The decline was the result of a complex set of social, political and economic factors, including stagnation in productivity growth, the breakdown of the capital-labor accord, and intensified competition. Many firms had decided to rationalize their production processes by relocating to places with lower production costs or more access to potential markets. Developing countries thus became hosts to branch or processing plants of the industries relocating from developed countries and related foreign investment gained importance in developing countries. Such significant industrial relocation was made possible by at least three conditions. First, many developing countries had practically inexhaustible reservoirs of disposable low-cost labor. Second, the division of the production process was so advanced that many operations or production processes could be carried out with unskilled workers. Third, advances in transportation and communications had created the possibility of producing good, completely or in part, at any site in the world while conducting central management of operations from headquarters in home countries (Frobel and others, 1980).

China's open door policy has had a strong spatial component. From the outset, it was recognized that development could not happen in all places at once, due to limited capital investment, and that certain policies needed to be experimented within limited areas before being implemented nationwide. Supported by growing local enthusiasm for such policies, particularly from Guangdong Province, radical reform policies were first introduced in the

SEZs in 1979 and the early 1980s. In essence, these zones were designed to serve as experimental sites as well as growth centers for China's new era of development. Fourteen more cities were designated as coastal open cities in 1984, with a special emphasis on promoting foreign investment.[1] The following year saw the declaration of the Yangtze River, Pearl River, and southern Fujian deltas as Open Economic Zones. In April 1988, the fifth SEZ was established in Hainan after its new designation as a province. In the same year, the coastal development strategy, officially called the "outward-oriented development strategy," was launched in the coastal areas under the firm endorsement of then premier, Zhao Ziyang (see Yang, 1991a). This policy had a much larger scale and wider range, embracing twelve provinces and cities under the direct control of the central government.[2] The coastal development strategy called for the more prosperous coastal provinces to be transformed into major centers of foreign economic activities and be integrated with the international economy. The strong spatial orientation of the reform policy was, however, de-emphasized to some extent after the 1989 democratic movement as inland areas pressed for more economic attention from the central government. In the Eighth Five-Year-Plan (for 1991-1995), the focus was placed more on the development of particular industries than regions.

The discussion of the SEZs in terms of official ideological orthodoxy relied primarily on Lenin's ideas about concessions and state capitalism, developed during the period of the New Economic Policy. Their central theme was inviting foreign capitalists to obtain concessions, and the granting of concessions was not considered dangerous to socialism. Following the classical tradition of Marxism, Lenin believed:

> [S]ocialism is inconceivable without large-scale capitalist engineering based on the latest discoveries of modern science. ... By 'implanting' state capitalism in the form of concessions the Soviet government strengthens large-scale production as against petty production, advanced production as against backward production. It also obtains a large quantity of the products of large-scale industry (its share of output) and strengthens state-regulated economic relations as against the anarchy of petty-bourgeois relations (Chan and others, 1986, p.94).

The particular conception of a "special economic zone" arose from discussions among individuals in Hong Kong, Guangdong, and Beijing around 1979. It was the invention of local planners, who played a key role in fleshing out the details of the SEZ policy. The Guangdong provincial Party Committee proposed to the central government that the province be given special treatment in making economic policy. The committee argued that, given the advantageous location of the province, allowing certain modifications to central policies on foreign trade and economic management would boost the local economy (Chan and others, 1986). This local enthusiasm coincided with the government's reorientation toward giving the coastal region the priority for development. A central work team was sent to investigate the possibility of setting up special zones in Guangdong and Fujian. As a result of the team's work, in mid-1979 it was announced that these two provinces were to be authorized to carry out a special policy and adopt flexible measures in external economic activities.

"Special" implies that the zone policy may not be extended to the rest of the country. "Economic" has two meanings. First, it distinguishes China's policy from EPZs in other Asian countries: China's SEZs would not merely be export zones, but would encompass a broader array of economic activities such as agricultural production and commerce. Second, they would not be "special administrative regions." The government at the time did not want to tie the success or failure of the zones too closely to non-economic questions.

Although Shenzhen is geographically far from the center of China, it is not politically peripheral. The central government in Beijing, and the reformists in particular, has made a tremendous political investment to ensure its success. In fact, Shenzhen has become one of the political battlefields between the reform and conservative factions in the central government. Its success or failure, at least in the early 1980s, would determine the fate of the reform. The SEZ promoters hoped to use Shenzhen not only to promote foreign investment and technology transfer, but also to learn how to adopt selected features of a market system into the socialist reform. Shenzhen, as well as other SEZs, represented in miniature the very essence of the new reforms (Pepper, 1988). Many top leaders took turns touring Shenzhen, using it as a tool to push for further reforms at various junctures. Shenzhen benefited enormously from that attention by China's top leadership. Each of the major reformist leaders, including Hu Yaobang (1983 and 1984), Deng Xiaoping (1984 and 1992) and Zhao Ziyang (1988), visited Shenzhen. In particular, Deng Xiaoping, the paramount leader of post-Mao China, used his two visits to advocate new measures of economic reform and endorsed SEZs' development several times during his tenure. Deng's first trip was a prelude to the designation of fourteen coastal open cities in 1984 and his second trip in 1992 signaled the intensification of market reform and the opening of Shanghai.[3]

Three major work conferences were organized to formulate and adjust development strategies for Shenzhen—in 1981, 1985 and 1990. The 1985 work conference made some drastic adjustments in the SEZ policy and consolidated the external orientation of Shenzhen (see Liu, 1992, for details on the criteria for such an orientation). The 1990 work conference further stressed SEZs' role as the foundation of the coastal development strategy and also their importance in generating foreign exchange through export promotion. At that time the central government took on the direct supervision of policy making and personnel appointments for Shenzhen. An office of Special Economic Zones was established within the State Council at the central level, and put in charge of major economic policies. Unlike the top officials in other cities in China, who were named by their provincial governments, the administrators for Shenzhen and other SEZs were appointed by the central government. The SEZs thus had direct access to the central government, often bypassing the provincial governments.

On the other hand, through much of its early life Shenzhen, as the brain child of the reformist leadership, was under constant attack from oppositional conservatives. When the national political and economic policy context was favorable, Shenzhen enjoyed enormous support from the central government; when national circumstances were working against reform, it often experienced policy fluctuations. But with the increasing dominance of reformists and the subsequent demise of conservatism, conservatives were only rarely able to collect enough clout to threaten the SEZ policy seriously. These occasions included mid-1985, when the Hainan auto scandal endangered SEZs' special status; early 1987, when the anti-bourgeois liberalization campaign roiled Shenzhen; and mid-1989, when student demonstrations for democracy shook the entire leadership circle in China (see Crane, 1992). After the 1989 leadership change in Beijing, Shenzhen went through a major reshuffling of top officials.

The debate over the SEZ policy also was fueled by fluctuations in Shenzhen's overall performance, particularly in the early 1980s. In addition to such economic shortcomings as high development costs and foreign exchange deficits, serious social and political problems arose: the proliferation of smuggling and corruption, and the deterioration of socialist morale (Harding, 1987). The debate became very heated between 1984 and 1986, as the economic and social costs of the SEZs, and of Shenzhen in particular, became apparent. The large corruption and smuggling scandal of Hainan exacerbated the doubts of some government leaders, who began to reconsider the extent of SEZs' openness to foreign investment and the effectiveness of the special policies. As a result, in late 1985 and early 1986 when central leaders agreed to cut back on state investment in the SEZs and Shenzhen was ordered to undergo a period of adjustment to try to improve its overall performance.

The year 1986, therefore, witnessed large-scale policy adjustments in Shenzhen. First, measures were introduced to reduce the economic costs. Shenzhen's budget for infrastructure development was reduced by a third. The central government ordered banks to enforce strict controls on credit and loans to Shenzhen. Shenzhen was held to its servicing obligations and required to repay the 700 million yuan loan used for infrastructure construction within three years of 1986 (Pepper, 1988). Second, new regulations limited the power of municipal officials and trading companies. One objective was to stop any trading in goods that allowed Shenzhen to undercut established inland suppliers. Another was to ensure that goods imported duty-free into Shenzhen were used there and not trans-shipped inland. A new "second line" administrative border along Shenzhen's northern boundary was built and staffed with customs officials to prevent unauthorized shipments and smuggling. Third, efforts were made to curtail corruption and black market trading of foreign currencies. To detect the allegedly pervasive practice of fraud and tax evasion, the first audit of all SEZ enterprises was conducted.

Despite all the political maneuvering and debate, however, the 1990 SEZ Work Conference announced that the SEZs would remain the foundation of the coastal development strategy. The SEZ policy also was unchanged: to establish an export-oriented economy based on foreign investment, industry, and imported advanced technology that would function as windows between China and the outside world. Deng Xiaoping's 1992 tour of Shenzhen and Zhuhai gave SEZs' status another major boost. On July 1, 1992, Shenzhen became the first city in China to be granted autonomous legislative power by the Standing Committee of the National People's Congress.[4] This move enabled the free-wheeling zone to make its own rules and regulations to cope with the needs of its growing economy.

Learning from the Experience of Asia's EPZs

The planning of China's SEZs to a large extent follows the experience of EPZs in other Asian countries, particularly those in Taiwan and South Korea (Falkenheim, 1986; Pepper, 1988; Wall, 1993b). Since the 1960s, many developing countries have implemented an export-oriented growth strategy—customs-free manufacturing—to promote industrialization. EPZs are perhaps the most common form of that strategy. Somewhat similar to the SEZs, an EPZ can be defined as an industrial enclave that engages in export manufacturing with the assistance of foreign investment and enjoys preferential treatment that is not generally available to the rest of the country. EPZs are a direct response to the growing tide of offshore assembly by firms from industrialized countries. Using their comparative advantage in low-cost labor, most EPZs are designed to increase foreign exchange earnings through manufacturing exports, to provide employment opportunities, and to promote foreign investment.

Such a zone policy became attractive to the Chinese government for two principal, economic reasons. First, in a purely economic sense, it was the second best method to a free trade regime. Although there is no such thing as completely free trade, a liberal trade regime can create an environment that facilitates flows of capital and goods, encourages competition both domestically and internationally, and allocates resources efficiently. Since China was unable to adopt a liberal trade regime nationwide, a zone policy offered the second-best and the quickest way to promote exports, by creating an enclave to attract FDI into labor-intensive manufacturing industries. EPZs could be used as a transitional strategy in an early stage of development, to experiment with new economic policies and facilitate the opening up of the economy, a path that China has apparently followed. Second, export processing could provide a gateway to the international community for China. Indeed, the SEZs were the key attraction China used to draw FDI from countries where globalization of production and industrial relocation had already increased the capital available for overseas investment. With the introduction of FDI also came the opportunity for China to enter global export markets.

An SEZ policy also was expected to offer some advantages over a large-scale nation-wide development strategy. The SEZs could be operated at much less costs than some other ways of attracting foreign investment, such as infrastructure upgrading, given the lack of adequate infrastructure or the resources for large-scale development. The administrative costs of operating a few zones also were lower than those required to streamline the entire antiquated Chinese bureaucracy. Furthermore, the SEZs presented a smaller domestic political risk, as compared to opening up the entire country to foreign participation. Here national sovereignty became relevant. Allowing foreign investment into the entire territory of China not only might have presented a threat to the domestic economy, but also could have stirred up widespread resentment and political resistance. By physically separating the SEZs from the vast inland areas, the Chinese government hoped to better control the extent to which foreign investment could penetrate the economy. The separation also helped slow the spread of capitalist ideology into the vast socialist interior of the country.

The experience of EPZs, particularly those in Asia, serves as a useful reference for evaluating China's zones (see Amirahmadi and Wu, 1995, for an in-depth discussion). EPZs in South Korea and Taiwan, as well as in Malaysia to some extent, are widely considered to be performing satisfactorily. The major gains from the operation of these zones are in employment and foreign exchange earnings. EPZs in South Korea and Taiwan realized their full planned capacity shortly after they were established. The share of foreign investment has remained high, and most products have been exported. Some domestic linkages also have been established and domestic value-added in exports has increased subsequently. In Taiwan, local supplies of materials and equipment have met almost half the needs of the industries in the three EPZs. Technology transfer has occurred largely by training workers. In addition, Kaohsiung EPZ in Taiwan has aided in the development of its surrounding region.

Several factors underlie the relatively satisfactory performance of these zones. Two of them are critical, but do not often exist in most other zones in Asia. First is a successful overall national industrialization strategy in the host countries, on which the success of zones depends. For instance, in South Korea, EPZs were established at the time when the country had just formulated its national industrialization strategy and made considerable headway in its export-oriented policy: a realistic exchange rate, a partially liberalized trade regime and a low inflation rate. It was these conditions that paved the way for the success of EPZs, not the other way around.

The second factor is the nature of governments in South Korea and Taiwan: they have successfully played the role of developmentalist states through strong interventions. They have had the legitimacy and ability to discipline the private sector and labor force by setting performance standards, providing subsidies, and controlling trade unions, particularly in the early stages of development. But they also have fostered the growth of the private sector—the engine of the rapid economic growth.

Despite some similar characteristics between EPZs and SEZs, such as customs-free manufacturing, export orientation, spatial enclaves, and preferential treatment, China's SEZs have some very distinctive features. They differ from other Asian EPZs in four major ways. First, most Asian EPZs have developed in free market economies. China, by contrast, has its own form of socialism and central control (Phillips and Yeh, 1989; Wong, 1985). Second, the objectives of the zones differ. The most important goals of the Chinese SEZs have been to attract foreign investment, earn foreign exchange via exports, and encourage technology transfer. Their role has been to serve as "four windows"—of technology, know-how, management skills, and open policy—for the rest of the country. Employment generation is only a remote, secondary objective. In fact, the then premier Zhao Ziyang noted during his tour to Xiamen that the SEZs were not being developed for the purpose of providing jobs.[5] Elsewhere, EPZs, while also aiming at attracting foreign investment and earning foreign exchange, have given priority to employment generation, and technology transfer has been only a subordinate purpose. Third, the development of the Chinese SEZs has proceeded with emphases not only on industrialization but also on agriculture, tourism, commerce and services, real estate, and science and education—a comprehensive approach. Fourth, the Chinese SEZs are usually on a much larger scale than all other Asian EPZs. Therefore, the SEZs have surpassed being simply EPZs and can be considered growth centers, particularly where three SEZs have been integrated into a larger regional framework—the Pearl River Delta region.

The rationale behind the concept of growth centers, which channel development resources and efforts to a few favored places, is that it is impossible to develop everywhere at once. This is especially true in developing countries, where such resources and efforts are scarce. A growth center strategy may be employed with the aim of maximizing national as well as regional growth (see Dewar and others, 1986; Glasson, 1978). Spread or trickle-down effects are often presumed to occur with growth centers, and are expected, in time, to radiate the dynamic growth of these centers into surrounding regions. Because such spread effects seem very appealing to policy makers, many developing countries have used growth center strategies. Since an overall development of export industries would not have been feasible for China, in the open-door era, a pragmatic alternative was to create special policy areas that allowed the growth of competitive export industries through joint ventures. But viewing the SEZs simply as growth centers would have potential pitfalls. Although the zones could be expected to produce a trickle-down effect in the future, that might never occur. On the contrary, the SEZs may have a tendency to become isolated enclaves, whose development could become disjointed from the domestic economy and fail to benefit surrounding regions.

Policy Innovations at the National and Local Levels

Establishing Adequate Legal and Administrative Frameworks

To attract foreign investment to the SEZs, China needed to establish an accommodating legal system and to streamline administrative procedures to cut down on red tape. In particular, a legal system that conformed to international standards was essential for foreign investors, and that had been virtually absent before the country opened up to the outside world. From

1979 on, however, the central government made great efforts to protect the legitimate rights and interests of foreign investors in China. In 1982, an entire article addressing this issue was added to the new Constitution, which has governed the legal system for foreign investment since then. The central government signed treaties on the mutual promotion and protection of investment as well as agreements to avoid double taxation and prevent tax evasion (Shenzhen Municipal Government, 1991a). It also entered into various foreign trade agreements, such as accords on industrial and technological cooperation.

In comparison to other Chinese legal branches, the area of foreign investment is better developed. There are now three major laws governing foreign investment at the national level (see Pearson, 1991, for detail). The 1979 Joint Venture Law marked the beginning of legislation on foreign investment. This law applied to all forms of foreign investment, although joint venture was viewed then as the basic form. The law legitimized the rights of foreigners to invest and profit. It contained fifteen articles addressing such fundamental areas as the legal status of joint ventures, foreign capital contribution, labor management, foreign exchange, taxation, and dispute resolution. Since it was the first such law in China, the 1979 Law was ambiguous in many aspects and vague in operational details. In September 1983, the second major law was released—the Joint Venture Implementation Regulations. These regulations, which were much more complicated and specialized than the 1979 law, were intended to improve the investment environment primarily by clarifying the rules. In particular, they provided greater detail about the government's policy on such important issues as profit repatriation, technology transfer, and foreign exchange. In 1986 the third major law appeared: the Provisions for the Encouragement of Foreign Investment. The 1986 Provisions went beyond the 1983 Regulations by liberalizing many aspects of the investment environment. Their most significant aspect was special incentives to encourage investment in advanced technology and export industries. The 1986 Provisions also further guaranteed the autonomy of joint ventures and relaxed requirements for short-term loans from the Bank of China. However, regarding wholly foreign-owned enterprises, the 1986 Provisions did not exclude the possibility of nationalizing or expropriating them when special circumstances arose.

Although certainly subject to these national laws, the SEZs also had the privilege of going further to induce investment. The Fifteenth Session of the Standing Committee of the Fifth National People's Congress in 1980 ratified the Regulations on Special Economic Zones in Guangdong Province, which gave the SEZs legal guarantees for development and clarified their nature, role, and goals. The 1980 Regulations also allowed the SEZs to give foreign investors preferential treatment in order to promote foreign investment and technology transfer, and defined the legal status and incentives available to foreign investors, as well as their obligations and responsibilities. Of subsequent regulations concerning general policies on the SEZs, one critical development was the central government's decision in 1981 to give Guangdong and Fujian provinces the power to make laws or regulations on the SEZs, in order to accelerate their development. The Shenzhen Municipal Government afterward formulated more than thirty regulations on foreign investment, most of which were approved by the Guangdong Provincial People's Congress. These regulations involved such issues as land control, business registration, personnel entry and exit, labor and wages, foreign participation in real estate, technology transfer, and foreign contracts (see Herbst, 1985; Wong and Chu, 1985). Shenzhen has been the forerunner of much important economic legislation in China.

Compared to the situation in the rest of the country, administrative procedures for contract approval were reduced substantially in Shenzhen. The lines of authorities and their responsibilities also were relatively more defined. The municipal government was given direct access to provincial and central government officials for approval of special contracts, without having to go through central ministries. It was permitted to approve contracts up to US$30 million for light industry, US$50 million for heavy industry, and US$100 million for other sectors, a power not enjoyed by most other cities.[6] Only projects with higher levels of investment, or with special purposes such as transferring advanced technology or producing import substitutes had to be approved by the central government. However, the contract approval process was still complicated and slow by western standards, involving several authorities and requiring anywhere from four months to two years. It was not until early 1993 that Shenzhen finally implemented a one-stop approval procedure for foreign investors, something practiced by many EPZs in other Asian countries.

In the early 1980s, the key organizational unit for foreign investment was the Shenzhen SEZ Development Corporation, which was established in 1981 and sponsored by the Guangdong Provincial SEZ Development Corporation. It acted on behalf of the Shenzhen Municipal Government as a medium for foreign and Chinese investors coming to Shenzhen, particularly in the sectors of infrastructure, transportation and communications. It also was responsible for seeking appropriate Chinese partners for joint ventures. Then, in 1984, the Shenzhen Bureau of Economic Development became the unit most responsible for foreign investment—especially two departments in the Bureau, the Sectoral

Planning Department and the Investment Clearance Department. The Shenzhen Bureau of Economic Development also oversaw the economic planning of Shenzhen, including both foreign and domestic investment projects. The Sectoral Planning Department controlled the amount of investment distributed to the various sectors and coordinated investment projects to avoid wasted efforts in any specific sector.[7] For instance, each year this department planned the number of FIEs allowed to be established in any sector or branch, and it had the power to approve or disapprove an investment proposal. The Investment Clearance Department would then examine the contract and other required documents, and either approve or disapprove the contract.

In 1993, with the new "one-stop" contract approval process, it was the Shenzhen SEZ Administration for Industry and Commerce that became the most powerful organization handling foreign investment. In accordance with China's regulations, contracts could be altered or dissolved only with the consent of the approval unit. This power was given to the Administration, and it also had the authority to supervise contract fulfillment, mediate disputes arising from a breach of contract, rectify illegal conduct by either party, and if necessary impose fines. Another organization, the Shenzhen Municipal Investment Promoting Center, also was given an important role in promoting foreign investment. Established by the municipal government to facilitate the investment process, it was an investment service organization that provided foreign investors with a variety of services, such as finding a Chinese partner, preparing contract documents, facilitating communications among enterprises, and providing legal consultation.

Searching for Effective Investment Guidelines

An adequate legal and administrative framework was gradually put in place, but implementing effective investment guidelines that would attract foreign investment into desirable sectors and activities proved to be difficult. It was proposed from the outset that manufacturing should be the key form of production and the basis of Shenzhen's economy. Investment was to be restricted in industries manufacturing these products: those with high output, but limited markets; low-end products made of raw materials in short supply in China; non-export products processed with imported raw materials; labor-intensive, low-end products processed with imported raw materials; products using obsolete technologies, consuming large amounts of water or energy, or causing serious environmental problems; and products proclaimed to be obsolete (Shenzhen Municipal Government,

1991a). Investment projects that had detrimental social or economic impacts, were heavy environmental polluters, or were hazardous to public health were forbidden. But to attract overseas capital and to establish the zone, the interests of investors were often given higher priority and more consideration than the needs of the zone were. This was particularly true in the beginning, when many Hong Kong investors set out to take advantage of the real estate market in Shenzhen. As of mid-1981, Shenzhen was experiencing a real estate boom as investors concentrated on property development. But the 1982/83 slump in the Hong Kong property market forced a painful realization for Shenzhen officials. They imposed restrictions on direct investment in residential buildings. It became evident that Shenzhen had to shift its development priority back to industry (Chan and Kwok, 1991). Early in 1982 Shenzhen amended its incentive package in order to appeal more to foreign investment in manufacturing.

The 1982 Shenzhen Social and Economic Development Plan was the first major effort to specify directions for industrial development. The plan conceded that although much investment would be used to finance infrastructure, public utilities and housing, industrial development would account for the lion's share of all economic activities. It also was expected that manufacturing industries would generate a significant amount of employment and absorb about 40 percent of the total labor force (Wong, 1985). The industrial groups selected as priorities included light consumer goods, textile and garment, electrical goods and electronics, food and beverages, metal and machinery, furniture, and crafts.[8] But the magnitude of industrial growth that followed was nonetheless small, partly because of Shenzhen's low industrial capability, and also because of the surge of retail and service activities. Retail, in fact, became a very profitable pursuit as the result of the price differentials between Shenzhen and inland areas. In addition, after the increase in organized tours from inland areas to Shenzhen in 1983/84 caused a temporary shortage of hotel accommodation, a wave of hotel development occurred the following year (Tang, 1990).

By 1985/86, Shenzhen had come to a turning point, displaying a pattern of problems similar to that seen in 1982: hyper-growth in capital construction, excessive amounts of investment in hotel and tourism, rising trade deficits as a result of large domestic sales, and stagnation in manufacturing capacity at the level of rudimentary processing. The subsequent policy changes made by the central government through its 1985 work conference reaffirmed the external orientation of Shenzhen and the emphasis on industrial development.[9] Three goals were set for Shenzhen: at least 50 percent of total industrial investment was to come from external sources; at least 70 percent of total commodity output was to be exported;

and a favorable balance was expected in foreign trade (Liu, 1992). These changes were crucial in promoting significant growth in industrial investment after 1986, because they once again weighted industrial development over trade and services.[10] As Liu (1992, p.12) asserted in the conference report:

> Only [by] develop[ing] industry can [the SEZs] integrate foreign funds, technology, knowledge, and management with Chinese realities and assimilate, change, and innovate them so they can be passed on to the interior; only so can [the SEZs] bring primary products from the interior, and process and package them according to world market needs with the foreign technology and equipment.

New standards were set for industrial development: the output of industries that used modern technology to manufacture new products was to make up 20 percent of Shenzhen's gross value of industrial output (GVIO), that of traditional industries using updated technology 60 percent, and that of labor-intensive traditional industries was limited to less than 20 percent. The 1985 conference also recognized that some processing/assembly activities, particularly in the electronics industry, had grown rapidly at the expense of other industries. As a result, investment in these activities began to be curtailed. By early 1994, incentive packages were no longer offered for foreign investment in processing and assembly operations, and in compensation trade (FBIS-CHI-94019, 28 January 1994, p.43).

In the early 1990s, Shenzhen government made a major change in its investment guidelines, proposing tertiary sectors as the pillar of zone development with advanced industrial activities as the base. The rationale was that the first decade of Shenzhen's development had laid a solid foundation for the local economy and paved the way for a new phase of development, which should further integrate Shenzhen with the international market and transform it into a multi-function trading center. Shenzhen was seen to have irreplaceable advantages in developing tertiary sectors: its proximity to Hong Kong—the regional center of trade and finance—good transportation and communications facilities, and the privileged status granted by the central government in making economic policy. The development of the financial sector in Shenzhen clearly benefited from these advantages. The Shenzhen foreign exchange center (swap market) was among the first established in the country and was allowed to offer the widest access for both foreign and domestic enterprises. In 1991, the Shenzhen Stock Exchange was set up and, except for the Shanghai Stock Exchange, was the only such stock market permitted in China since the Tianjin Exchange had been shut down in 1952. Shenzhen was encouraged to concentrate on technology-intensive industries, such as electronics and micro-electronics, software, bio-engineering, new materials, and refined chemicals, and to push out most of the heavy and labor-intensive industries (SCN, 17 March 1992). Moreover, Shenzhen benefited from foreign investment in such service sectors as banking and insurance, retail and services, and transportation and communications in the late 1980s, as shown in Chapter 4.

Summary

The creation of China's SEZ policy and the subsequent establishment of four SEZs in Guangdong and Fujian Provinces were a direct response to the leadership and policy changes around 1979. After being closed economically and politically for over two decades, China for the first time opened its door to the outside world. Learning from the successful experience of EPZs in some Asian neighbors, the Chinese government realized that it should take advantage of its vast reserve of low-cost rural surplus labor to engage in export manufacturing.

In order to attract foreign investment, China had to create a legal framework compatible to international norms and to reduce official red tape often associated with a planned system. However, the central government was not ready to adopt new economic, legal and administrative rules nationwide. The inevitable comprise was the relative autonomy and flexibility granted to the SEZs in policy- and law-making. A generous incentive package was designed to lure foreign investors. The government also devised investment guidelines, although their implementation proved to be difficult. These policy innovations paved the way for the SEZs to promote foreign investment and technology transfer.

2 Foreign Investment in Shenzhen: Proximity to and Complementarity with Hong Kong

A shift in China's domestic economic policy, coinciding with a conducive international environment, led to the creation of the Shenzhen SEZ, which drew enormous attention from both within and outside of China. In examining how well Shenzhen performed in promoting foreign investment from 1979 to 1994 and the primary factor in its performance,[1] this book's central argument is that Shenzhen's growth in foreign investment has been a positive function of proximity to major sources (in this case Hong Kong), in physical, economic, cultural and political terms. This analysis raises further questions: Has proximity to a neighboring territory with an advanced economy and higher factor costs favored Shenzhen's development over that of other cities in China? Has Shenzhen's success in attracting foreign investment, particularly that from Hong Kong, been a zero-sum game for China (i.e., gained at the expense of other cities)? Or has it captured inflows that might have otherwise bypassed China altogether? This chapter explores these questions.

A Center of Attraction for Foreign Investment

The overall performance of Shenzhen in attracting foreign investment was outstanding during the study period, which could be roughly divided into four phases: initial effort, 1979-1982; accelerated growth, 1983-1986; sustained development, 1987-1990; and rapid growth, 1991-1994. The first period was characterized by the growth of FDI and a large number of contractual joint ventures; the second period by the emergence of foreign loans; the third period by a growing number of equity joint ventures and wholly foreign-owned enterprises; and the fourth period by a significant increase in foreign loans (see Figure 2.1). Growth trends in the second and fourth phases were especially impressive. The amount of utilized foreign investment grew at an annual rate of over 40 percent each year, reaching over US$143 million for the first time in 1983 and peaking at US$489 million in 1986, a record that remained unbroken until 1990. From then until 1994, the annual magnitude of utilized foreign investment had more than tripled with close to US$1.73 billion attracted to Shenzhen in 1994 alone (see Table 2.1).

Shenzhen performed beyond the expectations of the central and local governments. The initial projections for the four SEZs to the year 2000 anticipated that Shenzhen would obtain US$1.50 billion in foreign investment during the period of 1980 to 2000.[2] By 1994, Shenzhen had already utilized than the targeted amount—close to US$5.35 billion of FDI and US$7.71 billion of all foreign investment (see Table 2.1). The inflows of foreign investment did not slow down even after the 1989 Tiananmen incident, which caused a halt at the national level.

Shenzhen was a major attraction for foreign investment, in particular FDI, in Guangdong Province and in China as a whole. From 1979 through 1994 it enjoyed an average share of 22.6 percent of the utilized foreign investment in Guangdong Province and 25.5 percent of the utilized FDI (see Table 2.2). At the national level, Shenzhen alone accounted for 5.1 percent of utilized foreign investment and 8.2 percent of FDI between 1985 and 1994. However, there were some wrinkles in this much acclaimed success of Shenzhen. First, in contrast to more stable growth at the national level, the growth of Shenzhen's utilized foreign investment was more volatile. Second, Shenzhen's role in attracting foreign investment at both the national and Guangdong provincial levels began to attenuate towards the end of the 1980s, as shown in Table 2.2. The decline was mainly the result of the gradual opening up of fourteen coastal cities since 1984, which meant that Shenzhen no longer enjoyed an exclusive, privileged status. Then, too, 1986 was a troubled year for Shenzhen, as the zone went into a serious economic crisis resulting from the overheated growth in previous years. A policy of readjustment was adopted accordingly, and was partially responsible for another low ebb in foreign investment (see Tang, 1990, for the readjustment in 1986).

The record of Shenzhen in utilizing FDI was outstanding compared to that of the other SEZs and most coastal open cities (see Table 2.3). In fact, only the city of Shanghai had a comparable magnitude of utilized FDI, but Shanghai was much larger and much more industrialized than Shenzhen. The performance of the other SEZs, though perhaps good on their own terms, was simply not comparable to Shenzhen's. Of course, their smaller sizes could account for part of the difference. It is worthwhile to note that

Table 2.1 Actually Utilized Foreign Investment in Shenzhen, 1979-1994
(millions of U.S. dollars, unless otherwise noted)

Type	1979	1980	1981	1982	1983	1984	1985	1986	1987	1988	1989	1990	1991	1992	1993	1994	Total
Loans	0.0	0.0	0.0	0.0	0.0	19.6	135.9	108.6	124.4	144.3	155.6	123.6	171.8	258.1	437.6	473.7	2153.2
FDI	5.5	27.6	86.2	57.7	113.2	186.4	179.9	364.5	273.8	287.2	292.5	389.9	398.8	448.8	989.0	1250.5	5351.3
EJVs	1.9	2.5	10.7	11.1	19.1	80.1	69.9	51.2	84.9	96.4	168.5	268.5	273.3	205.5	481.7	493.1	2318.6
CJVs	3.6	18.9	54.3	38.2	60.8	59.9	103.2	302.4	178.3	100.9	71.8	49.2	51.9	87.2	151.0	213.9	1545.2
WFOEs	0.0	6.1	21.2	8.3	33.3	46.4	6.8	10.9	10.6	89.9	52.2	72.3	73.6	156.1	356.4	543.5	1487.5
OFI	9.9	5.1	26.6	16.1	30.8	24.1	13.5	16.2	6.3	12.8	9.9	5.0	9.3	8.5	5.6	5.5	205.3
Leasing								0.3	4.1	10.1	5.7	2.8	3.8	3.0	1.8	0.0	—
Trade								1.6	1.9	1.5	2.9	1.3	3.5	2.4	0.9	0.8	—
Assembly								14.3	0.4	1.2	1.4	1.0	2.0	3.1	2.9	4.7	—
Total	15.4	32.6	112.8	73.8	143.9	230.1	329.3	489.3	404.5	444.3	458.1	518.6	579.9	715.4	1432.2	1729.6	7709.7

Composition (percent)

	1979	1980	1981	1982	1983	1984	1985	1986	1987	1988	1989	1990	1991	1992	1993	1994	Total
Foreign investment	100.0	100.0	100.0	100.0	100.0	100.0	100.0	100.0	100.0	100.0	100.0	100.0	100.0	100.0	100.0	100.0	100.0
Loans	0.0	0.0	0.0	0.0	0.0	8.5	41.3	22.2	30.7	32.5	34.0	23.8	29.6	36.1	30.6	27.4	27.9
FDI	35.7	84.4	76.4	78.2	78.6	81.0	54.6	74.5	67.7	64.6	63.9	75.2	68.8	62.7	69.1	72.3	69.4
OFI	64.3	15.6	23.6	21.8	21.4	10.5	4.1	3.3	1.6	2.9	2.2	1.0	1.6	1.2	0.4	0.3	2.7
FDI	100.0	100.0	100.0	100.0	100.0	100.0	100.0	100.0	100.0	100.0	100.0	100.0	100.0	100.0	100.0	100.0	100.0
EJVs	35.0	9.1	12.5	19.3	16.8	43.0	38.9	14.1	31.0	33.6	57.6	68.9	68.5	45.8	48.7	39.4	43.3
CJVs	65.0	68.6	63.0	66.2	53.7	32.1	57.3	83.0	65.1	35.1	24.6	12.6	13.0	19.4	15.3	17.1	28.9
WFOEs	0.0	22.2	24.6	14.5	29.5	24.9	3.8	3.0	3.9	31.3	17.8	18.5	18.5	34.8	36.0	43.5	27.8

— Not available.

Note: FDI, foreign direct investment; EJVs, equity joint ventures; CJVs, contractual joint ventures; WFOEs, wholly foreign-owned enterprises; OFI, other foreign investment.

Source: Shenzhen Statistical Bureau, *Shenzhen Socio-Economic Statistics, 1979-1985* and *1986-1990*; *Shenzhen Statistical Yearbook, 1992*; Ministry of Foreign Economic Relations and Trade, *Almanac, 1993 to 1995*.

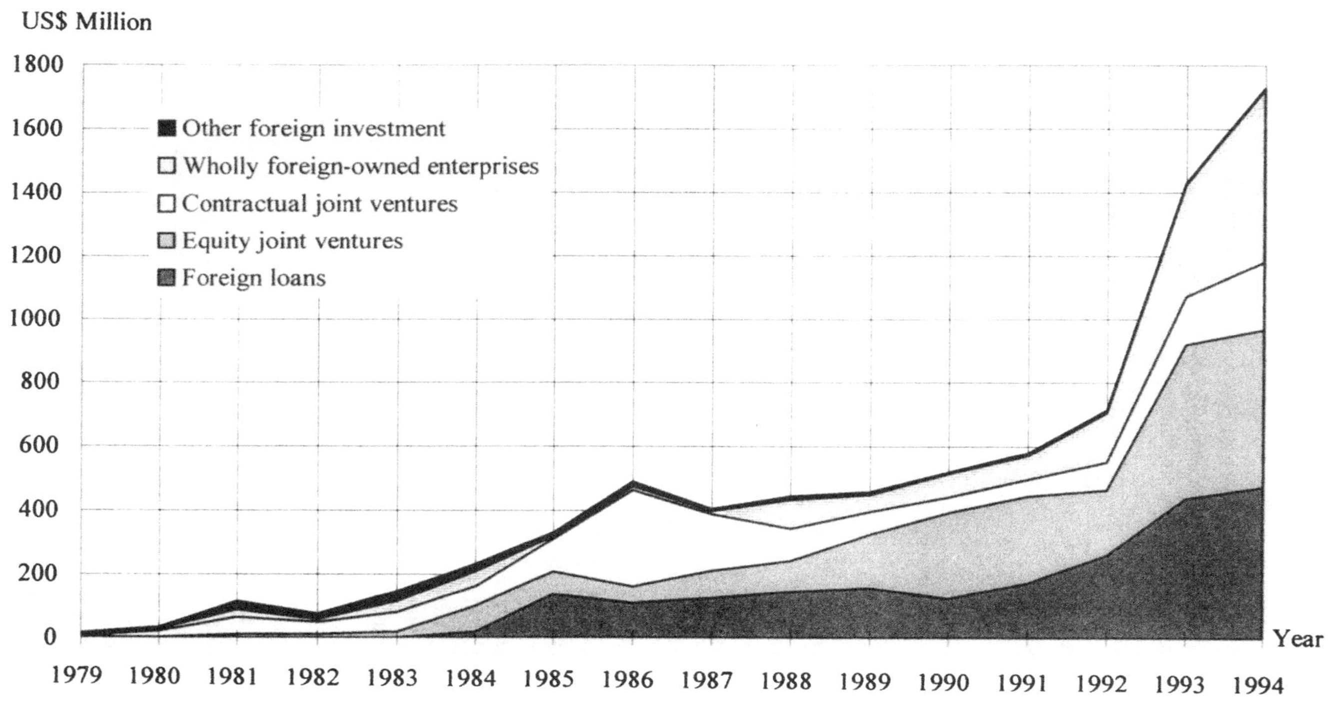

Figure 2.1 Actually Utilized Foreign Investment in Shenzhen, 1979-1994

Source: Based on Table 2.1.

Hainan, the newest SEZ, witnessed a drastic increase in utilized foreign investment as well as in FDI after 1988.

Table 2.2 Shares of Shenzhen's Foreign Investment in Guangdong Province and in China, Selected Years, 1979-1994
(percentage, unless otherwise noted)

	1979	1982	1985	1988	1991	1994	Average
Utilized foreign investment							
Guangdong Province	16.8	26.3	35.8	18.2	22.5	15.8	22.6
China	—	—	7.1	4.3	5.0	4.0	5.1
Utilized FDI							
Guangdong Province	17.9	33.7	34.9	31.2	21.9	13.2	25.5
China	—	—	10.8	9.0	9.1	3.7	8.2
Average size of FDI contract (US$ million)							
Shenzhen	0.5	2.7	2.8	0.7	1.1	1.3	1.5
Guangdong Province	—	—	1.2	0.8	1.1	1.8	1.2
China	—	5.0[a]	1.9	0.9	0.9	1.7	1.4

— Not available.
Note: FDI, foreign direct investment.
a. This is the aggregated figure for 1979-1982.

Source: Data on Shenzhen based on Table 2.1; Guangdong Statistical Bureau, *Guangdong Statistical Yearbook*, 1985, 1986, and 1992; State Statistical Bureau, *Historical Statistics*, 1949-1989; *China Statistical Yearbook*, 1986 to 1989, 1992 and 1996; *China Urban Statistical Yearbook*, 1995; Grub and Lin, 1991, p.78, Table 5.1; U.S.- China Business Council, 1990, p.11, Figure 4.

The composition of investment inflows to Shenzhen showed desirable patterns. First, Shenzhen attracted much more direct investment than foreign loans and credits, a pattern that conformed to the national priority. The rationale lay in the hope that FDI would not create large external debts and might bring technology, management skills, and market access in addition to capital.[3] FDI was the largest component of utilized foreign investment in Shenzhen, and its share remained above 60 percent except in 1979 and 1985 (see Table 2.1). Foreign loans did not come to Shenzhen until 1984, but grew steadily after 1985; between 1984 and 1994 close to 28 percent of utilized foreign investment was foreign loans. This growth was a direct result of financial decentralization initiated by the central government. In the early 1980s, most foreign loans to China, particularly loans from international financial institutions and official sources, were negotiated by and channeled through Beijing. So at that time, foreign loans made up a much larger share of the utilized foreign investment at the national level (over 66 percent). The central government also used foreign loans, overwhelmingly, as state subsidies to assist the development of backward interior regions. The situation changed somewhat towards the late 1980s; the SEZs were allowed to seek funding on their own, especially for infrastructure development, outside of the state channel.

The second desirable pattern was that equity joint ventures became the most common form of FDI, accounting for 43.3 percent of total FDI in the study period (see Table 2.1). Before 1988 (except in 1984), contractual joint ventures were dominant; but their importance declined significantly after 1987. In contrast to non-SEZ areas in China, wholly foreign-owned enterprises were allowed in Shenzhen from 1980 onward; their share in actually utilized FDI, on average, was about 27.8 percent.[4] By 1988 FDI was almost equally divided among the three forms—equity joint ventures, contractual joint ventures, and wholly foreign-owned enterprises, and since then the latter two forms have both experienced rapid growth. This was partly because the central government strongly encouraged investors to enter into equity investment contracts, which were likely to bind together the interests and risks of foreign investors and the Chinese, and to provide opportunities for technology transfer. The increasing dominance of equity joint ventures and wholly foreign-owned enterprises in Shenzhen also may show investors' growing confidence in the city.

A close look at the sources of investment reveals that Shenzhen's success in attracting foreign investment can be largely accounted for by the dominance of Hong Kong investment (see Table 2.4). Between 1986 and 1994, Hong Kong (together with Macao) contributed over three-fourths of all contracted foreign investment.[5] Another aggregate estimate by Shenzhen's Statistical Bureau showed that during the entire period of 1979 through 1991, Hong Kong was the source of over 64 percent of utilized foreign investment.[6] When the Shenzhen SEZ was first established, there was already a recognition that it would serve as a production site for firms relocating from Hong Kong. An official call to them in 1981 made this very clear: "Enterprises from Hong Kong which invested in the sixties and seventies have lost their advantages vis-a-vis other Asian countries due to increases in production costs based on wages and rent. They should come to Shenzhen." (*Jingji Yanju* or Economic Research, 20 June 1981, cited in

Table 2.3 Utilized Foreign Direct Investment in Selected Coastal Open Cities and Special Economic Zones (SEZs), 1985-1991 and 1994

City	Magnitude (US$ million)							As percentage of the national total						
	1985	1986	1987	1988	1989	1990	1991	1994	1985	1986	1987	1988	1989	1990	1991	1994
Coastal cities																
Dalian	14.3	30.5	49.6	74.9	80.6	201.3	261.1	758.5	0.9	1.6	2.1	2.3	2.4	5.8	6.0	2.2
Tianjin	32.5	42.8	127.4	16.7	72.4	83.2	93.9	1015.0	2.0	2.3	5.5	0.5	2.1	2.4	2.2	3.0
Yantai	1.7	4.4	4.6	10.2	11.4	30.2	52.9	356.1	0.1	0.2	0.2	0.3	0.3	0.9	1.2	1.1
Qingdao	2.3	10.7	14.0	12.3	58.0	45.9	46.5	416.5	0.1	0.6	0.6	0.4	1.7	1.3	1.1	1.2
Shanghai	102.4	147.6	212.0	364.2	422.1	177.2	164.2	3247.3	6.2	7.9	9.2	11.4	12.4	5.1	3.8	9.6
Ningbo	3.6	5.0	4.3	6.9	17.6	22.0	26.8	245.8	0.2	0.3	0.2	0.2	0.5	0.6	0.6	0.7
Fuzhou	15.1	14.7	14.6	23.6	50.4	101.9	138.1	421.3	0.9	0.8	0.6	0.7	1.5	2.9	3.2	1.2
Guangzhou	102.2	91.5	52.5	129.2	134.3	180.9	231.6	983.7	6.2	4.9	2.3	4.0	4.0	5.2	5.3	2.9
Zhanjiang	22.5	12.7	15.6	21.9	25.6	16.2	22.3	154.5	1.4	0.7	0.7	0.7	0.8	0.5	0.5	0.5
SEZs																
Shenzhen	341.4	495.3	370.1	540.2	762.7	756.2	1039.4	4033.8	20.6	26.4	16.0	16.9	22.5	21.7	23.8	11.9
Zhuhai	179.9	364.5	273.8	287.2	292.5	389.9	398.8	1250.5	10.8	19.5	11.8	9.0	8.6	11.2	9.1	3.7
Shantou	52.6	45.2	33.8	47.4	53.3	69.1	134.3	364.8	3.2	2.4	1.5	1.5	1.6	2.0	3.1	1.1
Xiamen	14.6	21.0	36.0	43.7	97.7	123.9	197.7	433.6	0.9	1.1	1.6	1.4	2.9	3.6	4.5	1.3
Hainan	73.3	33.9	17.5	47.7	209.8	72.7	132.6	1241.5	4.4	1.8	0.8	1.5	6.2	2.1	3.0	3.7
	21.0	30.7	8.9	114.2	109.4	100.6	176.1	743.4	1.3	1.6	0.4	3.6	3.2	2.9	4.0	2.2
National total	1661.0	1874.0	2314.0	3193.0	3393.0	3487.0	4366.0	33767.0	100.0	100.0	100.0	100.0	100.0	100.0	100.0	100.0

Source: Shenzhen Statistical Bureau, *Statistical Collection*, 1980-1986, 1988, 1989, and 1991; State Statistical Bureau, *China Statistical Yearbook*, 1986-1989, 1992, and 1996; *China Urban Statistical Yearbook*, 1995.

Table 2.4 Main Sources of Contracted Foreign Investment in Shenzhen, 1986-1994
(millions of U.S. dollars, unless otherwise noted)

Rank	Source	1986	1987	1988	1989	1990	1991	1992	1993	1994	1986-94	Percentage of Shenzhen total
1	Hong Kong & Macao	239.5	164.3	333.6	402.1	547.3	984.8	2059.4	4116.7	2450.1	11297.9	78.1
2	Taiwan	0.0	0.0	14.1	9.9	48.4	26.5	108.1	219.1	120.8	546.8	3.8
3	Japan	87.9	103.4	67.6	11.3	10.6	79.9	38.6	74.9	26.9	501.0	3.5
4	U.S.	10.5	7.8	34.4	22.9	12.5	9.8	47.6	182.9	80.1	408.6	2.8
5	Singapore	50.1	4.3	17.4	3.3	31.3	6.9	21.5	21.3	70.0	226.1	1.6
6	Britain	36.5	0.2	6.0	0.0	7.7	17.0	53.7	73.5	24.2	218.9	1.5
7	Canada	12.0	0.0	1.0	0.6	1.2	0.3	40.7	72.5	9.2	137.5	1.0
8	Australia	12.9	0.9	0.0	0.5	5.5	4.8	32.0	79.3	0.0	135.8	0.9
9	Thailand	0.6	1.1	0.0	25.9	10.9	0.7	0.0	52.8	14.2	106.2	0.7
10	Switzerland	25.0	0.0	0.0	0.0	8.1	0.8	0.0	0.0	0.0	33.9	0.2
	Total for top 10 sources	475.0	281.9	474.1	476.5	683.5	1131.5	2401.6	4893.1	2795.5	13612.8	94.1
	Shenzhen total	513.6	648.9	487.4	489.0	693.4	1151.6	2517.7	4977.4	2986.5	14465.6	100.0

Source: Shenzhen Statistical Bureau, *Shenzhen Socio-Economic Statistics, 1979-1985 and 1986-1990*; *Shenzhen Statistical Yearbook*, 1992; Ministry of Foreign Economic Relations and Trade, *Almanac*, 1993 to 1995.

Olle and Choi, 1988, p.118). Investors from Taiwan, although facing the same urgency to relocate to low-cost production sites, had to wait until the late 1980s, when the Taiwan government gave the green light for direct investment on the mainland.[7] In contrast, investment from industrialized countries such as Japan, the U.S. and Germany was slow in coming, a state of affair quite unsatisfactory to the Chinese government, as it was such investment that was expected to bring in advanced technology.

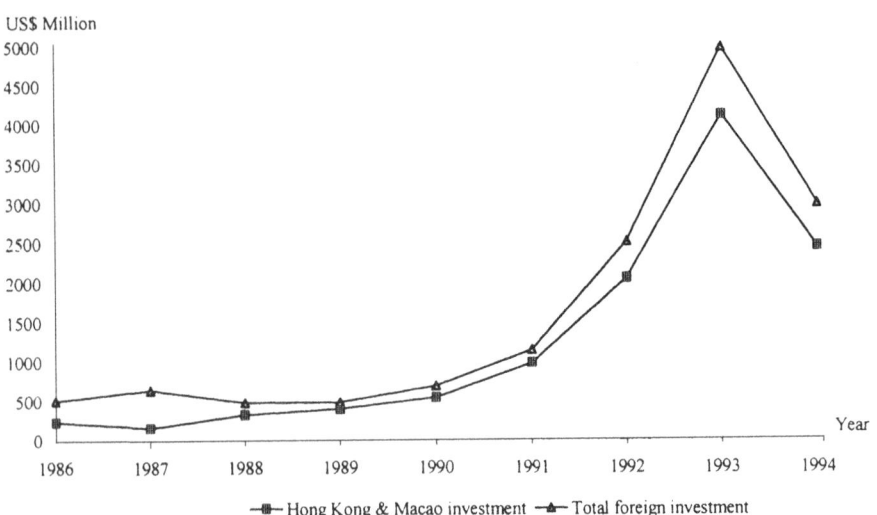

Figure 2.2 Dominance of Contracted Hong Kong Investment in Shenzhen, 1986-1994
Source: Based on Table 2.4.

Hong Kong investment dominated not only in Shenzhen, but also in Guangdong Province and in the nation as a whole. The sources of investment in Shenzhen, totaling eighteen countries, included industrialized countries such as Japan, Germany, France, Britain and the U.S., newly industrializing countries (NICs) including Hong Kong, Taiwan, Singapore and South Korea, and other developing countries such as Indonesia, Thailand, Philippines and Bolivia. The top ten sources made up a high 94.1 percent of all contracted foreign investment in Shenzhen between 1986 and 1994 (see Table 2.4).[8] Hong Kong alone signed contracts worth US$11.30 billion, about 78.1 percent of the total contracted foreign investment. This statistic shows that the investment patterns of Hong Kong determined the overall pattern of foreign investment in Shenzhen to a very large extent (see Figure 2.2).

The Primary Factor

Hong Kong has been the largest investor in Shenzhen's successful performance in attracting foreign investment; the question then is: Why is Shenzhen attractive to investors from Hong Kong? According to traditional investment theory, the primary factors determining foreign investment inflows, particularly those in labor-intensive industries, are labor costs and skills, domestic market potential or level of economic development, and government policies (see Frobel and others, 1980; Lipsey, 1994; Schneider and Frey, 1985). I argue, however, that these factors are not sufficient to explain the predominance of Hong Kong investment, since investors from other sources are not equally attracted to the zone. Rather, the primary determining factor has been Shenzhen's proximity to Hong Kong—geographically, economically, culturally and politically.

The industries invested in by all the major sources have had similar labor requirements, so low labor costs could not explain why Shenzhen has been uniquely appealing to Hong Kong investors. The sample of 1,621 FIEs provides an in-depth look at the composition and sectoral distribution of direct investment from each source between 1979 and 1990. Since the three largest sources—Hong Kong, Japan and the U.S.—accounting for over 85 percent of foreign investment in the sample (see Table 2.4), the sectoral distribution of their investments deserves close examination. Investments from all three sources were largely concentrated in such low-end, labor-intensive manufacturing as electronics, consumer electronics, chemicals, metal products, textiles & dyeing, garments, machinery, rubber & plastic products, and glass products (see Table 2.5).

Hong Kong has invested in the widest range of sectors and industries—sixty-six branches or industries—of all the participating countries or regions. Many of the areas most invested in by Hong Kong were labor-intensive industrial activities and usually of a very small project size (for example textiles & dyeing, metal products, garments, and rubber & plastics). In fact, over 96 percent of Shenzhen's joint ventures in textiles & dyeing, 78 percent of metal products, 95 percent of garments, and 86 percent of rubber & plastics were financed by Hong Kong investors.[9] Japanese direct investment was highly concentrated in the electronics industries, with electronics and consumer electronics together accounting for close to half of the total registered investment from Japan. Over 30

Table 2.5 Industrial Distribution of Hong Kong, Japanese and U.S. Direct Investment in Shenzhen, 1979-1990 (Cumulative)

Rank	Manufacturing industry	Number of projects	Registered investment Amount (US$)	Percent of each source	Average size of projects (US$)
Hong Kong					
1	Textiles & dyeing	122	169,639,846	8.9	1,390,491
2	Metal products	72	82,294,758	4.3	1,142,983
3	Garments	128	79,071,908	4.2	617,749
4	Rubber & plastics	79	74,828,315	3.9	947,194
5	Electronics	47	67,634,123	3.6	1,439,024
6	Computer & electronic systems	51	49,220,408	2.6	965,106
7	Consumer electronics	43	48,439,547	2.5	1,126,501
8	Glass products	17	44,233,346	2.3	2,601,962
9	Electrical machinery	48	42,352,250	2.2	882,339
10	Machinery	57	36,994,200	1.9	649,021
	Total for top 10 industries	542	571,128,905	30.1	1,053,743
	Hong Kong total (sample)	1427	1,900,132,195	100.0	1,331,557
Japan					
1	Consumer electronics	5	38,918,629	26.4	7,783,726
2	Electronics	4	33,639,492	22.8	8,409,873
3	Chemicals	1	5,852,592	4.0	5,852,592
4	Printing	2	4,806,867	3.3	2,403,433
5	Nonferrous metal	1	4,618,485	3.1	4,618,485

6	Computer & electronic systems	5	4,409,935	3.0	881,987
7	Metal products	1	2,982,268	2.0	2,982,268
8	Machinery	5	1,331,925	0.9	266,385
9	Electrical & lighting appliances	1	1,262,762	0.9	1,262,762
10	Rubber & plastics	1	593,379	0.4	593,379
	Total for top 10 industries	19	95,228,267	64.5	5,012,014
	Japan total (sample)	40	147,604,461	100.0	3,690,112
U.S.					
1	Glass products	1	17,282,948	11.7	17,282,948
2	Chemicals	7	17,233,888	11.7	2,461,984
3	Computer & electronic systems	12	15,297,997	10.4	1,274,833
4	Beverages	1	6,563,574	4.4	6,563,574
5	Oil refining	1	6,300,072	4.3	6,300,072
6	Metal products	5	5,922,010	4.0	1,184,402
7	Rubber & plastics	2	5,491,671	3.7	2,745,836
8	Machinery	2	3,772,690	2.6	1,886,345
9	Textiles & dyeing	1	3,097,797	2.1	3,097,797
10	Garments	6	2,955,422	2.0	492,570
	Total for top 10 industries	29	74,092,161	50.2	2,554,902
	U.S. total (sample)	69	118,907,548	100.0	1,723,298

Source: Shenzhen Bureau of Economic Development and Shenzhen Information Center, *Directory of Foreign-Invested Enterprises in Shenzhen*, 1991.

percent of FDI in the two electronics industries in Shenzhen actually came from Japan. Japanese direct investment had a larger project size than investment from most other sources did, and the projects in electronics were especially large (on average, about US$8 million). These projects included joint ventures by some major Japanese electronics manufacturers, such as Hitachi, Sanyo, and Crown. Both Hitachi and Sanyo had very profitable production in Shenzhen; Sanyo had, in fact, several joint ventures, with different Chinese partners.[10] The success of these ventures drew more Japanese investment to Shenzhen.[11] The U.S., like Japan, committed limited investment, with many projects in fact sponsored by Chinese-Americans. Most of the top ten industries that U.S. firms invested in were labor intensive.

Another finding further demonstrates that low labor costs could not be a primary factor underlying Shenzhen's attraction for Hong Kong investors: a large amount of Hong Kong investment has been in electricity (21 percent), and hotels and real estate (11 percent). Such investment projects often contained very low levels of labor inputs. Hong Kong's investment in electricity included two large power plants—a nuclear power plant and Huaneng Power Plant. Although another power plant in the zone, Shenzhen Shajiao Thermal Power Plant, was mainly financed by Japanese capital, Hong Kong investors also had shares in it. It would be difficult for Shenzhen to keep up with the energy supply needed by the booming development without the large investment from Hong Kong. Even so, energy remained one of the major bottlenecks in Shenzhen.[12] Moreover, Hong Kong contributed all the direct investment in hotels. With thirty-six projects, Hong Kong business people committed US$133 million in hotel development. Real estate was another major area of investment for Hong Kong, accounting for about 88 percent of all the real estate investment in Shenzhen.

The local policy environment, or government policies, also could not be shown to be the primary attraction for Hong Kong investors, since they received the same treatment as other investors did. Although the central government recognized the interests of Hong Kong compatriots in Shenzhen, it did not formally discriminate against investors from other countries or regions. For instance, all foreign investors were to be offered the same incentive package, including tax exemptions and holidays, duty-free imports for export production, relaxed foreign exchange controls, and reduced administrative procedures, as shown in detail in Chapter 3. Similarly, all foreign investors also were guaranteed their legitimate rights and exempted from double taxation, as discussed in Chapter 1.

Nor has domestic market potential appeared to have been essential for Hong Kong investors; they, as well as other investors, have been given only very limited access to this market. All FIEs were to export over 75 percent of their output value. Only with the approval of government authorities could they sell more products on the domestic market, often as import substitutes. Having excluded labor costs, government policies and domestic market potential as the primary factors, I argue that the significant growth of foreign investment in Shenzhen has been a positive function of Shenzhen's proximity to Hong Kong.

Proximity and Complementarity

First of all, physical proximity has been a significant draw for Hong Kong investors. Shenzhen is situated right next to the New Territory of Hong Kong, separated only by the Shenzhen River. Following the simplification of entry/exit procedures, Hong Kong workers and investors could apply for multiple-entry visas. In addition, new entry/exit ports have been established at the border with Hong Kong, with a new passenger line operating between Hong Kong and Shekou (part of Shenzhen).[13] All of these make it possible for many Hong Kong business people to commute easily from day to day, to supervise their branch facilities or joint ventures in Shenzhen. This proves to be a unique advantage for Hong Kong investors, allowing large savings in the costs of stationing expatriates in Shenzhen. According to an estimate made by a U.S. joint venture manager, such costs could easily go up to about a quarter million dollars per year per expatriate (personal interview). Management supervision by foreign investors was especially needed during Shenzhen's early years, because qualified management staff with appropriate technical training were hard to come by in Shenzhen and in China. Geographical proximity also has made it convenient for Hong Kong investors to coordinate supplies of components and parts. For instance, if something were to break down in their branch plants in Shenzhen, they could easily get spare parts from Hong Kong in an hour and fifteen minutes. Such convenience is particularly valuable for investors because China still lacks an integrated transport network. Shenzhen's proximity to Hong Kong also gives foreign investors access to Hong Kong's quality producer services that are not available in Shenzhen. They range from design, marketing, training, consulting, after-sale services, to banking and insurance.

The economic and cultural ties elaborated below are reinforced by a political connection: the agreement between China and Britain that returned Hong Kong to Chinese sovereignty in July 1997. In the Sino-British Joint

Declaration of 1985, China promised to maintain Hong Kong's capitalist system and way of life for at least fifty years after 1997 under the principle of "One Country, Two Systems." Beijing hoped to use economic interaction to facilitate political reunification, and the creation of the SEZs was part of Beijing's efforts to encourage commercial relations with Hong Kong. Hong Kong, on the other hand, regarded economic ties with the mainland as a means of cushioning its return to Chinese sovereignty in 1997, insofar as Beijing realized the importance of preserving the territory's political viability and economic prosperity throughout the transition (see Harding, 1993). So for strikingly different motives, political proximity across the border has accompanied increasing economic cooperation and particularly investment flows from Hong Kong.

This political dimension helps explain why no comparable Taiwan investment has come to the Xiamen SEZ during the same period, despite a physical, economic and cultural proximity similar to that between Hong Kong and Shenzhen. Although China has proposed the "One Country, Two Systems" idea as a way to unite Taiwan, that prospect remains unacceptable to Taiwan (see Jones and others, 1993). In fact, in view of the long-standing rivalry with China, Taiwan has kept many restrictions on investment and trade links with the mainland. Only since 1986 has the Taiwanese government allowed investment in China via third-country subsidiaries, although trading had begun earlier. Investment has been limited to primarily labor-intensive industries, and investment in high-tech and heavy industrial projects has been prohibited. In 1993, however, the Taiwanese government finally took an important step to facilitate investment in the mainland, by removing the requirement that firms had to first establish subsidiaries in third countries. In contrast to Hong Kong's motives for investment, Taiwan's interest in economic as well as cultural ties with the mainland has been in their value as an alternative to political reunification, not as a means of achieving it.

Economic Proximity

The most important aspect here is the high level of complementarity in factor endowments, both natural and human resources. Experience has demonstrated that highly favorable factor-resource conditions for complementary development and inter-territory division of labor under the outward processing arrangements, can lead to mutually beneficial dynamic economies of scale (see Ho and Kueh, 1993). To crowded Hong Kong, Shenzhen offers space, labor and energy for the expansion of its industries, services and tourism. Although China has large reserves of certain natural resources, it is not really a resource-rich country, especially in per capita terms. But in comparison to Hong Kong, China has relatively abundant and inexpensive land. And the most important advantage of Shenzhen is its human resources—a large supply of low-cost and disciplined labor. The labor force is mostly unskilled or at best semi-skilled, though with an elementary education, and consists mainly of surplus rural labor. Recently, excess workers from state enterprises have joined this labor pool. Manufacturing wages in Shenzhen are much lower than those in Hong Kong, due to differences in the quantity and quality of the labor force as well as capital investment per worker. In addition, Shenzhen's special status allows it to tap into the pool of gifted and skillful workers in China.

On its part, Hong Kong has strong advantages in capital, and in production, management, and marketing skills. As the financial center of the East Asian region, it has enormous capacity to raise productive capital and syndicated loans. For over three decades Hong Kong has been specializing in several manufacturing industries with great success; they include textiles, garments, electronics, and machinery. Its large trading companies and merchant houses have extensive experience in world markets. Hong Kong has thus served as a trading partner, financier, and middleman for China, and many of such contacts take place in Shenzhen (see Ash and Kueh, 1993; Sung, 1991). Meanwhile, Hong Kong's rapid process of industrialization could not be sustained without supplies of food, water, energy, and raw materials from across the river, generally at prices much lower than world levels.

The close economic ties between Hong Kong and Shenzhen also have been strengthened by industrial relocation based on joint production and a division of labor. Hong Kong was in a special position to take advantage of the opening up of China and the establishment of the Shenzhen SEZ. In the 1970s driven by the loss of price competitiveness resulting from high costs of labor and land (see Table 2.6), manufacturing industries in Hong Kong— particularly the textiles and clothing industries—began to restructure. Such restructuring mainly took the form of relocating production to lower-cost countries: Thailand, Indonesia, and China, where Shenzhen became an expansion outlet for Hong Kong's industries. The timing could not have been more perfect. The availability of outward processing facilities in Shenzhen has made it possible for Hong Kong to make a structural shift from domestic exports to re-exports, to maintain robust growth in exports.

The lower production costs in Shenzhen have helped to keep Hong Kong's exports competitive in the world market. The division of labor between Hong Kong and Shenzhen developed through this industrial relocation has had substantial gains for Hong Kong. Labor costs in

Shenzhen are 50 to 70 percent lower than those in Hong Kong, and factory rent is only about one-third that of Hong Kong (Sung, 1991). Firms in Hong Kong have therefore moved their labor-intensive production facilities or processes to Shenzhen, while concentrating on the more skill-intensive processes of design, testing, marketing and technical support. For instance, during the period of 1989 to 1994 Shenzhen alone accounted for 41.9 percent of all imports from China to Hong Kong related to outward processing (see Table 2.7). On the other hand, Shenzhen also has benefited because the large investment coming from Hong Kong has made possible Shenzhen's rapid industrialization. Moreover, though industrial processing often does not involve high technology, technology transfer is still evident, since Hong Kong has accumulated considerable skills in such export industries as garments, textiles, plastics, and electronics.

Table 2.6 Factors in Hong Kong Pushing Local Investors to Invest in the Pearl River Delta Area

Factor	Number of responses	Share (percent)
Labor related problems	542	60.2
Severe labor shortage	439	
Escalating wages	93	
High labor turnover rate	5	
Other problems	5	
Escalating land price and rent	268	29.8
Rapid increase in production cost	34	3.8
Strict government policy	13	1.4
Tight rules on pollution	8	
Restrictive labor legislation	5	
Operational convenience	12	1.3
Supporting industries relocated	6	
Customers' requests	6	
Keen competition in Hong Kong	6	0.7
Others	25	2.8
Total responses*	900	100.0

* Multiple responses were given by a total of 511 firms surveyed.

Source: Federation of Hong Kong Industries, 1992, p.34.

In addition to joint production, trade has been an aspect of the economic cooperation between Hong Kong and Shenzhen. There had always been a substantial direct trade link, with Hong Kong serving as an entrepôt (indirect trade and trans-shipment point) for China's products to the rest of the world.[14] Since 1979, it has become easier for Hong Kong to trade directly with China, because the transaction costs of establishing direct trade links have gone down. As China decentralized its foreign trade regime during the 1980s, Hong Kong regained its historical role as the entrepôt for China, which had been lost with the takeover of the mainland by the Communist Party. By 1989, the Hong Kong market represented 9 percent of China's exports, and imports from Hong Kong accounted for 9.4 percent of China's total imports, following Japan and U.S.[15] Close to 90 percent of the trade growth between Hong Kong and China, in fact, could be accounted for by entrepôt trade, and re-exports from Hong Kong were expanding at an average annual rate of 26 percent between 1980 and 1992. This pattern of trade resulted from the relocation of Hong Kong manufacturing activities, as over 80 percent of the output by Hong Kong-invested enterprises was shipped back to Hong Kong for re-export (Jones and others, 1993).

Table 2.7 Imports from China Related to Outward Processing,* by Processing Areas in China, 1989-1994

Processing area	1989	1990	1991	1992	1993	1994	1989-94
Estimated value (HK$ billion)							
Shenzhen	50.3	63.7	84.3	108.1	124.3	139.5	570.3
Guangdong Province	106.1	137.0	186.6	236.6	275.5	335.2	1277.0
Other provinces in China	7.5	8.1	10.8	17.4	19.7	19.7	83.2
Overall	113.6	145.1	197.4	254.1	295.2	354.9	1360.3
Share (percent)							
Shenzhen	44.3	43.9	42.7	42.6	42.1	39.3	41.9
Guangdong Province	93.4	94.4	94.5	93.1	93.3	94.4	93.9
Other provinces in China	6.6	5.6	5.5	6.8	6.7	5.6	6.1
Overall	100.0	100.0	100.0	100.0	100.0	100.0	100.0

* Refers to the importation of processed goods from China, all or part of whose raw materials or semi-manufactures have been exported from or through Hong Kong to China under contractual arrangement for processing.

Source: Hong Kong Census and Statistics Department, "Trade Involving Outward Processing in China, 1989-1994," *Hong Kong Monthly Digest of Statistics*, June 1995.

The cost differentials in land and housing have made Shenzhen an attractive location, as well, for housing and other real estate development by Hong Kong investors (personal interview with a Shenzhen official). This trend was particularly strong in the early 1980s when many compatriots from Hong Kong aimed to take advantage of the newly opened real estate market in Shenzhen. As of mid-1981, Shenzhen was experiencing a real estate boom. Between 1979 and 1985, the share of the construction & real estate sector in utilized foreign investment was close to 21 percent, trailing only behind the industry sector (32.7 percent). But the 1982/83 Hong Kong property market slumps forced a hard realization on Shenzhen officials. Restrictions were imposed on direct investment in residential construction, and in early 1982 Shenzhen amended its incentive package to attract foreign investment in manufacturing. As a result, the importance of real estate investment declined, particularly after 1986.

Another emerging trend has been Shenzhen's increasing use of Hong Kong's financial services. Hong Kong's financial industry grew substantially during the 1970s and 1980s. The growth of the financial service industry also was facilitated by the relocation of Hong Kong's manufacturing industries, which made labor available in a tight labor market. With the development of local-serving and internationally oriented banking and other services, Hong Kong has become a genuine financial center surpassed only by New York, Tokyo and London. Besides investing directly, Hong Kong firms have made or advised on many of Shenzhen's external financing arrangements. For instance, Hong Kong is the center for raising between 80 and 90 percent of China's syndicated loans (Sung, 1992). Since 1987 Chinese enterprises have begun raising capital on the Hong Kong stock market, and a number of Chinese enterprises have been listed for the first time. Portfolio investment also started to cross the border after the Shenzhen Stock Exchange introduced special B shares solely for purchase by foreigners in 1992.[16] In general, both foreign and Chinese enterprises in Shenzhen view Hong Kong as a good place to issue both short- and medium-term notes and certificates of deposit, and to obtain advice on arranging long-term loans. Hong Kong also serves as a bridge to Tokyo and European markets for larger financing needs. Furthermore, Shenzhen is learning about the world financial markets from Hong Kong. This benefit may prove to be even more important, since Shenzhen already leads the financial sector reform in China and in experimenting with new initiatives.

Hong Kong's process of industrial restructuring seems to have reached a point of no return, and its economy now seems inseparable from that across the Shenzhen River. Hong Kong's economic cooperation with the mainland has fed its growth. The expanding investment and trade links have given it a new and unique comparative advantage in the Asian region. In addition to the relocation of manufacturing from Hong Kong to Shenzhen and Guangdong, investment links have been established in transportation, communications, tourism, research, banking, insurance, utilities, and infrastructure. However, the economic cooperation has mainly taken the form of private and voluntary activities, with little official or institutional structure. Rather, it has been facilitated significantly by cultural and historical affinity.

Cultural Proximity

It is clear from the above discussion that the economic cooperation between Hong Kong and Shenzhen, and China as a whole, has been driven largely by market forces and functions. The cooperation appears rather informal when compared to such blocs as the Association of South East Asian Nations and the North American Free Trade Agreement, in which institutional integration has played an important role in creating the intensified trade and investment links among member countries. Research shows, however, that institutional arrangements such as tariff preferences may not be important for economic integration (Sung, 1992). Economic integration implies lowering transaction costs, and tariffs often are only a small part of such costs. Other human factors such as cultural affinity and government regulations may prove to be more important. In the case of Hong Kong and Shenzhen, cultural and historical affiliations have significantly facilitated mutual development.

The most important element of the cultural proximity is shared ancestry. According to official estimates, ethnic Chinese made up close to 98 percent of Hong Kong's population of 5.8 million in 1988. About 40 percent of the present population in Hong Kong were actually born in China, largely in Guangdong Province (Ho, 1992; Sklair, 1985). There are very strong links at the village and kin levels. Virtually all towns and villages in Shenzhen and southern Guangdong have abundant private connections with Hong Kong. In addition, the same dialect—Cantonese—is spoken in Hong Kong and Shenzhen as well as in Guangdong, but not elsewhere on the mainland. Many people in Hong Kong consider investment in Shenzhen as both a patriotic duty and a convenient way to help their relatives or friends. Some of the well-to-do, desiring the good will of the mainland, even choose to make donations, often for educational and training programs.[17]

Through the kinship network, Hong Kong investors have been able to obtain more favorable concessions from the local authorities in Shenzhen than could investors from other countries, often not on paper but nonetheless in reality. The advantage lies in the pre-existing social connections and the skilled use of reciprocal relations of gift exchange by Hong Kong businessmen, which requires familiarity with the local culture (see Smart and Smart, 1991). The kinship network can be a major tool for gaining access to local officials and developing social connections. Through a gift exchange system, either in material form or in the form of service, Hong Kong businessmen reinforce existing connections and cultivate new ones. In return, they receive favorable treatment by local officials, with information about or access to higher authorities or speedy handling of contract negotiation and approval. While Hong Kong investors benefit from this system, in which local officials feel obligated to provide concessions after receiving gifts, many investors from the west view the gift exchange system as a form of corruption. Chinese, including overseas Chinese, do not necessarily see it that way. They take for granted that a big gift is needed to do business and to maintain good relations (see Lockett, 1987).

Social connections may protect Hong Kong investment from many problems in production, personnel management, and marketing. Under normal circumstances, a network of friends and relatives and social connections convey a sense of security for Hong Kong businesses that other investors may achieve only through more formal, official channels. However, the gift exchange system is not without disadvantages. It can be difficult for investors to decide among many local officials, provide the needed concessions, and face extenuated gift requests once the system becomes institutionalized. Moreover, over the years abuse of the system has led to an increasing number of Chinese officials taking large bribes and committing economic crimes.

Because of their familiarity with the culture and business conduct on the mainland, investors from Hong Kong encounter fewer difficulties than investors from other countries do when operating in Shenzhen. Possible difficulties include cultural and language barriers, differences in negotiating practices, obstacles in administrative bureaucracies, incompatibility in enterprise and labor management, different perceptions of job definition, and an inadequate legal infrastructure for business as well as a cultural bias against litigation. Ever since acquiring Hong Kong as a trading post to facilitate links with China, the British had made no major attempt to isolate Hong Kong from China. As a result, local customs and traditions were kept largely intact (see Ho, 1992). Hong Kong and the mainland still share a wide range of cultural and business practices. One key common feature is management style: its characteristics include respect for seniority and hierarchy, group consciousness, the importance of saving "face," and the importance of personal connections (*guanxi*). Other similarities appear in negotiation practices, which can be characterized as slow in decision-making, manipulative in the use of friendship or *guanxi*, stressing patience, skillful in the use of pressure, and persistent in achieving mutual benefit. Hong Kong investors are more apt than others to use social connections and gift exchange to cultivate trust and to allow problems to be resolved as they arise, rather than pursuing the lengthy negotiations familiar to transnational corporations (TNCs) from other countries.

The small scale of Hong Kong-invested enterprises lets them fit well into the bureaucratic society on the mainland. First, small investment projects need to be negotiated only with local authorities, which enables Hong Kong investors to use their kinship network and social connections. Small projects are thus less likely to suffer from bureaucratic hold-ups and are relatively easier to negotiate. Projects with investments over US$30 million in light industry, on the other hand, must be approved by the central ministries. Second, small-scale enterprises, because of their flexibility, minimize the economic risks associated with production in a formerly planned economic system. Research indicates Hong Kong investors tend to set up several small ventures instead of one major venture, so that success depends largely upon cultivating good relations with local people (see Smart and Smart, 1991). There is also a preference for establishing joint ventures with collectively owned enterprises or for helping relatives and friends start their own private businesses.

Because of the cultural affinity described above, Hong Kong has been used as a middleman by many western countries and by those without formal diplomatic relations with China, such as Taiwan, and South Korea before 1993. Firms in these countries deal with China via a Hong Kong subsidiary or agent. Quite often the benefits well exceed the costs of establishing Hong Kong intermediaries. A survey conducted by Thoburn shows that in 22 percent of the joint ventures in Guangdong Province, western firms have used this form of entry (see X. Chen, 1993). This fact implies that the dominance of Hong Kong investment in Shenzhen may be overstated, as some of it could be disguised investment from other countries. Hong Kong also has been an intermediate agent for technology transfer. Investing directly in Shenzhen, Hong Kong firms bring with them technology they have absorbed from the west. Moreover, some TNCs that used to supply Hong Kong firms now face the relocation of their customers to the mainland for lower costs, as in the case of footwear, toys, garments, and chemicals industries. For instance, some American chemical companies have gone into China in order to keep their customers, and they often use their Hong Kong subsidiaries to supervise operations on the mainland (see FEER, 3 December 1992, p.46).

Another common socio-cultural feature shared by Hong Kong and Shenzhen is the lack of militancy in the labor force. As on the mainland, labor in Hong Kong has very limited organized political power. The union movement constitutes an active pressure; but without real decision-making power in the political arena, it has not had any significant effect on industrial relations (see Chiu, 1992). For instance, although there were over 300 trade unions in 1980, the majority of workers were not members of any union, and workplace organizations were close to nonexistent in the manufacturing sector. There is no unified labor movement, because of the political rivalries between pro-communist and right-wing trade unions. Except for unions in the civil service, unions have scant interest in better pay and benefits for their members; collective bargaining is not significant and applies to fewer than 5 percent of employees (Nyaw and Chan, 1982). Unions in Hong Kong, like those on the mainland, usually organize recreational, cultural and social activities, and provide educational, health care and medical services for their workers. With no minimum wage regulations and few political activities of unions, Hong Kong has been a heaven for export processing since the late 1950s.

Industrial relocation from Hong Kong has met with little opposition from labor because full employment has been maintained. Transferring industrial activities across the Shenzhen River has resulted in a decline in manufacturing employment in Hong Kong, in absolute terms, of about 230,000 manufacturing jobs lost between 1981 and 1992 (Ash and Kueh, 1993). But there was no significant increase in overall unemployment during the same period, which indicates that the surplus labor from the manufacturing sector has been largely absorbed by the service sector. Specifically, the employment share of the industrial sector (including manufacturing and construction) fell from 50 percent in 1980 to a mere 36 percent in 1991, while that of services rose from 48 to 63 percent. This shift displays the growing structural reorientation of the Hong Kong economy toward services, in line with its expansion as a financial and trading center. There has, in fact, been a labor shortage, particularly for technical personnel. In short, job security has never been a issue for most Hong Kong workers until the Asian financial crisis in 1998. Employment in every branch of the service sector, including financial services, trading services, transportation and communications, has grown steadily from 1980 to 1995, in sharp contrast to the decline in manufacturing employment

(Hong Kong Government Industry Department, 1996). The growth in real wages also has been much higher in the service sector than in the manufacturing sector. Hong Kong now has perhaps the most service-oriented economy in the world. The relatively fast transfer of manufacturing workers into the service sector and the weak institutional power of union movement have precluded any strong labor opposition resulting from unemployment.[18] This stands in sharp contrast to the situation in some industrialized countries, where the relocation of certain manufacturing industries has caused large-scale, prolonged unemployment and therefore has aroused strong labor opposition.

Summary

Overall, actually utilized foreign investment in Shenzhen during the period of 1979 to 1994, particularly FDI, reached amounts much beyond the central government's expectation. Shenzhen also was the major focus of FDI in Guangdong Province and in the nation as a whole, surpassing all other SEZs and coastal open cities except Shanghai. It attracted more direct investment, particularly equity joint ventures, than foreign loans and other types of foreign investment. The success of Shenzhen in attracting foreign investment can be largely accounted for by its ability to attract Hong Kong investors, who have contracted over three-fourths of all the investment. They are drawn to Shenzhen not just for the lower labor costs, large domestic market potential and open government policies, which would similarly appeal to investors from other countries. What Shenzhen uniquely offers to Hong Kong firms is a production site right next door with long-established trading and economic links, a people who share their language and culture, and a common political future. Such proximity is the primary factor underlying Shenzhen's success, and has made the establishment of Shenzhen as an SEZ a winning decision for the Chinese government.

It is the proximity to a neighboring territory with an advanced economy and higher factor costs that favors Shenzhen's development over that of other cities in China. Without investment from Hong Kong, Shenzhen might still be a small, backward town with little industrial development and, in particular, would not have seen the rapid growth of such industries as textiles, garments, rubber & plastics, and metal products, to which Hong Kong contributes over two-thirds of all foreign investment. Shenzhen also would not have become one of the major centers of clothing production and exports in the world without the investment from Hong Kong. The same situation has occurred in the real estate and hotel sectors, with capital from across the river fueling the almost overnight appearance of Shenzhen as the most modern city in China. Shenzhen's success has shown that joint production with Hong Kong can be a viable strategy for economic growth (Kwok, 1996). Moreover, the economic proximity between Shenzhen and Hong Kong contributes to Shenzhen's popularity among investors from other countries, because they can take advantage of the financial, trading and producer services that are offered in Hong Kong but absent in China.

In addition to economic complementarity, what seems to matter the most is historical affinity. Because of shared ancestry and language, Hong Kong investors enjoy abundant social connections in Shenzhen based on kinship networks, and so they often obtain more favorable concessions from local authorities than others can. Familiarity with business conduct in Shenzhen also enables them to transcend some formal barriers to investment and trade. The importance of historical affinity is reinforced by examining similar cases in other parts of China. For instance, as soon as the fourteen coastal open cities were designated in 1984, Japanese firms flocked to an old destination, Dalian; American and European investors to the previous treaty ports where they used to occupy concessions, such as Shanghai and Tianjin; and South Korean firms to the neighboring Shandong Province, mostly to the cities of Yantan and Qingdao (Table 2.3 shows the increasing attraction of these coastal cities to foreign investors).

It seems clear that Shenzhen's success in attracting foreign investment, particularly Hong Kong investment, is not at the expense of other localities and should not be considered a zero-sum game for the country as a whole. The opening up of China and the creation of the SEZs coincided with the needs of Hong Kong's manufacturing firms for restructuring and relocation in the late 1970s. Such relocation might otherwise have carried investment to other low-cost countries in the region, such as Thailand and Malaysia, but instead Hong Kong firms chose Shenzhen because of geographical, economic, cultural and political proximity. In other words, Shenzhen has captured investment flows from Hong Kong that might otherwise not have come to China at all.

3 Local Policy Environment and Labor Costs

Shenzhen's success in attracting large foreign investment has been primarily the result of Hong Kong's commitment. Hong Kong investors are interested in Shenzhen because of the physical, economic, cultural and political proximity. But investment from other sources, about a third of all utilized foreign investment in Shenzhen, also has been substantial. Why have these investors chosen Shenzhen over other Chinese cities that also have enjoyed the advantages of large domestic markets, low-cost labor forces and natural resource endowments—the classical factors underlying foreign investment inflows? This chapter proposes that, in addition to the primary determining factor—proximity to Hong Kong, the growth of foreign investment in Shenzhen is positively related to a favorable local policy environment and weakly responsive to labor cost differentials and domestic market potential. The favorable local policy environment is the aggregate of a number of elements, including policy openness and autonomy, liberal investment policies, and large government investment in infrastructure.

Shenzhen's Attraction for TNCs

In order to explain Shenzhen's attraction for TNCs, one must acknowledge their general concerns about investing in China. Regardless of investment orientations, TNCs invest according to their global strategy. By virtue of their size and massive capital resources, they can physically separate the various functions of the corporations and locate them differently, to maximize global profits. Major improvements in transportation and communications have reinforced this effect and made their global production more manageable. A critical determinant of a TNC's investment decisions is the possible rate of return in a particular country, which is enhanced by host government incentives and favorable policies but endangered by risks and uncertainty. But it is not clear that a country will attract more FDI simply by increasing incentives (see International Monetary Fund, 1985). If the overall investment climate is unfavorable, the inducement offered by special incentives is unlikely to encourage a large

TNC to change its worldwide investment strategy. A good example of this fact is the experience of EPZs established in many developing countries, which offer very attractive fiscal incentives, yet after many years have attracted only a few large TNCs.

By investing in a country with a socialist orientation, such as China, TNCs face some potential risks, including possible nationalization of foreign enterprises and possible financial loss resulting from political instability. But as the economic reform and open policy in China deepen and reach the point of no return, such risks appear to be less and less likely. The more realistic concerns of TNCs when investing in China are bureaucratic red tape, labor immobility, corruption, currency conversion difficulty, and rising operating costs (personal interviews). As an SEZ, Shenzhen has some incomparable advantages over other Chinese cities in its policy environment. Its relative autonomy in economic policy-making has made possible a more flexible labor management scheme, reduced bureaucratic procedures, relaxed foreign exchanges controls, and offered higher tax incentives. In addition, the government has invested tremendous amount of capital in Shenzhen's infrastructure, to support modern industries.

TNCs from different countries may have somewhat different concerns when deciding whether to invest in China. Since Japan and the U.S. have been the two major sources of TNCs in Shenzhen, it is worthwhile to look into how their companies have perceived such investment. On the whole, Japanese direct investment was slow in coming and remained virtually flat until the late 1980s, rising only after the signing of the Sino-Japanese Investment Protection Agreement in 1988. This trend had several underlying causes. First of all, it had much to do with the global investment strategy of Japanese TNCs. Japanese investment abroad has exhibited four major waves during the postwar period. The first wave of Japanese investment comprised of companies that went to countries in East Asia for such natural resources as oil and metals. The second and third waves were mainly garments and electronics firms in search of lower-cost labor and market access to industrialized countries through quota manipulation.

It was not until 1991, when the Japanese yen began to strengthen against the dollar again, that the fourth wave of Japanese investors, for the first time, started to aim at the markets in Asia and in China particularly (FEER, 9 June 1994, p.44). Even so, Japanese TNCs, overall, committed much less investment to China than to elsewhere in Asia. Taiwan and South Korea had been the traditional locations and the most reliable destinations of Japanese investment, and Thailand, Malaysia and Singapore had become major sites in the late 1980s. Unlike investors from Hong Kong, the fourth-wave Japanese TNCs had their eyes on the domestic market potential in China and tried to supply the growing demand of Chinese consumers.[1] But for many of them, the promise of China as a market had not come true during the 1980s. As a result, most early Japanese investment there was to process and assemble cheap electronics products for Third World markets, using outdated technology.

Unlike Hong Kong investors, Japanese companies were very cautious about investing in China because of an old uneasiness about the investment environment. Negative publicity and information portrayed China as an adverse investment environment. In particular, Japanese businesses regarded China's legal framework as inadequate to safeguard foreign investment, and they insisted on better protection. Their views became much more positive after the signing of the Sino-Japanese Investment Protection Agreement in 1988 (see Arnold, 1993). Nonetheless, because of socio-cultural differences, Japanese investors may run a gauntlet of country and operational risks in spite of the formal protection agreement. Many of them could not escape doing things strictly by the book and could not function flexibly as Hong Kong and overseas Chinese often could. As a result, many Japanese firms have preferred trading with, rather than investing in China. But China's austerity program, initiated in 1989 to replace imports with domestic-made products, has forced some Japanese firms to shift from trade to investment.

Similar to the Japanese case, outward investment from the U.S. had a long history in developing countries and in its own traditional locations, mostly in Latin America and several Asian countries, such as Taiwan and South Korea. China was a relatively new destination and the risks associated with it seemed high to many U.S. investors. To many of them, China was still a rather mysterious place, and Shenzhen became their choice of location largely because of its open policy (personal interview with the General Manager of an U.S. manufacturer). U.S. investors also were concerned about cultural differences, swings in economic policy, cumbersome bureaucracy, lack of infrastructure facilities, foreign exchange problems, and government control on foreign investment (see Grub and others, 1990). Many U.S. companies tended to first join force with firms in other Chinese-speaking countries such as Hong Kong and Singapore or to establish subsidiaries in those countries and then explore the possibility of investing in China. On the whole, U.S. investment in Shenzhen and China has been very limited, lagging behind that from Hong Kong and Japan.

Given such concerns of TNCs when making investment decisions, those locations in China that had favorable, open local policy environments possessed an edge over others and a unique attraction for TNCs. Cities without an open policy environment might not fare as well. Take the example of Guangzhou, the capital city of Guangdong Province, with about 6.4 million population in 1994. Prosperity in international trade and local commerce had made Guangzhou the largest city in China during the nineteenth century. It acquired a modest manufacturing base in the 1960s and 1970s, specializing in such industries as machinery, clothing, textiles, consumer electronics, household durables, transportation equipment, and food processing. Moreover, with the third largest seaport and airport in China, Guangzhou was only a short three-hour drive from the border with Hong Kong (about 80 miles).[2] When the Shenzhen SEZ was first created in 1979, Guangzhou was already the principal industrial node in south China, a leading trading post in the nation, and the administrative center of Guangdong Province. With a better urban infrastructure and stronger industrial base than Shenzhen's, Guangzhou appeared to be more ready to accommodate foreign investment.

How did Guangzhou perform as compared to Shenzhen? Not nearly as well. Between 1979 and 1991, Guangzhou was able to attract only slightly over half the amount of foreign investment that Shenzhen did (see Table 3.1). Guangzhou's record in promoting FDI was even less satisfactory, although its performance improved in 1994. Why was there such a difference between the foreign investment inflows to the two cities? I do not believe that the explanation lies with the two traditional factors—labor costs and market potential. Between 1988 and 1994, unit labor costs, as indicated by average annual salary, were consistently lower in Guangzhou—about 80 percent of Shenzhen's. As the largest industrial center in the region, Guangzhou also had better sea, air, and rail links to the rest of the country, which, coupled with its much larger population, made Guangzhou's own market potential and its access to the domestic market appear greater than those of Shenzhen. Nevertheless, all these factors in favor of Guangzhou were insufficient to attract TNCs. What Guangzhou did not have throughout the most of the 1980s was the local policy autonomy and liberal investment policies that Shenzhen had enjoyed since its creation.

Local Policy Environment

A critical factor in Shenzhen's success has been the government commitment to building a favorable local environment for investment through adopting open policies and building adequate infrastructure. Since it was designed to experiment with new economic policies and a market system, Shenzhen was granted a relative autonomy in policy-making that no

Table 3.1 Promotion of Foreign Investment in Shenzhen and Guangzhou, 1979-1991 and 1994
(millions of U.S. dollars, unless otherwise noted)

	1979-84	1985	1986	1987	1988	1989	1990	1991	1979-91	1994
Shenzhen										
Utilized foreign investment	608.7	329.3	489.3	404.5	444.3	458.1	518.6	579.9	3832.6	1729.59
Utilized foreign direct investment	476.5	179.9	364.5	273.8	287.2	292.5	389.9	398.8	2663.0	1250.5
Average annual salary (yuan)	—	—	—	—	3,388	3,858	4,303	5,015	—	10,572
Guangzhou										
Utilized foreign investment	343.6	155.3	178.2	82.8	255.2	298.4	267.4	377.4	1958.3	1214.6
Utilized foreign direct investment	264.8	102.2	91.5	52.5	129.2	134.3	180.9	231.6	1187.0	983.7
Average annual salary (yuan)	—	—	—	—	2,683	3,272	3,504	4,022	—	8,831
Guangzhou as percentage of Shenzhen										
Utilized foreign investment	56.5	47.2	36.4	20.5	57.4	65.1	51.6	65.1	51.1	70.2
Utilized foreign direct investment	55.6	56.8	25.1	19.2	45.0	45.9	46.4	58.1	44.6	78.7
Average annual salary	—	—	—	—	79.2	84.8	81.4	80.2	n.a.	83.5

n.a. Not applicable.
— Not available.

Source: Shenzhen Statistical Bureau, *Statistical Collection*, 1989 and 1991; Guangdong Statistical Bureau, *Guangzhou Statistical Yearbook*, 1994; State Statistical Bureau, *China Urban Statistical Yearbook*, 1995.

other cities had. As a result, it has been able to create an environment somewhat closer to western expectations. A set of liberal investment policies has further enhanced Shenzhen's attraction for foreign investors. Such policies include tax concessions, reduced customs duties, relaxed foreign exchange controls, and favorable land use fees. Substantial government investment has helped Shenzhen build its modern infrastructure and industrial base, and its self-financing capacity has grown over time, as well.

Policy Autonomy and Openness

Most importantly, Shenzhen was given the authority to determine its own socio-economic plan for approval by the State Council, and to prepare its own material supplies plan with leeway to acquire needed materials. Increasingly, the materials acquired by Shenzhen were subject to negotiated prices rather than fixed prices, which implied that market forces were playing a more important role in resource allocation (see Hsueh and Woo, 1988). Shenzhen also could retain all of its fiscal revenue for development, undertaking its own infrastructure and other facility investment with funds raised through taxation, enterprise profits, and bank loans. In addition, Shenzhen established companies that would bear their own profits and losses to manage the particular economic activities they specialized in. For instance, the Shenzhen Development Corporation was put in charge of urban infrastructure construction.

Reforms in the labor market were pioneered in Shenzhen. The 1980 SEZ Regulation had granted enterprises more autonomy for labor management. FIEs in Shenzhen were free to recruit their employees through advertisement and screening before submitting them to the Shenzhen Labor Bureau.[3] Upon approval by the Bureau, these enterprises also could recruit in Guangdong Province and, if necessary, recruit senior management and technical personnel throughout the country. Such a scheme enabled Shenzhen to overcome, to some extent, the problem of labor immobility and to gather the most talented from across the country. A "contract labor system" was first introduced in Shenzhen, with fixed-term contracts between employers and employees and thus no guarantee of permanent jobs for workers. Enterprises were given the right to draw up and sign contracts with their employees and to dismiss workers when they decided it was necessary. Workers were free to resign from their jobs and look for other ones. In addition, FIEs could turn to the Shenzhen Labor Services Company for help in worker recruitment and training.[4] Unlike the rest of the country, where wage scales were set by the central government and differed only slightly nationwide, Shenzhen had no wage controls. FIEs were free to set their wages according to their own assessment of the nature of the enterprise, type of work, level of skill, and performance. Bonuses accounted for a much larger percentage of income than they did in other types of enterprises or in non-SEZ areas, where fixed wages still made up a large for proportion of income.

Shenzhen was allowed to develop a regulatory scheme that differed in many ways from the rest of country. One major difference was the ownership control of FIEs. The SEZ regulations made it clear from the very beginning that wholly foreign-owned enterprises were welcome in the SEZs. China had broken with the common preference among developing countries for majority equity. The 1979 Joint Venture Law did not specify an upper limit for foreign equity, so in theory foreign ownership could be up to 100 percent. Nonetheless, Chinese officials often preferred either Chinese majority or fifty-fifty ownership for the comfort of having control over management (see Pearson, 1991). In Shenzhen, however, such official bias was much less prevalent, as shown by the sizable proportion of wholly foreign-owned enterprises (see Table 2.1). It was not until 1984, with the development of fourteen coastal open cities, that such enterprises were welcome elsewhere in China.

In 1985, the banking structure in Shenzhen was profoundly changed for the better and more efficient, when new legislation allowed foreign banks to establish full-service branches in Shenzhen.[5] Although foreign banks were still subject to approval and supervision by the head office and the respective SEZ branches of the People's Bank of China, they could carry out a full range of activities in both local and foreign currencies: granting loans, handling inward and outward remittances, settling of import and export transactions, handling of local and foreign currency investment, buying and selling stocks and securities, and accepting local and foreign currency deposits. Foreign banks also could provide FIEs with credits and loans via overseas channels. Foreign banks were, however, restricted to dealing only with FIEs, not state-owned enterprises. Nonetheless, the opening of the financial sector in Shenzhen to foreign banks gave FIEs access to quality financial services, when the state banking system was still antiquated.

After 1982, branch offices of the state banks in Shenzhen became more willing to support foreign investors with loans, and this opened the door to capital from domestic sources. Until then, most investors had had to rely on their own sources of capital.[6] In particular, the People's Construction bank was now prepared to support massive land development projects. Banks exercised a supervisory role over their clients, thoroughly investigating of a project's feasibility and investor's ability to repay before granting a loan. By minimizing the possibility of speculative investment, this process ultimately benefited all parties.

As an early launcher of reforms in labor management, ownership control, and banking services, Shenzhen over time has developed a complete system of policies and regulations similar to those in a market system. The immediate result of these policies has been a higher level of efficiency and flexibility for investors in Shenzhen. As pointed out by a Hong Kong manager in a U.S. invested joint venture, the most important concern was the social environment in which the company had to function. Efficiency and supportive policies were critical, and Shenzhen was definitely better in those respects. A manager in a Singaporean joint venture listed three advantages of Shenzhen, compared to other coastal open cities: pioneering reform, high efficiency, and a new attitude (personal interviews).

Investment Policies

Another distinction benefiting Shenzhen is that the central government has offered a variety of preferential policies and procedures for FIEs in the SEZs. Many foreign firms have been lured to Shenzhen by these incentives first made available in 1979. Shenzhen's incentive package includes tax concessions, reduced duties, favorable fees, and relaxed controls on foreign exchange and profit repatriation. Their purpose has been to increase the profit margin of investment or the rate of return. Even when compared to other similar zones in the Asian region, Shenzhen's package is very generous and attractive.

Tax concessions   Corporate income tax. The rate of corporate income tax for FIEs is an example of Shenzhen's policies favoring foreign investment. The 15 percent corporate income tax is among the lowest in the world and even lower than that in Hong Kong (18.5 percent) (see Hsueh and Woo, 1988). It is less than half that (33 percent) in non-SEZ areas. Furthermore, no local tax is levied. Firms with contracts of more than 10 years in industry, transportation, agriculture, forestry, and livestock farming are exempted from income tax for two years, commencing with the first profit-making year, and are allowed a 50 percent reduction for the next three years.[7] After this five-year period, FIEs whose export value exceeds 70 percent of their output value in any year can claim a 10 percent tax reduction in that year. Enterprises in tourism and service sectors are exempted from corporate income tax for three years. Technologically advanced enterprises can enjoy a three-year extension of the 50 percent reduction. Enterprises that reinvest their net profits in China for at least five years may, upon approval by the tax authorities, obtain a 40 percent refund of the income tax paid on the reinvested amount. Those who reinvest such profits in establishing or expanding export enterprises or technologically advanced enterprises for a period of at least five years, may get a complete refund of the income tax on the reinvested amount.

<u>Value-added tax</u>. Export products made by FIEs with imported materials are exempted from value-added taxes, as are export products made with local materials (except for a few products subject to special state provisions, such as crude and refined oil). If these enterprises sell their products inside Shenzhen, a five percent value-added tax is collected for most products. If these enterprises sell their products in inland areas, tax must be paid retroactively on the reduced or exempted amount. This tax policy has been designed to encourage FIEs to export their products.

<u>Personal income tax</u>. Foreign repatriates, with monthly income over 800 yuan, are subject to a personal income tax at half of the progressive rates, which are between 5 and 45 percent. Incomes earned in the SEZs from royalties, rent, interests, dividends, and bonuses are taxable at a fixed rate of 10 percent. Interests on deposits in banks inside Shenzhen were exempt from personal income tax until 1995.

<u>Consolidated industrial and commercial tax</u>.[8] Almost all goods imported by FIEs, with a few exceptions given a 50 percent reduction (including mineral oil, cigarettes, liquors and other necessaries of life), are exempt from this tax. So are export products and products to be sold within the zones. If FIEs' products, upon approval, are sold to domestic markets, then the tax has to be paid retroactively. Incomes of enterprises in banking and insurance are exempt from this tax for five years, and afterwards are taxed at the rate of 3 percent.[9]

Reduced duties   Imports and exports. Machinery, equipment, parts, accessories, raw materials, transportation utilities and other production inputs used by FIEs for export production can be imported without any import license and be exempt from import duties.[10] If their products, upon approval, are sold to domestic markets, such duties have to be paid retroactively. Neither import license nor import duties are required for necessary office equipment imported by those enterprises invested in by Hong Kong, Macao, Taiwan or overseas Chinese. Import duties for most consumer goods used by FIEs also may be exempt or reduced if all the items are used within Shenzhen. Export products of these enterprises, except those restricted by the government, are exempt from export duties.[11]

Import substitutes. FIEs that provide advanced technology needed in China and are developing new products or upgrading existing ones may apply for quotas to sell their products on domestic markets as import substitutes.[12] These products may be considered as exports with regard to duties if they would otherwise have to be imported, they meet the specifications and standards of imported ones, and they have reasonable prices. FIEs can charge foreign exchange for such products, and domestic purchasers are told to give priority to the import substitutes over imported foreign products.

Favorable land use fees Although the government controls the ownership of all land, land use rights can be bought, with the rate of payment depending on such factors as the purpose of its use, the location, and tenure.[13] The maximum allowed period of land use depends on the type of investment. For instance, industrial use can lease for thirty years, and commercial for twenty years; fifty years is allowed for residential as well as for scientific, cultural and educational activities; twenty years is allowed for agriculture, and thirty years for tourism. A foreign investor may acquire land use rights through bidding or auction. Upon approval by the Shenzhen Bureau of Science and Technology, FIEs with advanced technology may be allowed a 50 percent reduction in land use fees for five years. Those with high technology may even apply for an exemption from land use fees. FIEs involved in scientific, cultural and educational activities also enjoy preferential land use fees. The rule is that land use fees are kept lower than those in other potential sites overseas.[14]

Foreign exchange and profits Foreign exchange. Initially, foreign exchange flows in the SEZs, as elsewhere in China, were subject to state planning, and transactions could be made only through the Bank of China. But by early 1986, FIEs in Shenzhen and other SEZs were allowed to make bilateral swaps of foreign exchange on a bilateral basis at a swap market.[15] Such swap markets were later established in other cities where large markets for foreign exchange existed. Shenzhen swap market allowed the widest access for both foreign and Chinese enterprises, as well as individuals. Shenzhen, furthermore, tried an exclusive foreign exchange experiment, which allowed a foreign currency—the Hong Kong dollar—to circulate as a means of exchange, or a virtually legal tender.[16] Shenzhen's FIEs also enjoyed privileged access to foreign exchange earnings. They retained the right to use a large proportion, 70 percent, and in some cases 100 percent, of the foreign exchange they earned.[17] FIEs with advanced technology or involved in transportation, energy and telecommunications are allowed to purchase from domestic markets and re-export to earn foreign exchange, if they do not have their own export products available and have temporary difficulties in balancing their foreign exchange accounts.

Profits. After-tax profits of foreign investors, or funds obtained at the expiration or discontinuation of contracts could be remitted abroad through the Bank of China or other registered overseas banks in Shenzhen. No income tax is levied on such profits or funds. Foreign expatriates also can remit their incomes from salary or other legitimate sources abroad, after paying personal income tax.

Government Infrastructure Investment

To build Shenzhen's urban infrastructure and industrial base, the Chinese government made enormous financial investment there.[18] Between 1979 and 1991, close to US$0.8 billion was invested in capital construction and infrastructure development by central as well as provincial allocation, state ministries, and other provinces, accounting for about 10.2 percent of the total infrastructure investment in Shenzhen (see Table 3.2). The central government was a major sponsor, especially in the first few years. Financial resources allocated from Beijing allowed Shenzhen to build a modern city out of a farming village in a short time, as the concentration of investment in productive activities and adequate provision of infrastructure favored steady growth. The Shenzhen Municipal Government also allocated substantial funding for infrastructure construction. It alone financed about 12 percent of all infrastructure investment in Shenzhen between 1979 and 1991. Compared to other cities in China such as Beijing, Shanghai and Tianjin, Shenzhen's own municipal expenditure allocated a much large share for infrastructure investment (see Table 3.3). Overall, funding from central, provincial and local governments for infrastructure development amounted to almost US$1.7 billion during the period of 1979 through 1991.

Government infrastructure investment (the sum of central, provincial and local government funding) was positively correlated with the quantity of actually utilized foreign investment in Shenzhen, particularly in the early 1980s (see Figure 3.1). The rapid rise in government infrastructure investment was accompanied by the accelerated growth of foreign investment between 1979 and 1985. But as a result of the policy adjustment stemming from the 1985 Work Conference, in 1986 there was a one-third reduction in Shenzhen's budget for infrastructure development. Such a sharp dive was felt shortly afterwards, and the level of utilized foreign

Table 3.2 Investment in Shenzhen's Capital Construction and Infrastructure Development, 1979-1991

Source of investment	1979	1980	1981	1982	1983	1984	1985	1986	1987	1988	1989	1990	1991	Total
Magnitude (US$ million)*	33.3	81.6	154.5	329.5	447.4	555.2	862.9	514.8	579.8	933.6	922.5	948.2	1225.8	7589.3
State allocation	15.9	21.6	13.0	24.7	22.1	7.5	13.4	13.3	7.3	7.3	2.5	2.0	3.7	154.3
State ministries and provincial fund	8.2	8.6	14.0	30.2	35.5	53.5	118.3	81.4	67.3	112.4	10.1	55.7	27.0	622.1
Local government allocation	4.2	6.3	19.1	33.3	39.4	76.1	140.7	92.9	69.1	103.1	125.9	108.8	93.8	912.6
Domestic bank loans	0.0	4.6	18.1	105.7	168.7	228.5	176.1	73.1	101.7	151.1	107.8	170.7	428.7	1734.8
Foreign capital	3.6	35.2	77.3	99.7	112.2	94.6	112.7	93.2	92.7	140.0	287.3	338.1	269.1	1755.8
Local enterprise self-financing	1.4	5.3	11.4	26.0	49.0	77.7	229.0	80.4	186.6	245.2	293.5	189.2	392.9	1787.6
Other investment	0.0	0.0	1.7	9.9	20.6	17.4	72.8	80.4	55.1	174.5	95.4	83.6	10.7	622.1
Share (percent)	100.0	100.0	100.0	100.0	100.0	100.0	100.0	100.0	100.0	100.0	100.0	100.0	100.0	100.0
State allocation	47.8	26.4	8.4	7.5	4.9	1.4	1.6	2.6	1.3	0.8	0.3	0.2	0.3	2.0
State ministries and provincial fund	24.5	10.5	9.0	9.2	7.9	9.6	13.7	15.8	11.6	12.0	1.1	5.9	2.2	8.2
Local government allocation	12.5	7.7	12.3	10.1	8.8	13.7	16.3	18.0	11.9	11.0	13.6	11.5	7.6	12.0
Domestic bank loans	n.a	5.6	11.7	32.1	37.7	41.1	20.4	14.2	17.5	16.2	11.7	18.0	35.0	22.9
Foreign capital	11.0	43.2	50.0	30.3	25.1	17.0	13.1	18.1	16.0	15.0	31.1	35.7	22.0	23.1
Local enterprise self-financing	4.1	6.5	7.4	7.9	11.0	14.0	26.5	15.6	32.2	26.3	31.8	20.0	32.0	23.6
Other investment	n.a.	n.a.	1.1	3.0	4.6	3.1	8.4	15.6	9.5	18.7	10.3	8.8	0.9	8.2

* These figures are converted from the Chinese currency (RMB), based on market exchange rates.

Source: Shenzhen Statistical Bureau, *Shenzhen Statistical Manual*, 1991.

Local Policy Environment and Labor Costs 63

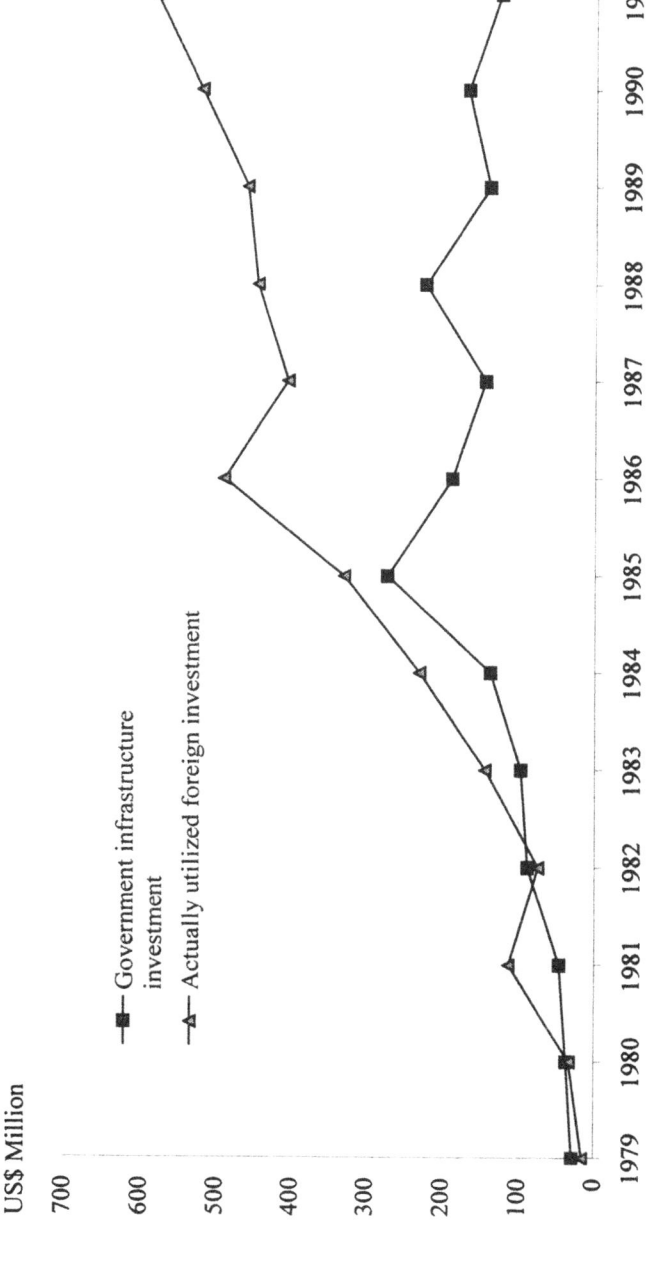

Figure 3.1 Government Infrastructure Investment and Actually Utilized Foreign Investment in Shenzhen, 1979-1991

Source: Based on Table 2.1 and Table 3.2.

investment dipped to a low ebb in 1987. Since then, government infrastructure investment has fluctuated and has never exceeded the 1985 level. Meanwhile, Shenzhen did not experience notable growth in utilized foreign investment until several years later in 1990. As shown in Chapter 2, the gradually attenuated role of Shenzhen in attracting foreign investment could be attributed to the opening up of other coastal cities in China. I believe, however, the significant reduction in government infrastructure funding was partly responsible, as well.

Table 3.3 **Municipal Infrastructure Investment as Percentage of Expenditure, Selected Cities, 1979-1989**

City	1979	1980	1981	1982	1983	1984	1985	1986	1987	1988	1989	Average
Shenzhen	30.0	45.3	49.8	37.3	38.3	41.0	53.4	50.9	48.0	45.0	45.0	44.0
Beijing	50.2	38.0	40.1	38.4	33.0	37.1	32.8	25.3	21.1	19.9	19.6	32.3
Shanghai	47.0	32.1	28.4	24.0	21.4	26.3	30.9	24.0	18.6	8.6	7.5	24.4
Tianjin	44.9	31.2	34.3	51.7	48.7	42.3	41.8	21.2	16.7	12.7	12.5	32.5

Source: Shenzhen Statistical Bureau, *Shenzhen Socio-Economic Statistics*, 1979-1985 and 1986-1990; State Statistical Bureau, *Historical Statistics*, 1949-1989.

Shenzhen has benefited significantly from government infrastructure investment. As pointed out by a manager in a Singaporean joint venture, Shenzhen had the best investment environment in the country, especially in production facilities. Modern, standardized factory buildings were constructed and equipped with adequate utilities, ready for leasing to FIEs. In addition, in the earlier years Shenzhen's self-financing capacity also was strengthened gradually with the help of government investment. By 1991, close to a third of infrastructure investment was raised through local enterprise self-financing. A major channel was sales of land use rights or land leasing. Recently, Shenzhen has tried to raise funds by selling license plates, import & export quotas, and duty-free quotas. Foreign investment, too, has been a major source of infrastructure investment, making up about a quarter of the total investment. Domestic bank loans made up a similar share (see Table 3.2).

The importance of having a supportive local policy environment can be further demonstrated by the rise of a number of coastal open cities as new centers of attraction for foreign investment after they were granted status similar to Shenzhen's. In Guangdong Province, the capital city of

Guangzhou is such a case. Already the largest industrial node in south China, after a decade of unimpressive performance, Guangzhou took off rapidly at the end of the 1980s, and by 1994 was closing the gap with Shenzhen (see Table 3.1). At the national level, the rise of Dalian and the lower Yangtze River Delta is most noticeable (see Table 2.3). Located in the Northeast region, Dalian has a long history of industrialization and of historical affiliations with both Japan and Korea. The designation as a coastal open city has enabled Dalian to renew such affiliations and benefit from both the rapid growth of Japanese direct investment in China in the late 1980s and the establishment of diplomatic relations with South Korea.[19] In addition, the lower Yangtze River Delta region, which embraces Shanghai, Nanjing, Ningbo and Suzhou, may have already been a major attraction for foreign investors as the central government finally opened up this region completely in the early 1990s. This region also benefits from a strong industrial base, large market potential, abundant natural resources, better quality of the labor force, and strong technological capabilities.[20] This spatial redistribution of foreign investment reflects, in general, a shift from the south, mainly the Pearl River Delta region, along the coast to new northern frontiers, noticeably the Bohai Gulf in the Northeast and the Yangtze River Delta in the East.

In addition to its proximity to Hong Kong and its attractive policy environment, Shenzhen also has benefited from two other factors: (1) the availability of a low-cost, disciplined and non-militant labor force, and (2) many foreign investors' perception of a large domestic market in China, and their willingness to forego some short-term profits in return for long-term market shares. Although only weakly responsible for the growth of foreign investment in Shenzhen, these two factors have made China as a whole appealing to the investment community.

Labor Costs

Firms involved in industrial relocation and offshore assembly tend to establish such facilities to carry out the labor-intensive stages of production, as elaborated in the next chapter. They often are highly mobile, since the investment usually requires small amounts of capital and equipment and uses a specific standardized technology (see Behrman, 1988). The existence of a pool of disciplined, low-skilled or semi-skilled labor can, depending on the level of product standardization, influence their location decision. When labor costs rise and reach an unprofitable level in terms of both physical and social costs, these firms often close down their production facilities and move to lower-cost locations. This has already happened in the footwear industry, where major offshore production sites have shifted from South Korea and Taiwan to China and Thailand. As a result, the industries using offshore assembly are often considered foot-loose: they change locations relatively easily and are forever on the run for lower labor costs. They tend to have rather strong bargaining power vis-à-vis host countries, because they bring in foreign exchange through outward processing.[21]

Labor in Shenzhen and in China as a whole was attractive to such industrial relocation in several ways: low wage costs, low social costs in the absence of government regulations, and a low level of militancy. A survey of 10,000 Japanese companies in 1990 revealed that one of the top motivations for companies interested in investing in China was the low cost of labor.[22] These companies considered labor in China abundant, cheap, and relatively good in quality. Another characteristic of this labor force made it even more attractive for foreign investors—namely, its non-militancy or lack of organized power. Many firms from industrialized countries decided to relocate offshore partly to avoid unionized labor at home. So the unassertiveness of the labor force has become a main factor contributing to the steady growth of export-led industrialization in some developing countries. On the other hand, most Latin American countries have lost out in the competition for foreign investment in offshore assembly despite their relatively low costs of labor, since organized labor had played an important part in previous import-substitute industrialization (see Wilson, 1991).

Most FIEs believed that the unit cost of labor in Shenzhen and in China was almost always lower than in other countries, according to a 1992 survey of selected enterprises in coastal provinces and cities by the U.S.-China Business Council.[23] For instance, in 1992 unskilled labor costs on the mainland were reported to be only one-tenth the going rate in Taiwan. The Chinese government also imposed some control, formally or informally, on the wages paid by FIEs. In general, the basic wage should be above 120 percent, but not exceed 150 percent of that in state enterprises in the same region.[24] The rationale of limiting the wages of FIEs' employees was to maintain the attractiveness of China as an investment location. Another concern was that high wages in these enterprises could put pressure on state enterprises to match them up in order to keep the best workers. From this perspective, China's approach was distinctively Asian, in that the government played a major role in controlling the labor force and its competitiveness. The continuing devaluation of the Chinese currency served to reinforce such a competitive advantage.

The social costs of labor also tended to be very low in Shenzhen, due to the lack of labor laws and regulations. Although in the post-Mao reform era new labor laws governing FIEs were formulated, they were meant mainly to attract foreign capital by creating a labor system similar to the western model. There was less effort to safeguard workers' rights and workplace security, and to deal with workplace abuses; the approach to those issues was piecemeal and reactive. Only in the late 1980s did the government begin to issue a series of regulations, mandating a 16-year minimum age for hiring, an eight-hour workday, labor protection, and the institution of social welfare benefits when applicable. It was not until the spring of 1991 that the Regulations on Banning the Use of Child Labor were issued.[25] These regulations, moreover, were essentially stop-gap measures, reflecting the lack of a comprehensive labor law in China.[26] A draft labor law was finally issued in January 1994 and then ratified by the National People's Congress in July 1994.[27]

The absence of organized labor movements also has kept social costs of labor low. The only organized institution close to representing workers' rights and interests in China—the trade unions—has been politically week, for a host of historical, political, ideological, and economic reasons. The first had to do with the nature of the communist revolution that took power in 1949. The revolution succeeded by using a peasant-based strategy in an agrarian society. The virtual exclusion of the proletariat from the revolution placed trade unions out of the mainstream of the communist movement (see Wilson, 1986). Second, lacking any history of industrialization, unions also had no tradition of autonomous action. Once the Chinese Communist Party (CCP) took power, it established central control over all other institutions, including the government and trade unions. The 1984 All China Federation of Trade Unions (ACFTU) Regulations explicitly said that national, transregional and transindustrial mass activities should by every means be discouraged. Third, there has been a strong ideological bias against trade unions representing workers' rights and interests, which was seen as posing an unacceptable challenge to political authority. The situation changed somewhat after 1979 because of reform efforts to restructure the role of the party in labor allocation and to increase labor mobility. But by the late 1980s, it was evident that few of the basic goals of union reform had been met. The unions had not managed to free themselves from subservience to the party. In a survey conducted by ACFTU in 1988, over 60 percent of the 640,000 respondents gave very little credence to the value of trade unions. They complained that the unions did not represent workers' opinions and did no more than pass on government decisions (see Chiang, 1990).

As a result, trade unions at all levels have very limited roles. At the national level, the major function of ACFTU has been to mobilize workers to support China's industrialization efforts under the leadership of the party.[28] The two major national organizations representing labor and trade unions, ACFTU and the Ministry of Labor, have been left out of most of the economic policy-making process unless labor issues are its main focus.[29] Moreover, collective bargaining, the main activity of unions in western countries, has not been the function of trade unions in China. Created as a modern organizational mechanism for mobilization and socialization, trade unions have been assigned primarily to maintain discipline and ensure the production commitment of the work force (see Lee, 1986).

Just as at the national level, at the enterprise level unions are not generally involved in major decision-making. Their functions are confined to organizing social, recreational and educational activities and providing health, childcare and consultation services. In addition, union officials have seemed prepared to give up control of the work force to foreign investors. A local union official has asserted: "[F]oreign investors do not understand the role of our trade unions. We have to convince them that trade unions are to unite workers to contribute to the well-being of the enterprise, unlike those in foreign countries which aim at defeating their bosses."[30] Unions have exhibited a lower level of institutional development compared to those in other socialist states, and a substantial proportion of workers has not been unionized. For instance, in 1982 in units where there were unions, the participation rate was about 85 percent. However, not all units had a union. It was estimated that, as of 1982, 23 percent of all wage-earners in China worked in units without union organization. Only about 67 percent of all wage-earners belonged to unions (see Wilson, 1986).

Domestic Market Potential

A classical factor underlying foreign investment inflows, domestic market potential, has proved to be of minimal importance for Shenzhen. Restrictions imposed by the government on market access were a major deterrent and were often set in the form of export quotas for FIEs, stipulated in the negotiation process. Most FIEs were allowed to sell only a limited share, around 20 percent, of their products on the domestic market. Beijing also set up a general export target for Shenzhen as a whole, of at least 70 percent of the total commodity output value in Shenzhen to be exported (see Liu, 1992). Over the course of the 1980s, the government relaxed some restrictions in an attempt to lure more investment. But there were still two conditions that FIEs had to meet to gain preferential access to the domestic market. First, if their products were urgently needed by China, the products could be considered import substitutes, and a large proportion, or even all, could be sold on the domestic market. Second, the technology of such enterprises had to be advanced and be able to benefit China's technological development. Sales had to be conducted through certain channels set by the government and had to comply with plans.

Therefore, from the very beginning, domestic market potential was not built into the SEZ policy framework as an attraction for prospective investors. In fact, the very restricted market access discouraged many potential U.S. investors, who often viewed the large potential domestic market as the biggest attraction, more important than cheap labor (personal interviews). The tension between U.S. investors and the Chinese government grew until an agreement on market access was signed in the early 1990s. But even in 1997, when China struggled to join the World Trade Organization (WTO), it was still criticized for seriously restricting access to its domestic market. As Kueh (1992, p.638) correctly pointed out:

> The essential feature of the Chinese approach is that it has simultaneously moved away from "import-substitution" to "export-oriented" foreign investment, while retaining the basic elements of an inwardly-oriented industrialization strategy, the antithesis of opening up the vast domestic market to foreign competition.

Regardless of these restrictions, investors' perception of a large Chinese market has proven to be far from accurate. According to traditional investment theory, the domestic market potential of a host country is most important for "weight-gaining" industries or market-oriented investment (see Root, 1990). Examples of such industries are automobiles, construction, food stuff, beverages, and durable goods. They aim to locate close to their prospective markets in order to secure market shares. The demand for consumer goods is essential, since such demand is the driving force behind the demand for all commodities, including producer goods.[31] In addition to the size of the population in the host country, the income level and distribution, consumer expenditure and consumption pattern, and consumer tastes and preferences all contribute to domestic market potential. For those investors producing luxuries for a country, the existence of a certain market segment, namely the high income proportion of the population, is crucial.

However, per capita GNP or income level in China was low throughout the 1980s. According to the World Bank, China's GNP per capita was only US$370 in 1990, despite an impressive annual growth of over 8 percent

Table 3.4 Macro Indicators for China and Selected Developing Countries, 1979 and 1990

Country	Per capita GNP (US$)[a]		GDP annual growth 1979-90 average (%)	Private consumption per capita, 1990 (1987 US$)	Population (millions)		GNP (US$ billion)	
	1979	1990			1979	1990	1979	1990
China	260	370	8.5	160	969.0	1,134.0	251.9	419.6
Indonesia	400	570	5.9	290	145.0	178.0	58.0	101.5
South Korea	1,520	5,400	8.1	2,130	37.5	42.8	57.0	231.1
Malaysia	1,400	2,320	6.4	1,260	13.4	17.9	18.8	41.5
Thailand	590	1,420	7.4	740	45.7	55.8	27.0	79.2
Mexico	1,810	2,490	2.9	1,270	68.8	86.2	124.5	214.6

Note: GNP, gross national product; GDP, gross domestic product.
a. The calculation of GNP is based on the atlas method.

Source: Compiled from the World Bank, *World Tables* (Washington, DC, 1992).

between 1979 and 1990 (see Table 3.4).[32] China was thus ranked in the middle of the low-income economies, whose average GNP per capita was US$350. In spite of the enormous population (over 1.2 billion) in China, consumer purchasing power was seriously limited by the low income level. Compared to its Southeast Asian neighbors, such as Indonesia, Malaysia and Thailand, China lagged behind in both GNP per capita and personal consumption. However, using another well recognized method—the purchasing power parity approach—to take into account the domestic purchasing power of currencies, gives results ranging from US$1,400 to US$1,990 GNP per capita for China in 1990. The consensus is that a proper estimate of GNP per capita in China would be somewhere between the two results, at two to three times higher than the official statistics. This would put the level of GNP per capita in China at between US$740 and US$1,110 in 1990. It has been generally agreed in the business world that when per capita income exceeds US$1,000, consumption will begin to be stimulated or formation of a consumption society will start (see Okumura, 1993; Shaw and Woetzel, 1992). Thus, at best, by 1990, China was only on the verge of becoming a major market for consumer goods.

The high-income segment of China's population was very small, because the relatively even income distribution, particularly within urban areas. According to a 1988 study by the Research Program on the Chinese Economy, the Gini coefficient—a commonly used measure of income distribution—for urban and rural areas was between 0.23 and 0.34 respectively, with an overall Gini ratio of 0.38.[33] By international standards, the income distribution in China was relatively equal, and China compared favorably with most developing countries, although the economic reform has allowed some places, particularly those in the South, to get rich first.[34] The top decile group of the population had about 27 percent of the country's total income. As of 1990 China had about 16 million well-to-do consumers, just over 1.3 percent of the total population.

According to international standards, China's consumption level in the 1980s could be considered poor. The Engel coefficient, a common measure of consumption level, was about 56 percent for China between 1985 and 1990.[35] For most Chinese in the 1980s, the bulk of disposable income was spent on food (between 50 to 60 percent), followed by daily goods and other consumer durables (about 25 percent) and clothing (between 10 to 15 percent). Despite some shift in the pattern of consumption during the decade, the rank order and magnitude of these major consumption categories in urban areas remained fairly stable (see Chai, 1992). Urban and rural expenditure patterns also were strikingly similar for most of those categories, regardless of the large difference in these two income levels.

But per capita expenditure in urban areas was much higher than that in rural areas. Unlike many other developing countries, the expenditure patterns for high and low income groups in China were quite similar. Since a large portion of disposable income was used to purchase food, general consumption of non-durable goods (such as clothing and shoes) and durable goods was low.[36] Spending on housing and services was very limited, since both were heavily subsidized by the government. Such a consumption pattern resembled that of Japan in the late 1950s and Taiwan in the late 1960s.

Due to the low level of per capita GNP (hence disposable income), the very small size of the high-income segment of the population, a relatively even distribution of income, and a low consumption level, China's domestic market potential for consumer goods was very limited in the 1980s. Demand for consumer goods was largely confined to food stuff, clothing, and basic household items. China was not yet a mass consumption society, particularly for foreign-made, high-price or luxury items, and did not turn out to be a huge market of millions upon millions of consumers for market-oriented investment. Moreover, reaching China's consumers was difficult, as the transportation network and infrastructure facilities to support the burst of industrial growth and consumer spending were not there. Many foreign investors with ambitious marketing plans for China, particularly those producing expensive consumer goods, had to reassess their initial rush of enthusiasm about the "China market." Some came to the realization that their hope for securing markets in China might lie in the long run rather than the short run.

However, rapid economic growth and large household savings are underpinning a recent surge in spending, and China's consumer market may be ready to come of age in a decade or so. Although the growth of Chinese consumption depends on the future population growth and rate of accumulation, China should be able to double its living standard between 1990 and 2000, and reach a moderately comfortable level if the current growth rate can be sustained. By then the consumption pattern in China will be comparable to that of Taiwan in the late 1970s and Japan in the late 1960s. One rapidly growing category of consumption is likely to be such consumer durables as refrigerators, washing machines, air conditioners, vacuum cleaners, and automobiles, some of which are already popular in urban households but still scarce in rural areas.[37] Chinese consumers will prefer small and energy-saving household electronic appliances. Demand for housing and services also will increase rapidly. Because of poor roads and space limitations, however, the demand for cars will probably remain small. In some cities in south China, such as Shenzhen, Guangzhou and

Shanghai, there is already a group of high-income people who consume mostly foreign goods and represent a market segment that warrants major attention from foreign investors.[38]

As a byproduct of the relatively even income distribution and a very large population, a small increase in per capita GNP or income can lead to a much larger increase in demand for certain consumer goods. This can be thought of as a "staircase" pattern of consumption. When the average level of income surpasses a threshold, a large number of households will all of sudden be able to afford major household items. Therefore, a moderate growth in China's income level will have a much larger impact on its consumer market potential than a large income growth would have in small but more developed countries such as Taiwan and South Korea. Of course, changes in real consumer expenditure in different categories of consumer goods will depend not only on income growth, but also on the price and income elasticity of demand. Nevertheless, rising consumer spending as a result of rapid income growth may increase the attraction of the domestic market potential for future investors. The attraction will be further enhanced when China eventually permits wider market access. A successful bid for the WTO will be helpful in this respect.

Summary

In addition to large inflows of Hong Kong investment, Shenzhen also has attracted a sizable number of TNCs from other countries, including Japan and the U.S. Compared to other major coastal open cities, Guangzhou for example, Shenzhen had no advantage in labor costs or access to the domestic market; in fact, the average annual salary of workers was constantly higher in Shenzhen. What really made the difference was the policy autonomy and openness Shenzhen enjoyed, in both general economic policy and investment incentives. These were no doubt the fruits of the SEZ policy, without which Shenzhen would be no different from other cities in China. In particular, Shenzhen had the authority to prepare its own development plan and was given priority in acquiring needed materials. Employment, wage, and ownership policies were much more flexible for FIEs. Given freedom to recruit across the country, these enterprises were much less circumscribed by the problem of labor immobility that often hampered enterprises elsewhere.

A package of preferential incentives also was offered to FIEs in Shenzhen. They enjoyed one of the lowest corporate income tax rates in the world, at 15 percent, and one of the most generous tax holidays, up to five years. Enterprises excelling at export production and using advanced technologies could claim even longer periods of tax exemptions or reductions. To boost export performance and, ultimately, foreign exchange earnings, Shenzhen exempted FIEs from value-added tax and duties on exports, and from duties on imports of capital goods and materials to be used for export production. To partially overcome the inconvertibility of the Chinese currency, in 1986 the first currency swap market in the country was set up in Shenzhen, which allowed the widest access by both foreign and Chinese enterprises. Compared to elsewhere in China, FIEs in Shenzhen also enjoyed the most favorable retention rates for their foreign exchange earnings. Those with difficulty in balancing their foreign exchange accounts were allowed to purchase from the domestic market and re-export. There were also preferential treatments in the areas of land use fees and profit repatriation.

Besides the open policy and liberal incentives, Shenzhen has benefited from the central government's tremendous investment in infrastructure development, as well as from investment by the provincial and local governments. In fact, actually utilized foreign investment in Shenzhen was positively correlated with government infrastructure investment. A rising level of government funding prior to 1986 was accompanied by a phenomenal growth in utilized foreign investment; but a halt in such funding that year was reflected in a sharp dive of foreign investment inflows in 1987. Compared to other major cities in China, the Shenzhen Municipal Government allocated the largest share of expenditure to infrastructure construction. As a locale favored by government infrastructure investment and special investment policies, Shenzhen fared better than other cities in attracting foreign investment.

Shenzhen also has benefited from the availability of a low-cost, disciplined labor force, resembling the trends in other similar zones in Asia. Unit costs of labor in Shenzhen were almost always lower than those in other countries, largely because of the low wage rates. The social costs of labor were very low due to the lack of government regulations, the absence of labor movements, and the lack of union power. Despite the residual importance of low labor costs in Shenzhen's case, their draw was stronger than that of the domestic market potential. Government restrictions significantly limited FIEs' access to the domestic market. Because of a low level of per capita income, a limited consumption pattern, and the small size of high-income segments, the domestic market potential for consumer goods was very limited in the 1980s. China's market potential has proven to be long-term, not short-term, for the investment community.

Although TNCs have accounted for a limited share of the investment in Shenzhen during the study period, their importance is bound to increase in the near future. TNCs have emerged as the major agent of global economic activities and can now be held responsible for most FDI inflows to developing countries. They are controlling between a quarter and a third of all world production and are especially active in processing and marketing. For most TNCs, China is an attractive investment location in the long run, and Shenzhen is the gateway to this large territory. Most TNCs in Shenzhen have perceived it as one of the most attractive locations in China (personal interviews). In one joint venture executive's view, Shenzhen now even has several advantages to attract high-tech industries, including locational advantages, preferential policies, high living standards to entice the talented, a good market, and high efficiency. Shenzhen's experience also has served as proof that an open door policy for the investment community can succeed. Its favorable policy environment, consisting of policy openness and autonomy, liberal investment incentives, and strong government commitment, is a critical factor in its success. As the country gradually moves into an overall liberal investment regime, TNCs will in time overcome their concerns about the risks traditionally associated with investing in a socialist country.

Many TNCs believe that their ability to form "strategic alliances," mainly through joint ventures, is crucial for their long-term access to the Chinese market. They expect their Chinese partners to help them overcome specific obstacles to operation within China. For instance, Chinese partners could obtain important information on local markets, which is useful for commercial success.[39] As a newly opened market with large potential, China represents one of the last niches in the global investment competition. Some TNCs are even willing to invest a minimum amount in the beginning just to establish a foothold in this market. A 1986 survey by the Ministry of Foreign Economic Relations and Trade of China has shown that one of the main objectives of TNCs is to gain access to the huge potential Chinese market, and to use China as a production base to serve other Asian countries in the long term. Short-term profit maximization is not their primary objective. In this situation, a gradual opening up of the domestic market will be a significant attraction for foreign investors. Some locales have begun to allow a high proportion of FIEs' products to be sold on the local market. For instance, Chengdu, the capital city of Sichuan Province, has led the nation in opening its market to foreign investors by allowing them 100 percent domestic sales (CND, 1 April 1994). But for the SEZs, which have been designed to be export-oriented, restrictions on domestic sales are likely to continue.

4 Technological Content of Foreign Investment

Given that Shenzhen has been successful in attracting large volumes of foreign investment, what has been the technological content of such investment? Has the proximity to Hong Kong biased the composition of foreign investment inflows to Shenzhen? One of the original goals of the SEZ policy was to promote the transfer of advanced technology, particularly through projects and enterprises that could produce the following outcomes: competitive exports, import substitutes, technologically advanced products, quality-improving and energy-saving processes, and high domestic value-added. How successful has Shenzhen been in technology transfer? Has the goal of using foreign investment to promote technology transfer been undermined by the lack of an effective framework for intellectual property rights and by Shenzhen's underdeveloped capabilities? These are the questions to be answered in this chapter.

Technological Content and Technology Transfer

The industrial sector received the largest share of foreign investment in Shenzhen between 1979 and 1991 (see Table 4.1).[1] The total amount of contracted foreign investment in industry was US$4134.3 million, out of which US$2109.7 million was actually utilized. Before 1986, industry's dominance was not significant; it had accounted for about a third of all utilized foreign investment. In the early years, the criticism that "real estate was the major pursuit of foreign businessmen" had some truth (Crane, 1990, p.62), as the share of the construction & real estate sector was over 20 percent, trailing slightly behind industry. It was only after 1986 that industry became the preeminent sector for foreign investment (see Figure 4.1). Between 1986 and 1991, close to two-thirds of all foreign investment went to industry, far more than other sectors attracted together. The second largest amount went to the banking & insurance sector in that period.

Industrial direct investment was largely concentrated in several low-tech, labor-intensive manufacturing industries: textiles & dyeing, electronics, metal products, consumer electronics, rubber & plastics, garments, and glass products (Table 4.2).[2] The main beneficiaries of FDI inflows were two manufacturing industries: textiles and garments industries, together, received over 10 percent of investment; and electronics and consumer electronics, together, received over 8 percent. This pattern resembled that of many other similar zones in Asia, where the two most important industries have been electronics, and textiles and garments. The electronics industries in Shenzhen attracted a fairly significant amount of direct investment from Japan (about a third of those industries' investment), and consumer electronics drew investment from the Netherlands (about 12 percent).[3] But unlike many zones, which formed industrial monocultures, Shenzhen was able to attract investment to other manufacturing industries.[4]

Most industrial FIEs in Shenzhen were characterized by assembly operations and simple processing, with foreign firms sending raw materials, parts or components to Shenzhen and exporting products back home for sale or to a third country for further processing into finished goods. This was demonstrated by the surge of capital goods imports from Hong Kong, the rise of re-exports through Hong Kong, and the low value-added of these enterprises. It was estimated that about three-fourths of Hong Kong's domestic exports to the mainland were products shipped for further processing. Meanwhile, Hong Kong's re-exports of Chinese origin to overseas markets expanded by 26 percent annually between 1980 and 1992. Almost 80 percent of such re-exports were products of outward processing arrangements with Hong Kong firms (see Jones and others, 1993; Sung, 1991).

Net output ratios of these enterprises were very low, ranging between 20 and 30 percent (see Table 4.3). As the ratio of net output value to gross output value, net output ratio could be an approximate indicator of value-added. A low ratio would show that the local industry's input was mainly labor that performed assembly and processing dictated by the technology embedded in the production lines (see Chan and Kwok, 1991). That was the case for several major manufacturing industries in Shenzhen that received large foreign investment inflows: electronics, textiles & dyeing, metal products, and rubber & plastics. Foreign enterprises in only two manufacturing industries—pharmaceutical and crafts—had net output ratios higher than 30 percent in 1991. The net output ratio for industrial FIEs (or FIIEs) as a whole was lower than the average for all industrial enterprises in Shenzhen, clearly pointing to the strong tendency of foreign enterprises to engage in outward processing.

Among all foreign-invested manufacturing activities, electronics, machinery, and garments, in that order, were the dominant producers, as measured in net as well as gross output value (see Table 4.3). Selected as a

Table 4.1 Sectoral Distribution of Actually Utilized Foreign Investment in Shenzhen, 1979-1991 (millions of U.S. dollars, unless otherwise noted)

Sector	1979-1985 Amount	1979-1985 Percent	Sector	1986-1991 Amount	1986-1991 Percent
1 Agriculture	8.2	0.9	Agriculture	11.2	0.4
2 Industry	306.5	32.7	Industry	1803.2	62.3
3 Tourism & hotel	66.0	7.0	Geology & prospecting	3.7	0.1
4 Construction & real estate	193.6	20.6	Construction		
5 Transportation & communications	30.8	3.3	Transportation & communications	41.7	1.4
6 Retail & services	113.3	12.1	Retail & services	56.5	2.0
7			Real estate & utilities	292.3	10.1
8			Health care & welfare	2.0	0.1
9			Education & culture	1.4	0.0
10			Research & technical services	0.2	0.0
11			Banking & insurance	497.8	17.2
12			Government agency		
13 Others	219.6	23.4	Others	184.7	6.4
Total	938.0	100.0	Total	2894.7	100.0

Source: Shenzhen Statistical Bureau, *Shenzhen Socio-Economic Statistics, 1979-1985 and 1986-1990*; *Shenzhen Statistical Yearbook, 1992.*

Technological Content of Foreign Investment 79

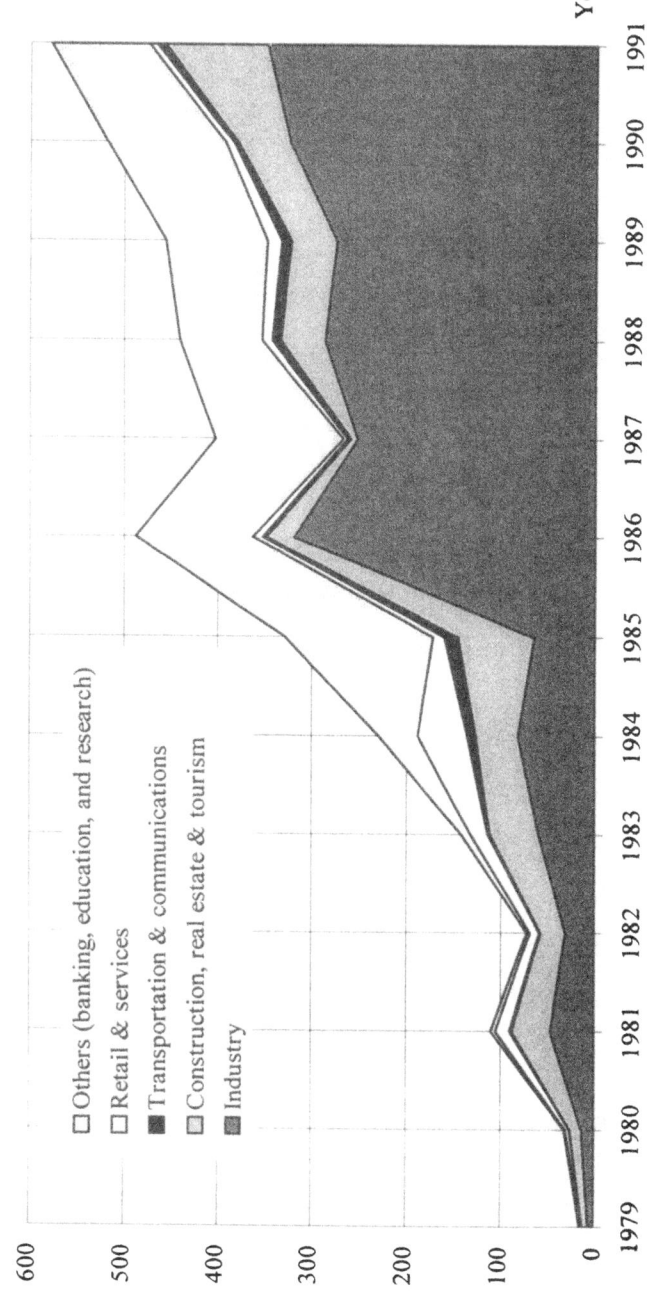

Figure 4.1 Sectoral Distribution of Actually Utilized Foreign Investment in Shenzhen, 1979-1991

Source   Shenzhen Statistical Bureau, Shenzhen Socio-Economic Statistics, 1979-1985 and 1986-1990; Shenzhen Statistical Yearbook, 1992.

Table 4.2 Shenzhen's Top Ten Manufacturing Industries Receiving Foreign Direct Investment, 1979-1990 (Cumulative)

Rank	Manufacturing industry	Number of projects	Registered investment Amount (US$)	Percent	Average size of project (US$)
Ranked by registered investment					
1	Electricity	3	444,034,635	17.6	148,011,545
2	Textiles & dyeing	129	176,402,969	7.0	1,367,465
3	Electronics	55	108,670,718	4.3	1,975,831
4	Metal products	81	105,473,938	4.2	1,302,147
5	Consumer electronics	50	100,681,792	4.0	2,013,636
6	Rubber & plastics	86	87,033,987	3.4	1,012,023
7	Garments	137	83,231,791	3.3	607,531
8	Computer & electronic systems	73	71,074,267	2.8	973,620
9	Glass products	18	61,516,294	2.4	3,417,572
10	Chemicals	49	51,909,074	2.1	1,059,369
	Top 10 manufacturing industries	681	1,290,029,465	51.1	1,894,316
	Total for the industrial sector	1,329	1,877,949,988	74.4	1,413,055
	Shenzhen total (sample)	1,621	2,523,203,285	100.0	1,556,572
Ranked by number of projects					
1	Garments	137	83,231,791	3.3	607,531
2	Textiles & dyeing	129	176,402,969	7.0	1,367,465
3	Rubber & plastics	86	87,033,987	3.4	1,012,023
4	Metal products	81	105,473,938	4.2	1,302,147
5	Computer & electronic systems	73	71,074,267	2.8	973,620
6	Machinery	68	47,489,365	1.9	698,373
7	Footwear & headwear	63	38,830,030	1.5	616,350
8	Electronics	55	108,670,718	4.3	1,975,831
9	Electrical machinery	55	49,689,149	2.0	903,439
10	Consumer electronics	50	100,681,792	4.0	2,013,636
	Top 10 manufacturing industries	797	868,578,008	34.4	1,089,809
	Total for the industrial sector	1,329	1,877,949,988	74.4	1,413,055
	Shenzhen total (sample)	1,621	2,523,203,285	100.0	1,556,572

Source: Shenzhen Bureau of Economic Development and Shenzhen Information Center, *Directory of Foreign-Invested Enterprises in Shenzhen*, 1991.

priority industry from the outset, electronics was readily the single largest manufacturing industry in terms of output value. Its priority was based on several factors, including Shenzhen's inability to develop heavy manufacturing activities rapidly, Shenzhen's proximity to one of the world's primary electronics production centers—Hong Kong, and the rising domestic demand for consumer electronics. By 1987, Shenzhen's electronics industry had developed into the second largest in the country, next only to Shanghai, and accounted for 6 percent of China's gross output in electronics (see X. Chen, 1993). In 1993, Shenzhen's electronics industrial output reached 18 billion yuan, making up 12.9 percent of the country's total. The export value of the industry was nearly 11 billion yuan, over 15 percent of China's total electronics exports (FBIS-CHI-94098, 20 May 1994, p.65). The electronics industry in Shenzhen also witnessed the formation of one of the first large industrial groups, Shenzhen Electronics Groups, which served as an institutional umbrella for over 100 domestic and foreign enterprises. This conglomerate was China's pioneering effort to adopt a new corporate structure, characterized by vertical and horizontal integration.

If foreign investment inflows to Shenzhen have been largely low-tech, has technology transfer happened at all? A general classification of transferable technology includes product, process, equipment, information, managerial know-how, and training. FDI is the channel of technology transfer most often used.[5] Obtaining technology through FDI appears the most effective way, particularly in high-tech industries whose technology is often exclusive or proprietary. Technology transfer through FDI sometimes comes with know-how, personnel training, and shop-floor cooperation between foreign and Chinese technicians, all of which help the actual absorption of the technology.

Technology transfer in Shenzhen was limited due to the fact that most FDI projects were low-tech and very small in size.[6] Technology embedded in small-scale, mature manufacturing or processing could not have been very advanced. Between 1979 and 1990, over half of Shenzhen's FIEs had registered investment under US$0.5 million, and another 23 percent were between US$0.5 to US$1 million, so about three-quarters of FIEs had less than US$1 million each in registered investment (see Figure 4.2). The likelihood of advanced technology transfer in these projects was very small, as it would often entail large amounts of capital. This situation left Shenzhen with only about a quarter of all FIEs possibly involved in advanced technology transfer.

Technology transfer did happen in some of these enterprises, in the form of product, process, know-how, management skills, or training. Although very limited, successful cases of transfer were not unseen, as shown in the case studies presented in this chapter.[7] Some unsystematic numbers also are indicative. It was estimated that the contribution of technology transfer to the growth of Shenzhen's industrial output in 1990 was around 30 percent. According to customs statistics, in the late 1980s and early 1990s, complete plants and technology often headed the list of major import items; they amounted to somewhere between US$60 million to US$100 million annually.[8] Recently, there has been a sizable increase in the number of joint ventures in large, modern industrial activities.

Table 4.3 Net/Gross Output Value of Shenzhen's Selected Manufacturing Industries Receiving Foreign Investment, 1991
(billions of yuan, unless otherwise noted)

Manufacturing industry	NVIO [1]	[1] as % of all FIIEs' NVIO	GVIO [2]	[2] as % of all FIIEs' GVIO	Net output ratio [1]/[2]
Electrical machinery	101.2	2.9	706.3	4.1	14.3
Electronics	1038.4	30.3	6481.5	37.3	16.0
Wood products	24.6	0.7	152.2	0.9	16.2
Textiles & dyeing	207.2	6.0	1250.7	7.2	16.6
Leather	58.6	1.7	310.8	1.8	18.9
Papermaking	74.8	2.2	387.4	2.2	19.3
All FIIEs	3431.9	100.0	17372.7	100.0	19.8
Plastics	113.3	3.3	525.1	3.0	21.6
Metal products	104.6	3.0	474.4	2.7	22.1
Rubber	11.6	0.3	52.3	0.3	22.2
Printing	71.1	2.1	319.8	1.8	22.2
All industrial enterprises	5517.3		23608.3		23.4
Food	54.2	1.6	230.4	1.3	23.5
Chemicals	124.4	3.6	509.7	2.9	24.4
Beverages	65.4	1.9	262.3	1.5	24.9
Garments	362.9	10.6	1438.7	8.3	25.2
Sporting goods	108.9	3.2	428.9	2.5	25.4
Furniture	28.9	0.8	109.5	0.6	26.4
Machinery	443.9	12.9	1671.9	9.6	26.5
Building materials	113.4	3.3	418.2	2.4	27.1
Transportation equipment	29.7	0.9	105.0	0.6	28.3
Pharmaceuticals	46.8	1.4	134.3	0.8	34.8
Crafts	32.0	0.9	79.6	0.5	40.2

Note: FIIE, foreign-invested industrial enterprise; NVIO, net value of industrial output; GVIO, gross value of industrial output.

Source: Shenzhen Statistical Bureau, *Shenzhen Statistical Yearbook*, 1992.

High-tech industrial activities initially appeared in computers and software, micro-electronics and its basic devices, new materials, and biological engineering. In 1991, eleven out of the nineteen newly approved, technologically advanced enterprises involved foreign investment.[9] There

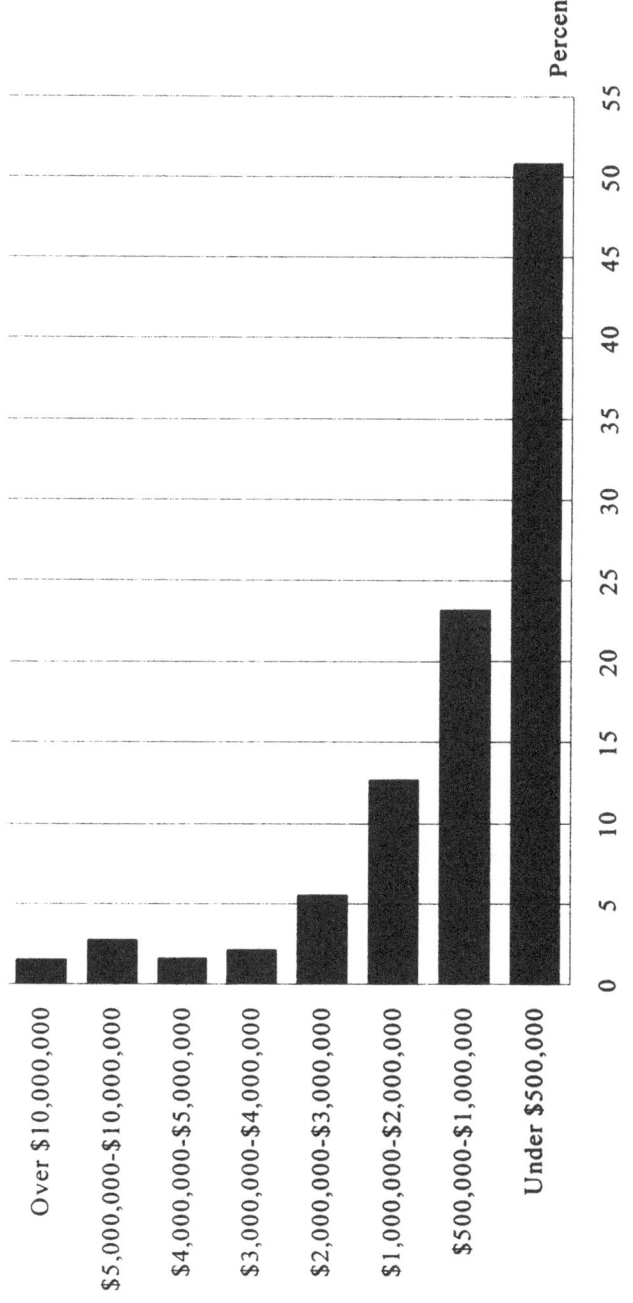

Figure 4.2 Size Distribution of Shenzhen's Foreign-Invested Enterprises, 1979-1990 (Cumulative)

Source: Shenzhen Bureau of Economic Development and Shenzhen Information Center, *Directory of Foreign-Invested Enterprises in Shenzhen*, 1991.

were also reports of some technology being further diffused to inland enterprises. For instance, in 1983, Shenzhen provided over 100 sets of modern instrument and equipment for non-SEZ areas.[10] But more often than not, such diffusion occurred through personnel transfers. After working for a few years in Shenzhen, some workers from inland areas would return home, bringing experience, skills, techniques, and market information. There they would set up enterprises that could further the development of the local economy.

The case of Joint Venture One is a good example of how technology transfer proceeded in some FIEs.[11] A flat glass manufacturer, it was one of the largest U.S. manufacturing joint ventures in China. The total amount of investment specified in the contract was US$100 million, but the initial registered investment was only US$20 million in the form of equity. The rest of the venture's funds came from a syndicated loan arranged by foreign banks. The venture ran a loss during the first three years. According to the current General Manager, who was involved in the initial negotiations, three major factors led to the losses: an unbalanced investment structure (heavy bank loans), lukewarm markets, and high production costs (including raw materials, technology and bonuses). In 1991, changes in the contract arrangement and management structure reduced losses substantially. The venture was profitable in 1992, with over 70 percent of products exported.

An immense amount of technology transfer occurred through this joint venture: the entire production process, marketing, and packaging. The U.S. partner qualified as the twentieth largest firm in Fortune's Global 500 chemicals group, with an even higher rank in the building materials group. It supplied all the technologies, and most of the critical raw materials were imported.[12] Over twenty patents were involved in the transfer, through licensing agreements and patent payments spanning ten years. With the advanced LB float glass technology, the venture produced flat glass of international standards, for the first time in China. The production line was highly automated and monitored around the clock by a computerized control room. The process included a proprietary technology for protecting glass surface from corrosion. The contract negotiations had discussed the issue of technology renovation, but without settling it. Basically, the joint venture would not have the right to obtain new technology beyond what was transferred according to the contract. Both sides fulfilled contract arrangements well, particularly in keeping the confidentiality of the transferred technology. There also was a management and training agreement. In the first few years, the U.S. partner stationed several expatriates in Shenzhen, including the first General Manager, to ensure the smooth transfer of technology and establishment of a management system.

U.S. personnel also occupied all key technical posts and were on site to help with the plant start-up.[13] They trained the Chinese management staff and carried out training whenever a new technology was transferred. Overall, the joint venture was one of the successes and became a show case. It was also by far the largest and most sophisticated glass producer in China.

The foregoing analysis of the technological content of foreign investment in Shenzhen shows that such investment was mostly concentrated in small, low-tech, labor-intensive, processing/assembly activities, and hence technology transfer was very limited. These trends were shaped primarily by the industrial structure of Hong Kong investment, which was the largest source. The investment pattern or structure of TNCs from other countries could explain the rest. Two additional factors hampered Shenzhen's promotion of technological transfer: the lack of an appropriate regulatory framework for technology transfer, and Shenzhen's low industrial capabilities.

Industrial Structure of Hong Kong Investment

As the largest source of investment, Hong Kong has significantly influenced the composition of foreign investment inflows to Shenzhen, particularly in manufacturing industries. With the exception of consumer electronics and chemicals, Hong Kong investment accounted for over 60 percent of FDI in the top ten foreign-invested manufacturing industries in Shenzhen (Figure 4.3). Specifically, over 96 percent of textiles & dyeing, 78 percent of metal products, 86 percent of rubber & plastics, 95 percent of garments, and 85 percent of electrical machinery joint ventures in Shenzhen were financed by Hong Kong investors. All of those industries were low-tech and labor-intensive, and four of them—including textiles & dyeing, metal products, garments, and rubber & plastics—were the top investment areas in by Hong Kong (see Table 2.5). Those four industries also were among the top six manufacturing industries (garments, textiles, electrical machinery, plastic products, metal products, and watches & clocks) in Hong Kong at the end of the 1970s, as measured by gross output value. Clearly, Hong Kong's industrial structure was the key factor shaping the technological content of Shenzhen's foreign investment.

Hong Kong began industrializing in the late 1950s, and to a large extent its rapid course of development was spurred by U.S. mass merchandisers, such as Sears Roebuck, J.C. Penney, Montgomery Ward, and other leading chain stores (see Henley and Nyaw, 1985). Because of their small domestic market and limited resource endowment, Hong Kong's

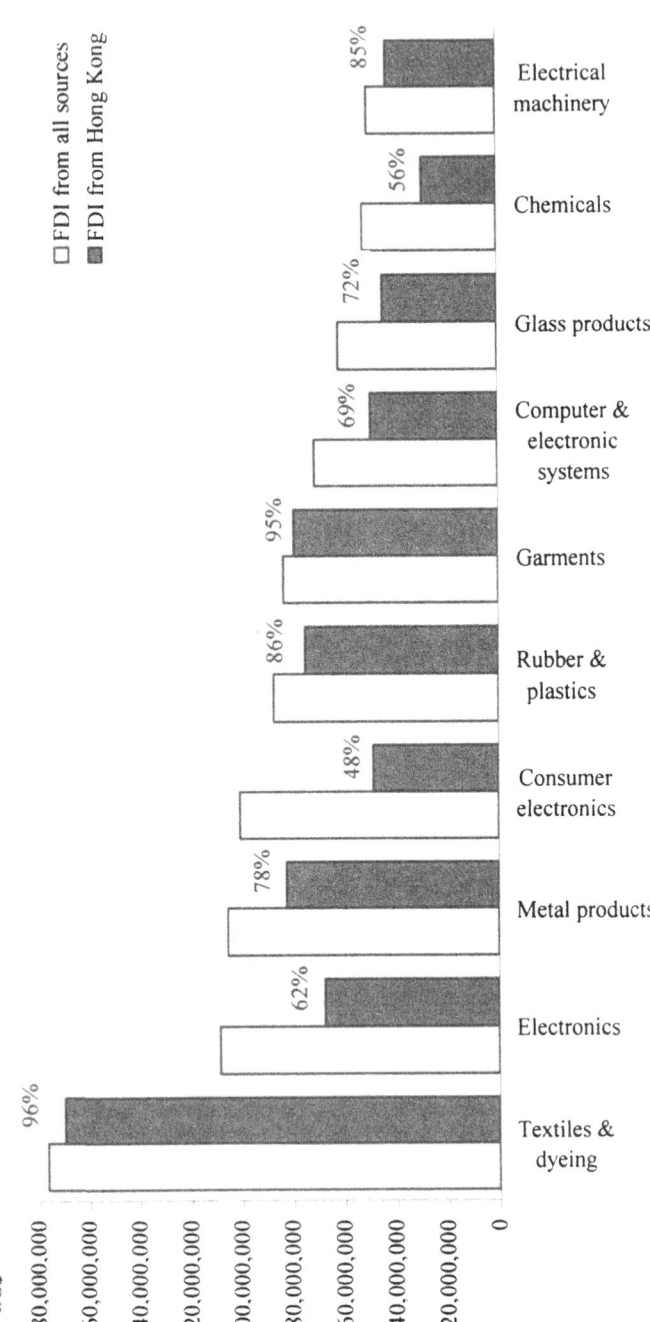

Figure 4.3 Hong Kong's Impact on Foreign Direct Investment (FDI) in Shenzhen's Manufacturing Industries, 1979-1990 (Cumulative)

Source: Shenzhen Bureau of Economic Development and Shenzhen Information Center, *Directory of Foreign-Invested Enterprises in Shenzhen*, 1991.

Technological Content of Foreign Investment 87

Table 4.4 Structure of Hong Kong's Manufacturing Sector, Selected Years, 1970-1995

Rank	Manufacturing industry	1970 Amount	1970 Percent	1980 Amount	1980 Percent	1985 Amount	1985 Percent	1990 Amount	1990 Percent	1995 Amount	1995 Percent
Employment (thousands)											
1	Clothing	158.0	28.8	275.8	30.9	292.8	34.5	251.7	34.5	111.9	29.0
2	Printing	18.4	3.3	26.4	3.0	30.4	3.6	37.5	5.1	44.8	11.6
3	Electronics	38.5	7.0	93.0	10.4	86.1	10.1	85.2	11.7	44.1	11.4
4	Textiles	77.1	14.0	88.8	10.0	65.9	7.8	68.6	9.4	28.2	7.3
5	Metal products	35.6	6.5	62.8	7.0	47.9	5.6	41.8	5.7	22.3	5.8
6	Food & beverages	13.7	2.5	22.4	2.5	21.2	2.5	23.4	3.2	21.1	5.5
7	Machinery	6.8	1.2	12.4	1.4	20.6	2.4	26.9	3.7	19.3	5.0
8	Plastics	71.0	12.9	86.3	9.7	84.7	10.0	53.1	7.3	16.0	4.1
9	Watches & clocks	9.8	1.8	49.5	5.5	36.7	4.3	27.2	3.7	12.1	3.1
10	Jewelry	2.6	0.5	10.9	1.2	13.4	1.6	17.5	2.4	11.2	2.9
Domestic exports (HK$ billion)											
1	Clothing	4.3	35.1	23.3	34.1	44.9	34.6	72.2	31.9	73.8	31.9
2	Electronics	1.1	8.7	13.4	19.7	27.0	20.8	58.6	25.9	64.3	27.7
3	Textiles	1.3	10.3	4.5	6.7	7.8	6.0	16.9	7.5	14.0	6.1
4	Watches & clocks	0.2	1.7	6.6	9.6	9.6	7.4	19.1	8.5	13.6	5.9
5	Chemicals	0.1	0.8	0.5	0.8	1.3	1.0	6.7	2.9	9.2	4.0
6	Jewelry	0.1	0.9	0.8	1.1	2.5	2.0	6.1	2.7	5.7	2.5
7	Machinery	0.03	0.2	0.4	0.6	1.3	1.0	4.0	1.8	5.5	2.4
8	Printing	0.09	0.7	0.7	1.1	1.7	1.3	3.6	1.6	5.1	2.2
9	Plastics	1.5	12.3	6.1	9.0	10.7	8.2	8.2	3.6	5.0	2.2
10	Metal products	0.3	2.8	2.0	3.0	2.9	2.3	4.5	2.0	4.7	2.0

Note: Percent denotes the percentage share of all manufacturing industries in each year. Ranking is by the 1995 amount.

Source: Hong Kong Government Industry Department, 1996.

manufacturers took the route of export processing early on, producing goods to others' designs and quality standards at minimum costs and maximum efficiency. Adopting a strategy of specializing in only a few of the several stages of the manufacturing process, they found a niche in the global structure of several labor-intensive industries by developing a high level of proficiency in the management of large batch and mass production technology. The strategy also was left largely in the hands of private enterprises since Hong Kong was deeply committed to a philosophy of "positive non-interventionism" (Nyaw and Chan, 1982, p.461). The role of government in industrial development was confined to providing an efficient infrastructure. By the 1970s, the combination of consistent economic policies of free enterprise and free trade, an industrious work force, a well-founded industrial infrastructure, an excellent network of world-wide transportation and communications, and a fast-growing export market had made Hong Kong a leading manufacturing export center.

Export orientation, however, led to concentration in a rather narrow range of industries, in which the factor resource endowment of the economy would have a comparative advantage. As a result, light and labor-intensive manufacturing industries, producing mainly consumer goods, continued to dominate Hong Kong's industrial sector. In 1977, the top six manufacturing industries in terms of gross output were all from the labor-intensive group, including garments, textiles, electrical machinery, plastic products, metal products, and watches & clocks. In 1979, the first five of those industries accounted for over 76 percent of Hong Kong's manufacturing employment (Nyaw and Chan, 1982). The textiles and garments (clothing) industries were Hong Kong's largest, together employing about 41 percent of the total manufacturing work force in 1980, and 36 percent in 1995 (see Table 4.4). They also were the dominant exporting industries, turning out between 38 and 45 percent of domestic exports during the period of 1975 to 1995. Electronics, as the second largest exporter and the third largest employer, held shares of about 20 percent of domestic exports and 10 percent of manufacturing employment on average. Towards the end of that period, the importance of electronics in both employment and domestic exports increased, but that of clothing and textiles steadily declined. Domestic exports then consisted almost entirely of manufactured goods, and the majority were low value-added products tailored to the lower end of markets and mainly from two industries—textiles and clothing, and electronics.

By the late 1970s and early 1980s, Hong Kong's competitiveness in the export markets for consumer goods was seriously challenged by several other developing countries in the region with lower costs, including

Thailand, Malaysia and Indonesia. The rising costs of labor and land in Hong Kong indicated that its export-led economy had reached a point where further growth could not depend solely on domestic factor inputs. Coincidentally, China then began its course of opening. This made Shenzhen, as well as south China, the perfect destination for Hong Kong's industrial relocation, and labor-intensive industries and/or low-end processing operations (including garments, textiles, electrical machinery, electronics, toys, plastics, and metal products) immediately made the move.[14]

The fact that domestic exports of producer goods from Hong Kong to China outstripped those of consumer goods reflected the increasingly important role of Hong Kong-based outward processing in the mainland. Between 1989 and 1994, over 75 percent of all exports from Hong Kong to China in several commodity groups (clocks & watches, garments, toys, and textiles) were related to outward processing in China (see Table 4.5), and most of these industries were, again, Hong Kong's top investment areas in Shenzhen. It was reported that by the early 1990s, most electronics and toy manufacturing had been relocated to China (FEER, 28 April 1994, p.68). While labor-intensive industries moved their production to Shenzhen, such technology- and knowledge-intensive stages as designing, testing and marketing, tended to be kept in Hong Kong. Moreover, the manufacturing that stayed in Hong Kong started moving decisively away from labor-intensive production into high value-added exportable products that could compete on quality.[15] Instead of expanding horizontally as in the past, Hong Kong manufacturing had to move vertically by raising skill levels and productivity.

Hong Kong's manufacturing industries were characterized by their many small and medium-sized firms, which was indirectly confirmed in Shenzhen by the fact that Hong Kong investment produced the smallest contract (US$0.7 million) among all major sources, and one well below Shenzhen's average.[16] By comparison, Japanese and Singapore investment resulted in contracts averaging US$3.0 and US$3.1 million. Hong Kong's small size had limited the amount of land available for industry and had precluded the development of large-scale or land-intensive industries. In 1975, firms with fewer than 50 workers constituted 91 percent of Hong Kong's total manufacturing establishments and provided about 37 percent of total manufacturing employment (see Table 4.6). About 7 percent of firms were medium-sized, and they employed over 30 percent of manufacturing workers. The remaining 2 percent were large-scale establishments, accounting for 33 percent of employment.

Table 4.5 Exports from Hong Kong to China for Outward Processing, by Commodity Group,[a] 1989-1994

Commodity group	1989	1990	1991	1992	1993	1994	1989-94	Share (percent)
Estimated value (HK$ billion)								
Textiles	23.1	28.0	35.6	43.7	44.3	51.8	226.4	29.6
Machinery & electrical equipment	10.4	11.5	13.9	20.6	24.0	28.2	108.6	14.2
Plastics	8.5	10.8	13.2	16.8	17.8	20.7	87.7	11.5
Audio & video products	9.5	11.2	11.7	12.7	16.4	20.6	82.0	10.7
Metal products	3.8	4.6	6.8	8.2	10.4	11.5	45.4	5.9
Clocks & watches	4.0	5.2	6.0	7.2	7.9	8.2	38.5	5.0
Garments	2.3	2.7	3.5	4.6	5.3	6.0	24.3	3.2
Toys	1.7	1.9	2.0	2.4	2.6	2.4	13.1	1.7
Others	13.5	16.1	21.2	25.5	31.6	31.8	139.7	18.2
Overall	76.9	91.9	113.9	141.6	160.2	181.2	765.7	100.0
Estimated proportion (percent)[b]								
Clocks & watches	96.2	97.1	97.2	98.1	98.6	98.2	97.6	n.a.
Garments	85.8	87.4	87.6	86.8	89.1	87.7	87.4	n.a.
Toys	87.5	89.9	86.2	87.5	88.8	83.5	87.2	n.a.
Textiles	74.1	77.4	78.2	82.7	81.8	78.4	78.8	n.a.
Plastics	68.1	75.7	64.8	67.6	67.0	62.3	67.6	n.a.
Audio & video products	69.1	75.2	69.9	64.6	56.0	57.1	65.3	n.a.
Metal products	44.6	52.7	53.7	40.8	40.4	42.5	45.8	n.a.
Machinery & electrical equipment	32.8	39.6	34.7	34.1	30.8	33.8	34.3	n.a.
Others	35.1	37.6	36.9	32.9	30.4	27.3	33.4	n.a.
Overall	53.0	58.8	55.5	52.4	47.9	47.7	52.6	n.a.

n.a. Not applicable.
a. Refers to the exportation of raw materials or semi-manufactures from or through Hong Kong to China for processing, with a contractual arrangement for subsequent re-importation of the processed goods into Hong Kong.
b. Indicates the share of estimated value of outward processing trade in the value of overall trade in each commodity group.

Source: Hong Kong Census and Statistics Department, "Trade Involving Outward Processing in China, 1989-1994," *Hong Kong Monthly Digest of Statistics*, June 1995.

This dominance of small-scale firms gradually increased throughout the 1980s, and by 1995 they accounted for close to 96 percent of manufacturing establishments and over half of manufacturing employment. Most of Hong Kong's small firms were family or individual businesses,

Table 4.6 Hong Kong's Manufacturing Establishments by Employment Size, Selected Years, 1975-1995

Employment size (persons engaged)	1975 Amount	1975 Percent	1980 Amount	1980 Percent	1985 Amount	1985 Percent	1990 Amount	1990 Percent	1995 Amount	1995 Percent
Number of establishments										
Small (1-49)	28,331	91.3	41,836	92.1	44,627	92.8	46,500	94.7	29,821	95.8
Medium (50-199)	2,219	7.2	3,006	6.6	2,920	6.1	2,188	4.5	1,101	3.5
Large (200 and over)	484	1.6	567	1.2	518	1.1	399	0.8	192	0.6
Total	31,034	100.0	45,409	100.0	48,065	100.0	49,087	100.0	31,114	100.0
Persons engaged (thousands)										
Small (1-49)	249.5	36.8	368.2	41.3	365.6	43.1	354.1	48.5	194.4	50.4
Medium (50-199)	205.4	30.3	267.7	30.0	259.8	30.6	205.0	28.1	98.3	25.5
Large (200 and over)	224.0	33.0	256.2	28.7	223.4	26.3	171.2	23.4	93.4	24.2
Total	678.9	100.0	892.1	100.0	848.9	100.0	730.2	100.0	386.1	100.0

Source: Hong Kong Government Industry Department, 1996.

often operating from premises in multi-story buildings, with start-up capital coming from personal or family savings and private borrowing. Many were devoted almost entirely to production, to the exclusion of marketing or research and development (R&D), a pattern made possible by Hong Kong's vibrant marketing network of trading companies and merchant houses with extensive experience in world markets.[17]

Hong Kong's technological capabilities were limited by the small size of the capital goods sector, whose development in turn was severely constrained by the territory's limited land and natural resources, as well as by the small size of firms.[18] Moreover, in accordance with its laissez-faire economic policy, the Hong Kong government never actively undertook industry-specific R&D activities or the development of strategic industries. As a result, by the 1980s, Hong Kong's technological development lagged well behind that of Taiwan and South Korea. Hong Kong firms rarely exported technology in the form of turnkey projects or licensing agreements, as their technology was relatively unsophisticated. Technology was transferred mostly through direct investment in the form of process, product, and software, including management, marketing and training. Hong Kong firms also were not usually innovators, and their technological development could be considered intermediate at best. Much of the machinery and equipment used in joint production or processing in Shenzhen was either imported from industrialized countries or taken from factories in industries being phased out in Hong Kong. Thus, technology transfer from Hong Kong to Shenzhen through industrial processing, while tangible, was of limited sophistication.

Some service investment from Hong Kong followed manufacturing industries to Shenzhen, in an attempt to retain established customers. These firms were mostly producer services, including banking, insurance, consulting, and marketing. This trend, too, reflected the changing structure of the Hong Kong economy. For many years, manufacturing had been both the territory's largest employer and its most important sector, but its dominant position was lost in the late 1980s. Now, with the tertiary sector accounting for almost 77 percent of output and 68 percent of employment, Hong Kong has become the most service-oriented economy in the world.[19] Yet the scope of such service investment in Shenzhen was limited because the service sector was not open for foreign investment until the late 1980s. Thus, only after 1986 did Shenzhen's foreign investment in banking & insurance begin to grow. Moreover, the growing income level in Shenzhen attracted Hong Kong investment in such consumer services as retail, catering, real estate, tourism, and construction, clearly shown by Hong

Kong investment's absolute dominance in Shenzhen's real estate and hotel sectors.

Investment Structure of Other Sources

Investment from sources other than Hong Kong also was limited to those of a low-tech nature because TNCs relocated three types of industrial production to Shenzhen: standard or automated production lines such as plastics, textiles, metal products, machinery, and certain electronics assembly; the most labor-intensive stages of some labor-intensive industries that had difficulty automating (e.g. sewing and cutting in the garment industry); and the labor-intensive stages of such capital-intensive industries as chemicals, and computer & electrical systems. In this respect Shenzhen was no different from other export-processing facilities in developing countries around the world, where textiles and garments, and electronics were the two dominant industries. One indication of the labor-intensive nature would be a lower capital intensity in these affiliates as compared to their parents' production. It was estimated that the capital intensity of the manufacturing affiliates in developing countries was only about 40 percent of that of affiliates in developed countries (see Lipsey, 1994). TNCs also tended to use small-scale operations for which only labor-intensive methods of production were available, or to operate in a labor-intensive way by adopting different technologies Many Hong Kong firms reported that their subsidiaries used technology different from that of the parent firms. Often the subsidiaries adopted a less complicated or modified version of the parents' technology (see Chen, 1984).

Over the past several decades, technological changes have led to the standardization of some products and production processes, and less use of skilled labor on the shop floor, as some or all of the production process has become automated. In other industries where automation was technically impossible or very difficult, the incentive to move to areas with low labor costs was even stronger. Since the share of labor costs in total production costs was high, the decentralization of production was largely motivated by labor costs and control problems (see Schoenberger, 1988). This could be seen in the sectoral distribution of FDI from Japan and the U.S. in Shenzhen: many of their top investment areas were such standard labor-intensive industries as electronics, metal products, plastics, textiles, and machinery (see Table 2.5).

Industrial relocation was aided by the feasibility of breaking down the production process into clearly separated stages of production, seen in such industries as garments, electronics, automobile, machinery, textiles, chemicals, and electrical engineering. The production process often could be divided into three hierarchical levels, with technology or knowledge-intensive engineering and technical functions at the top, an intermediate level of skilled production activities, and low-skilled and standardized production operations at the bottom. In the garment industry—a leading area of U.S. investment in Shenzhen—production could be conceptually divided into three stages: pre-assembly (designing, pattern grading and marking, and cutting), assembly (sewing), and post-assembly (finishing, inspection and packaging), each performed at a different level of skill and labor intensity. Functions performed by skilled labor, including design, pattern making and inspection, usually were kept at home bases. However, the sewing and finishing stages of production, which would use between 80 to 90 percent of the total labor, were relocated to far-flung countries with low-cost labor (see Frobel and others, 1980). The required skills for sewing (assembly), an activity for which automation has been virtually impossible, had not changed and could be learned quickly and without much difficulty.[20]

Similarly, such relatively capital-intensive industries as automobile, chemicals, and electrical engineering were able to relocate overseas the production stages that required more labor inputs.[21] The production stages requiring advanced technology and skilled labor, and sometimes proximity to the market, were again kept in the home countries. For example, in the semi-conductor industry, mask-making and wafer fabrication—the two high-technology processes—remained in developed countries.[22] In Shenzhen, that was the case with U.S. and Japanese investment in the chemical, and computer & electrical systems industries (Table 3-5). So, with the exception of a few resource-oriented industries—including nonferrous metal, glass products, and oil refining, the industries most invested in by Japan and the U.S. in Shenzhen had labor-intensive and low-tech production lines or stages. These production/activities also were low in value-added and tended not to have strong multiplier effects on other industrial sectors.

Since the majority of manufacturing activities was low-tech and labor-intensive, and used simple processing, little complex technology had to be transferred. Often, technology was already embedded in the parts to be assembled or processed. Even when some production did use complex technology, it by no means implied access to that technology by the joint venture in Shenzhen, since the technology was not developed on site. Technology transfer also was hampered by TNCs' tendency toward internalization as a means of overcoming transaction cost imperfections.

The most direct way for TNCs to prevent disclosure of technology and thereby earn monopoly profit was to internalize knowledge assets and apply that knowledge only to production under their control. So, TNCs were very cautious about how their technology, whether hardware or software, was transferred to their subsidiaries or joint ventures, and under what conditions. This caution would be particularly strong for a location where intellectual property laws and protection were not appropriately enforced (Miller and Rushing, 1990). Often TNCs would intentionally keep some part of a technology from being transferred, so that the subsidiaries could not have a complete mastery of the technology, as shown in the following case study.

Joint Venture Two was a manufacturing joint venture initiated by a Chinese technology research institute; a Chinese electronics company and the Shenzhen SEZ Development Corp. (10 percent share); and a U.S. electroplating manufacturer (45 percent share) that was one of the oldest and largest in the industry.[23] During the negotiations, several factors had to be considered, including the potential, standing and market prospects (particularly in China) of the product technology; channels for raw material supplies; and the possibility of export sales. The venture manufactured nearly two hundred electroplating additives and over ten phosphating materials. Unlike most joint ventures, which had to target export markets, over 80 percent of its products were sold domestically as import substitutes because of large demand. The contract had to be approved by the central government, since a much greater domestic market access was to be granted. The venture later opened three branch offices—in Shanghai, Tianjin, and Chengdu.

A major component of the contract involved technology transfer. Over 260 patents and more than 460 compositions were imported from the U.S. and Britain. The U.S. partner did not want to transfer the entire production line. First, much more investment would be required if the entire line was transferred. Second, the production cycle would be much longer. Third, a complete set of raw materials would have to be imported. Fourth, a skilled labor force would be needed, but was lacking at the time. More importantly, the U.S. partner worried about a potential hazard, that the Chinese partners would not be able to maintain confidentiality. The final arrangement was that the joint venture would take semi-processed products, which had been finished to between 50 and 80 percent by the U.S. parent company, and complete them. The advantages of doing so were fast returns and smaller equipment requirements. But the disadvantages were that the Chinese side developed little knowledge of the critical technology and became dependent on the foreign company. Some training of workers and staff in the application of technology took place; but it did not extend to management skills.

Up until 1990, the lack of large investment projects in advanced manufacturing industries had a direct, negative impact on technology transfer in Shenzhen. Investment from such developed countries as Japan and the U.S. lagged far behind Hong Kong investment, and it was concentrated in small, processing operations. In recent years, however, there has been a notable increase in direct investment from highly industrialized countries, and particularly since 1990 when investment from Japan and the U.S. increased rapidly. U.S. firms reportedly have been in the forefront of technology transfer, particularly in the fields of transportation equipment, communications devices, computers, and microelectronics. But even as investment in advanced industries rose and the willingness of TNCs to transfer technology increased, was Shenzhen ready to absorb and diffuse advanced technology? I believe that its ability to do so was seriously hindered by the lack of an appropriate regulatory framework for technology transfer, and by its underdeveloped industrial capabilities.

The Regulatory Framework for Technology Transfer

The regulatory framework for technology transfer in Shenzhen, as well as in China in general, was far from adequate. Most significantly, the protection of intellectual property rights was a key point of dispute between foreign investors and the Chinese government, since such protection would be central to effective technology transfer.[24] As the main sources of new technology, industrialized countries vigorously demanded adequate laws and their enforcement, in view of the rising costs of developing technology and the decreasing expectancy of the useful life of some technologies. The Chinese government, however, had long regarded technology as a public good. This especially was the case from 1949 to 1979 under a centralized research system, when state institutes and research sectors held complete control over the development of new technology. In Shenzhen, enterprises were allowed to use the already developed technology (see Watanabe, 1993), and often the Chinese partners of joint ventures would unilaterally disclose the imported technology to affiliated domestic enterprises. Moreover, state ministries allowed enterprises to do so in order to cut costs (FEER, 18 July 1991, p.62). Foreign investors complained that the Chinese did not respect intellectual property rights, while the Chinese would complain about the unwillingness of foreign investors to disclose the latest technology.

The Chinese government made some efforts to strengthen the laws in this area, issuing the 1982 Trademark Law, the 1985 Patent Law, and the 1990 Copyright Law (*Beijing Review*, 3-9 June 1991, p.31). But these laws were criticized by many westerners as incomplete. For instance, the Patent Law did not include pharmaceuticals and chemicals industries because of the interests of many domestic enterprises. It was amended only in 1993 after strong pressure from the U.S. (FEER, 18 July 1991, p.62; *The China Business Review*, July-August 1993, p.10). Even the pioneering Shenzhen Technology Regulation, released in 1984, contained no element of intellectual property rights protection. Moreover, the enforcement of these laws was inadequate because many Chinese officials held a sharply different viewpoint, and because of the lack of an effective monitoring mechanism.

Shenzhen also suffered from the lack of a formal system for managing the acquisition of foreign technology. In its absence, two unfavorable trends developed: confusion over the importance of advanced versus appropriate technology, and a bias toward transfer of hardware rather than software (skills and training). Throughout the 1980s, the Chinese government repeatedly stressed that new and advanced technology would be the emphasis for technology transfer (see Simon, 1992). It was sensible, on the one hand, that China was trying to learn from the best of the west to boost its own research capacities and improve the quality of export products. On the other hand, in many cases advanced technology was not the only solution. The importance of appropriate technology has not registered in the minds of many Chinese officials. Neither has the importance of attempting to maximize benefits and minimize costs when making investment decisions.

In addition, the indispensable balance between hardware and software acquisitions was inadequately understood. A great deal of emphasis was placed on importing complete plants, production lines, machinery, and equipment; but not enough was placed on know-how, management skills, and training. Without the acquisition of software along with hardware, the effectiveness of the transferred technology could be markedly reduced. Many technology transfer agreements in Shenzhen were one-time transactions, and foreign investors were not obligated to update the technology. Training, a vital element of technology absorption, often was absent throughout the Chinese system. In some enterprises, no formal training took place; in others, the depth of training was so limited as to preclude long-term follow-up through redevelopment.

Moreover, technology import activities were uncoordinated and fragmented in Shenzhen. Instead of sharing technology across enterprises, the same kind of technology transferred by one enterprise also might be imported by another. Take the example of floppy disk manufacturing. By 1993 there had already been over seventy enterprises in Shenzhen engaged in such production, using imported assembly lines. But more companies were still being set up because floppy disk manufacturing appeared quite profitable due to its relatively high value-added and large market demand (personal interviews). What resulted was a great deal of duplication and, consequently, waste of foreign exchange and sometimes under-utilization of production capacity. In addition, no explicit link was made between economic development priorities and guidelines for technology transfer. No organization seemed to have the authority for overall planning for technology importation. The end result was that some sectors that were in desperate need of technological upgrading, such as energy, transportation, and communications, barely received the necessary technology. Meanwhile, such consumer goods industries as color TV and refrigerator manufacturing imported numerous production lines, which resulted in an over-supply.

Shenzhen's Industrial Capabilities

Shenzhen started from an initial manufacturing capacity well below that of most of the fourteen coastal open cities, particularly Shanghai, Tianjin and Dalian. By the late 1970s, these cities had already developed a full range of industrial activities, from capital goods or heavy industries to light industries. When the Shenzhen SEZ was first established, it was literally a farming village. The area had about two hundred small factories producing small-scale farming tools, hardware, and some daily consumer goods (see Tang, 1990). Despite the rapid industrial growth in the 1980s, Shenzhen turned into what Hong Kong was in the 1970s: a zone specialized in a few stages of the manufacturing process, characterized by small and medium-scale enterprises, and dominated by such labor-intensive light industries as electronics, machinery, garments, and textiles. In 1991, small-scale enterprises produced over 53 percent of Shenzhen's industrial output, and medium-size ones over 18 percent. The top manufacturing industries in terms of output were electronics (about 41 percent), machinery (over 12 percent), garments (over 6 percent), and textiles (about 5 percent), which together accounted for about two-thirds of Shenzhen's 1991 industrial output.[25] In Shenzhen's formative years, its success depended on investment from Hong Kong; but, in turn Shenzhen was not able to attract investment from the more sophisticated industries of developed countries.[26]

Shenzhen also was characterized by the lack of efficient industrial support facilities, such as skilled workers and engineers, and local supplies and services. It was reported that only two industrial engineers were working in the entire city when the Shenzhen SEZ was first established (People's Daily, 10 September 1991). At the county level, there were only four research institutes, which specialized in agriculture, forestry, agrimachinery and fishing, and had fewer than thirty research staff members. Although Shenzhen enjoyed a preferential status in recruiting workers and engineers from all over the country, it nevertheless often ran into difficulty getting qualified technical personnel because of restrictions stemming from the household registration system and resistance from enterprises in inland areas. Even when workers with appropriate skills were obtained, some were lured away by the seemingly profitable trading activities in Shenzhen. Many industrial enterprises also found it hard to replace lost personnel promptly because of the difficulty in providing housing, and obtaining household registration and employment quotas.[27] Another disadvantage of Shenzhen was its small capital goods sector, and hence its dependence on inland areas for many raw and intermediate materials. Resources for any large-scale industrial development, particularly heavy industries, were very limited. This shortage was in a sharp contrast to the cities of Shanghai, Tianjin and Dalian, all located in regions endowed with natural resources and industrial supplies. Since Shenzhen did not have a large industrial base and capital goods sector, the need for technological upgrading was limited.

The low level of manufacturing capacity and the lack of support systems in Shenzhen can best be illustrated by its inability to attract foreign investment to the automobile industry. Transport industries, particularly the auto industry, have been considered one of the leading sectors in many economies, having the most significant linkages, setting the technological pace, and generating the most employment.[28] The growth of such industries could provide a source for technical progress and increased productivity in other core industries such as basic metals, engineering, chemicals, and electronic components. However, cheap and semi-skilled labor has never had as important a role in these industries as in garments and electronics production. Instead, productivity, organization and quality would be the major considerations in auto production and assembly (see Mody and Wheeler, 1990). The Shenzhen government apparently recognized the importance of auto manufacturing in boosting its industrial capabilities and aimed to promote related industries by establishing an auto manufacturing center. In its plan, auto manufacturing would become one of Shenzhen's pillar industries by the year 2000, accounting for 10 percent of the total industrial output. But up until the early 1990s, direct investment in transport industries was confined to several maintenance and repair shops, and a few component manufacturers. It would take a long time to build a competitive auto industry from scratch because of the low level of industrial capability and the lack of a sophisticated component industry in Shenzhen.

The revealed comparative advantage (RCA) of Shenzhen remained in low-tech, labor-intensive manufacturing industries, such as electronics, textiles, and garments. This was much more similar to Hong Kong than to some of the major industrial centers in the country. China as a whole also displayed a similar pattern in exports, as shown by the changes in its RCA in the 1980s.[29] In 1989/90, China had an aggregate RCA index of only 0.24 in capital-intensive items, compared to 0.41 in 1979/80. Many of the export products that had high individual RCAs were actually cross-classified as natural resource-based (see World Bank, 1994a, Annex 7.2). Therefore, for the near term, major export and investment opportunities in Shenzhen and China would be mainly in labor-intensive products. China has apparently followed the route taken by South Korea and Taiwan, building an economy by exporting cheap and labor-intensive products and gradually introducing more sophisticated products. This route would be feasible as long as labor costs could be kept low. Otherwise, productivity would need to compensate for rising labor costs.

Moreover, the absorptive capacity of Shenzhen remained low in terms of the skill levels of the work force, R&D facilities, and institutional infrastructure. The general level of education of production workers was comparable to that of other developing countries at a similar stage of development. Some foreign investors admitted that the Chinese had an inherent capacity to learn and a tradition of hard work (personal interviews). What often made these investors uneasy was the job definition held by Chinese workers, who tended to remain narrow in their focus and to lack the initiative found in workers of many industrialized countries. Shenzhen also did not have strong R&D facilities, largely because it had been developed from a greenfield, with little prior industrial base. It lacked not only a pool of qualified technical personnel, but also the established research institutions or universities capable of undertaking technological innovation and redevelopment. Often, technologically advanced enterprises in Shenzhen had to look for R&D partners in inland research institutions to develop new products. The experience of Joint Venture Three described below demonstrates the importance of a capacity for technological innovation and redevelopment, which many joint ventures did not have. Shenzhen's institutional infrastructure—training institutes, consulting services, advisory centers, financial services, and legal services—also was far from adequate. For instance, it was not until recently that the Shenzhen

Bureau of Science and Technology started to realize the importance of technical consultation and allowed the Association of Science and Technology to offer such services to the public (personal interview with the Chairman of the Association).

Joint Venture Three was initiated by a Singapore computer manufacturer, a Chinese microelectronics company, and Shenzhen Science & Technology Industry Park Corp.[30] Engaging in the production of peripheral equipment for microcomputers, the joint venture targeted floppy disk drives (FDDs) as the main product. Investment from the Singapore company included purchases of equipment and introduction of products. Both process and product technologies were transferred to the venture without service fees. Three production lines were introduced: FDD, power supply for PC/AT, and printed circuit board assembly (PCBA).[31] Production started in June 1986, and the venture employed about 140 people. The cumulated profit for the first three years (1987-1989) was over US$1 million. The joint venture sold most of its FDDs (over 90 percent) to the Singapore company and then to export markets, the largest being the U.S. It filled a gap in the production of FDDs domestically, but was less competitive in international markets, where the major competitor was Japan.

The venture survived a major market shift because it was able to develop some new products. The initial production of FDDs operated very smoothly. Soon the enterprise was doing well enough that the Singapore company removed its personnel and the venture was on its own. Then, markets for FDDs soured in 1989. While the Singapore investor failed to introduce any new products after 1989, the venture began to develop its own products, including game machines, computer shelter disks, and floppy disks (assembly only). As a result, the joint venture agreement became essentially a marketing partnership. The venture's own product—game machines—scored first in production and export volume in China. It sold products in three ways: direct sales to the U.S., Indonesia, and Australia; domestic sales; and indirect sales through the Singapore company. According to its management chief, in order for a joint venture to be successful, the venture should first take advantage of foreign technology to catch up with international standards and quality. Then, the Chinese partner must redevelop the transferred technologies or develop new ones so that reliance on the foreign investor is limited. This case could, in fact, be a role model for many joint ventures in promoting technology transfer.

Summary

A major trend in Shenzhen during the study period has been a high concentration of direct investment in labor-intensive, low-tech manufacturing industries and simple assembly/processing operations, including textiles & dyeing, electronics, metal products, consumer electronics, rubber & plastics, garments, and machinery. Among them, textiles and garments, and electronics drew the most investment, and electronics also produced the largest output value. Most of these industries showed very low net output ratios, indicating a low level of value-added. There was a significant rise in the level of investment in such service sectors as banking & insurance after 1990. As foreign investment was mostly confined to low-tech, small projects, technology transfer was very limited, although there were some successful cases.

The proximity to Hong Kong has significantly biased the technological content of foreign investment inflows to Shenzhen. As the single largest source of investment, Hong Kong has dominated all but two of the top ten manufacturing industries in Shenzhen receiving foreign investment. Hong Kong investment predominated in those industries that had been important in Hong Kong; the five Shenzhen manufacturing industries that felt the greatest impact of Hong Kong investment were the same industries that had been the top producers and employers in Hong Kong. The causal relationship here is very convincing: Shenzhen's FIEs, much like Hong Kong firms a decade earlier, came in time both to specialize in a few stages of the manufacturing process and to be dominated by low-tech and labor-intensive light industries. Limited by the small size both of the capital goods sector and of the majority of its enterprises, Hong Kong's technological capabilities were lagging behind other Asian NICs. As a result, the technology transferred through industrial relocation to Shenzhen tended to be low in sophistication. Most production technology was already embedded in the parts or components to be assembled. Some Hong Kong firms also used less complicated versions of their technology in joint ventures in Shenzhen.

Resembling similar export processing facilities around the world, Shenzhen's investment from other sources has been concentrated in three low-tech types: standard or automated production lines such as plastics, textiles, metal products, machinery, and certain electronics assembly; the most labor-intensive stages of labor-intensive industries that are difficult to automate, such as sewing and cutting in the garment industry; and labor-intensive stages in such capital-intensive industries as chemicals, and computer & electrical systems. As a result, little complex technology needed to be transferred. The transfer of advanced technology also was limited by the strong tendency of TNCs to internalize knowledge assets. Often they would intentionally keep some part of a technology from being transferred. This was clearly the case with Joint Venture Two, which involved the transfer of technology for electroplating production by a U.S. firm. On the whole, the growth of foreign investment in Shenzhen did not result in meaningful technology transfer.

Moreover, the goal of using FDI to promote technology transfer has been undermined by the lack of an effective regulatory framework and by Shenzhen's underdeveloped industrial capabilities. TNCs from industrialized countries often demanded laws covering the protection of intellectual proper rights and their enforcement, which neither Shenzhen nor China as a whole provided. Even the pioneering Shenzhen Technology Regulation, released in 1984, had no such provisions. As a result, firms interested in transferring some advanced technology to their subsidiaries in Shenzhen were very cautious as to how technology was transferred and under what conditions. Shenzhen also suffered from the lack of a formal system for managing technology acquisitions. It was not quite ready to absorb and diffuse advanced technology because of its underdeveloped industrial capabilities—the aggregate of its manufacturing capacity, supporting systems, and absorptive capacity. In particular, it lacked a pool of qualified technical personnel and established research institutions or universities capable of undertaking technological innovation and redevelopment.

Shenzhen's future course is to attract more investment in advanced manufacturing industries and operations, such as auto production, and to attract more investment from highly industrialized countries, such as Japan and the U.S. Recently, some researchers at the municipal government have proposed that heavy and processing industries should be moved out, and Shenzhen should cultivate its competitive edge in such industries as electronics, biological engineering, and refined chemicals.[32] Any such efforts should not undermine existing gains, mainly from Hong Kong investment. Although Hong Kong firms are not themselves innovators in technology, their technology may nevertheless be appropriate for China. Since advanced technology is not necessarily the only solution, Shenzhen needs to recognize the importance of using appropriate technology.

In recent years, technological innovations in developed countries have increased the technological content of some mature manufacturing production processes. Many of these innovations, such as robotics and artificial intelligence, are labor-saving. They also are changing the structure of production systems and patterns of sourcing for goods and labor since they lead to reductions in production costs, particularly those of the labor component. The implications of these technological innovations are twofold. First, it is possible for some industries to reorganize production at home without relocating overseas.[33] Second, developing countries with skilled labor forces, conducive supporting services, and adequate infrastructure will become more attractive to foreign investors from technologically advanced industries. On the whole, technological changes appear to reduce the comparative advantage held by many developing countries in low-cost labor.

Facing this new trend, Shenzhen still has at least two locational advantages over other cities in China that possess greater industrial capabilities: (1) its proximity to Hong Kong, which enables many investors to use high-quality producer services there; and (2) its policy openness, which has created a more efficient business environment. But Shenzhen cannot play these two cards for very long. As China develops its national transportation networks and gradually adopts an overall liberal investment regime, other cities will catch up. Therefore, raising the level of Shenzhen's industrial capabilities will be critical if Shenzhen wants to remain competitive and attract more high-tech investment. For some labor-intensive and low-end industries, notably garments and electronic manufacturing, Shenzhen does offer the potential for upgrading, which should be exhausted before it moves on to other industries.

5 Export Performance and Domestic Linkages

Foreign investment has been a major source of the capital behind Shenzhen's growth. By 1994, there were about 11,200 FIEs registered.[1] These enterprises have been the building blocks of Shenzhen's economy, and their performance has significantly affected Shenzhen's overall performance. After an extensive debate in the early 1980s, it was made clear in the work conference of 1985 that Shenzhen should develop an externally oriented economy, and at the same time provide demonstration effects for and establish linkages with inland areas. Three major criteria were set for measuring the external orientation:

1. Investment sources should be primarily external, reaching at least 50 percent of total industrial investment;
2. Products should be sold mainly abroad, reaching at least 70 percent of the total value of commodity; and
3. There should be a favorable balance in foreign trade (Liu, 1992, p.11).

FIEs have been expected to lead Shenzhen's effort to fulfill one of its original goals: to promote exports and, ultimately, increase foreign exchange earnings. At the same time, these enterprises have been encouraged to create linkages with inland enterprises and to source their production inputs domestically. To encourage exports, Shenzhen has offered more attractive incentives to export-oriented enterprises, those producing solely for export or import substitution and having a positive foreign exchange balance. Such incentives include extended tax breaks, and priority in obtaining utility supplies and receiving short-term bank loans. Another effective way to encourage exports has been by requiring that FIEs maintain a foreign exchange balance. Because of the inconvertibility of the Chinese currency prior to 1997, domestic sales could not meet the needs of these enterprises for foreign currency with which to import production inputs. Therefore, until 1997, most of them would have had to export their products to earn foreign exchange. Have Shenzhen and its FIEs, in particular, performed satisfactorily in export promotion? Have such enterprises at the same time created extensive domestic linkages with inland areas? If not, why? These are the questions this chapter attempts to answer.

Trends

Shenzhen's export performance could best be considered mixed. Gross exports grew steadily, but net exports were not as substantial. Total exports between 1979 and 1985 totaled only US$0.95 billion. After 1986, annual exports grew steadily from US$0.73 billion to US$5.10 billion in 1992, and to US$18.31 billion in 1994 (see Table 5.1). The bulk of the exports were contributed by the industry sector, whose share averaged over 78 percent, and which was growing steadily over time. Shenzhen was able to maintain a positive trade balance after 1987, whereas the nation as a whole did not achieve this until 1990.[2] On average, Shenzhen contributed 4.1 percent to the nation's exports between 1986 and 1991. In 1993, Shenzhen became China's largest exporting city, for the first time surpassing even Shanghai, which had continued to dominate exports (FBIS-CHI-94009, 13 January 1994, p.73).

Compared to other industrial enterprises in Shenzhen, foreign-invested industrial enterprises turned out a better export performance. Between 1986 and 1991, about 77 percent of all industrial exports were contributed by foreign enterprises (see Table 5.2). The dominance of these enterprises in industrial exports was much more significant than their share of output value (about 64 percent). An average of about 70 percent of their output was exported, on a par with the goal of 70 percent and significantly higher than the Shenzhen average. State enterprises had a very disappointing performance, exporting only 23.7 percent of their output value. The export performance of foreign-invested industrial enterprises also varied with the sources of investment. In 1990, industrial enterprises with Japanese investment had the highest ratio of exports to output value—84.2 percent. They were followed by industrial enterprises with investment from the U.S.—80.9 percent, Taiwan—79.7 percent, and Hong Kong—75.3 percent (Shenzhen Municipal Government, 1991b).

Since foreign exchange earnings are the real goal of export promotion, net exports is a much more appropriate indicator than gross exports. Shenzhen was not successful in producing a large quantity of net exports, and FIEs in particular had low net export ratios. In contrast to a total of US$17.70 billion exports between 1986 and 1992, Shenzhen's net exports only amounted to not quite US$4.39 billion. This represented a 24.8 percent net export ratio, or the net foreign exchange earnings derived from gross exports (see Table 5.1). Shenzhen's performance in this respect did not compare well with successful EPZs elsewhere in Asia. EPZs in Taiwan, South Korea and Indonesia had net export ratios of over 45 percent in the 1980s (Amirahmadi and Wu, 1995). In 1994, Shenzhen's net exports were only 9.0 percent of total exports.

Net exports in Shenzhen were drastically reduced by large imports during the same period. About US$13.31 billion worth of goods were imported to Shenzhen between 1986 and 1992 (see Table 5.1). According to customs statistics, each year since 1984, between 70 to 80 percent of all imports to Shenzhen were reported to be equipment, and raw and intermediate materials for production. Major import items included electronics components and parts, metals and minerals, instruments, petrochemicals, machinery, wool, auxiliary materials for garments and textiles, and complete plants.[3] The low net export ratio also may suggest that Shenzhen served more or less an import processing function for the large domestic market.

Nonetheless, Shenzhen did see the formation of some leading export industries, products, and enterprises. For instance, in 1989, several manufacturing industries exported more than 75 percent of their output value, including garments, textiles, leather products, entertainment and sporting goods, rubber products, arts and crafts, wood products, and paper products (Tang, 1990). All of these industrial activities were labor-intensive, and some were simple processing/assembly. Therefore, the role of such assembly activities in promoting exports should not be underestimated. In the early 1980s, such activities were the mainstream in Shenzhen and contributed to the marked rise of manufactured exports.[4] Major export products were garments, plastics, color TVs, bicycles, cotton yarn, fabrics, telephones, and stereos. Exports of those industries with higher levels of capital and technology, such as chemicals, oil refining, and communications devices, were less than 70 percent of their output value. Several manufacturing industries with large foreign investment, including electronics, metal products, and consumer electronics, produced more for domestic sales; less than 70 percent of their output was exported. The case of the electronics industry is particularly illustrative. Only about a third of its output value was exported in the late 1980s, and it was the major producer of color TVs, tape recorders, stereos, and calculators for the domestic market (X. Chen, 1993).

FIEs dominated the list of industrial enterprises with exports over US$5 million, which were considered the leading export enterprises. These included Guangming Overseas Electronics Co., Sanyo Electric (Shekou) Ltd., Huaqiang Sanyo Electronics Co., Huafa Electronics Co., Shenzhen

Table 5.1 Shenzhen's Export Performance, 1986-1994
(billions of U.S. dollars, unless otherwise noted)

	1986	1987	1988	1989	1990	1991	1992	1986-92	1993	1994
Exports										
Shenzhen total	0.73	1.41	1.85	2.17	3.00	3.45	5.10	17.70	5.89	18.31
Foreign-invested enterprises	0.26	0.51	0.56	1.01	1.66	1.87	3.01	8.88	3.05	8.60
(as percentage of Shenzhen total)	35.6%	35.9%	30.1%	46.6%	55.5%	54.2%	59.0%	50.1%	51.8%	47.0%
Local exports	0.51	0.82	0.98	1.37	2.13	2.35	3.54	11.71	—	—
(as percentage of Shenzhen total)	70.3%	58.1%	52.9%	63.1%	71.2%	68.3%	69.4%	66.1%	n.a.	n.a.
Industrial exports	0.44	1.03	1.28	1.60	2.46	2.80	4.35	13.95	—	—
(as percentage of Shenzhen total)	60.1%	73.0%	69.2%	73.4%	82.0%	81.3%	85.3%	78.8%	n.a.	n.a.
Imports										
Shenzhen total	1.12	1.14	1.59	1.58	2.48	2.52	2.88	13.31	3.14	16.67
Foreign-invested enterprises	0.64	0.51	0.53	0.87	1.83	1.63	1.81	7.82	—	—
(as percentage of Shenzhen total)	57.4%	44.6%	33.1%	55.4%	74.0%	64.6%	62.8%	58.8%	n.a.	n.a.
Net exports										
Shenzhen total	-0.40	0.27	0.26	0.60	0.52	0.92	2.22	4.39	2.75	1.64
Foreign-invested enterprises	-0.39	0.00	0.03	0.14	-0.17	0.24	1.20	1.05	n.a.	n.a.
Net exports as percentage of exports										
Shenzhen average	-54.6%	19.0%	13.9%	27.4%	17.4%	26.8%	43.5%	24.8%	46.7%	9.0%
Foreign-invested enterprises	-149.5%	-0.8%	5.3%	13.8%	-10.2%	12.9%	39.9%	11.8%	n.a.	n.a.

n.a. Not applicable.
— Not available.

Source: Shenzhen Statistical Bureau, *Shenzhen Socio-Economic Statistics*, 1986-1990; *Shenzhen Statistical Yearbook*, 1992; Ministry of Foreign Economic Relations and Trade, *Almanac*, 1993 to 1995; State Statistical Bureau, *China Statistical Yearbook*, 1992.

Table 5.2 Export Performance of Shenzhen's Industrial Enterprises, 1986-1991

	1986	1987	1988	1989	1990	1991*	1986-91
Magnitude (1980 constant prices, millions of yuan)							
State enterprises	171.6	407.8	740.7	1284.9	1422.3	1531.5	5558.7
Collective enterprises	199.2	318.2	518.1	691.7	797.7	887.4	3412.3
Joint enterprises (state with collective)	7.0	11.5	14.8	21.6	20.1	112.7	187.7
Foreign-invested enterprises	1441.2	2332.2	3477.9	4801.7	8022.5	10523.5	30598.9
Shenzhen total	1818.8	3069.7	4751.4	6799.9	10262.7	13055.2	39757.6
Share in Shenzhen total (percent)							
State enterprises	9.4	13.3	15.6	18.9	13.9	11.7	14.0
Collective enterprises	10.9	10.4	10.9	10.2	7.8	6.8	8.6
Joint enterprises (state with collective)	0.4	0.4	0.3	0.3	0.2	0.9	0.5
Foreign-invested enterprises	79.2	76.0	73.2	70.6	78.2	80.6	77.0
Share of industrial exports in gross output (percent)							
State enterprises	17.6	25.1	27.4	34.9	33.1	27.5	29.5
Collective enterprises	65.4	72.1	73.6	73.3	77.3	77.0	74.6
Joint enterprises (state with collective)	33.3	39.3	38.7	14.6	19.2	66.5	36.8
Foreign-invested enterprises	63.6	63.6	64.0	69.8	75.0	71.2	70.0
Shenzhen average	51.0	53.3	53.5	58.4	63.6	60.2	58.8

* The 1991 deflator based on 1980 constant prices was calculated by the author, using the 1990 deflator based on 1980 constant prices and the 1991 deflator based on 1990 constant prices.

Source: Shenzhen Statistical Bureau, *Shenzhen Socio-Economic Statistics*, 1986-1990; *Shenzhen Statistical Yearbook*, 1992.

China Bicycles Co. Ltd., Konka Electronics Co., and Zhongguan Textiles & Dyeing Co. In 1992, Shenzhen China Bicycles Co. Ltd. and Konka Electronics Co. were awarded the second and third prize in the Fifth National Appraisal of Foreign-Invested Industrial Enterprises (SSZD, 6 May 1992). In 1993, three foreign-invested industrial enterprises from Shenzhen—Huaqiang Sanyo Electronics Corp. Ltd., Shenzhen China Bicycles Co. Ltd., and Yexin Technology (Shenzhen) Corp. Ltd.—were the top three on the list of the ten largest FIEs in China in terms of exports and foreign exchange earnings (People's Daily, 24 June 1994). Shenzhen China Bicycles Co. Ltd. alone accounted for one-third of the nation's total bicycle exports in the 1980s and became the largest bicycle exporter in China.

The creation of linkages between Shenzhen and inland areas was directly affected by its export performance and import trends, in at least two aspects. First, the heavy reliance on imported raw and intermediate materials for production implied that very few inputs would be supplied from domestic sources, in the form of backward linkages. Second, Shenzhen served as an entrepôt for the rest of China. On the one hand, Shenzhen was a mid-point for re-exports from the rest of the country with at least over a third of its exports deriving from non-local sources (see Table 5.1).[5] Many enterprises were believed to be re-exporting products or materials purchased domestically, which often were not related to the actual business nature of the enterprises. The practice was particularly popular among those enterprises producing largely for domestic markets with imported raw or intermediate materials, but having to balance their own foreign exchange accounts as required by the central government.[6] On the other hand, because of the much simplified customs procedures there, foreign consumer goods moved through Shenzhen for sale in inland areas. Shenzhen also remained a hot spot throughout the 1980s for people from the inland areas purchasing foreign goods. Among imported consumer goods, the highest volume was found in air conditioners, automobile spare parts, clothing, foodstuff, and TV sets. Smuggling made the situation even worse, and it could not be captured by any official statistics.

Domestic linkages between Shenzhen's FIEs and inland areas can be classified into five types: backward purchases for production in Shenzhen, backward linkage in the form of subcontracting, direct sales on the domestic market, equity investment in inland enterprises, and repatriated wages of migrant workers. As shown in Table 5.1, FIEs largely relied on imported materials for their production; the proportion was as high as 80 percent. Consequently, purchases from domestic sources could not be substantial.[7] This has, in fact, been a common problem in similar zones in other countries. Even in South Korea, where the local economy was relatively developed, the domestic share of total raw materials used in Masan EPZ was only around 35 percent in 1985, which was largely accounted for by intra-EPZ purchases.[8] Backward linkages in the form of subcontracting also were limited in Shenzhen. FIEs established subcontracting to take advantage of the even cheaper labor available in the surrounding region. Only a few industries had a significant proportion of their production subcontracted, including machinery with 33 percent, textiles with 28 percent, and electronics with 18 percent (Wu, 1991). A major disadvantage for subcontractors was that they were not given the same kind of incentives and concessions as those enjoyed by FIEs, such as duty-free imports, tax breaks and holidays, and access to subsidized credits.

Theoretically, direct sales by FIEs on the domestic market were restricted, with the exception of those producing import substitutes. The 1979 Joint Venture Law barely mentioned the possibility of domestic sales, although such likelihood was legally approved in the 1980 SEZ Regulations. FIEs could sell a large proportion of their products domestically only if approved by the appropriate authorities and they met one of the following conditions: (1) they would provide equipment and technology that China urgently needed; (2) they would use large amounts of domestic materials and parts; (3) China was importing similar products in large amounts; or (4) their products would be either unique or superior in quality to those made domestically (Grub and Lin, 1985). In reality, however, sizable portions of FIEs' products in some industries were sold domestically because of the lack of competitiveness on the export market and the large domestic demand for such products. In addition, Shenzhen's industrial exports confronted barriers on the international market such as the technological gap with advanced foreign manufacturers, the already saturated export markets for many products, and an absence of China's own marketing channels. Again, the case of the electronics industry is a good example. Taking advantage of the short supply of certain electronics products on the domestic market, Shenzhen's electronics industry sold products domestically at very attractive prices. Shenzhen-made color TVs found their way into millions of Chinese households, and personal computers manufactured in Shenzhen were purchased by thousands of working units in the interior.

There were at least two positive aspects to the creation of domestic linkages: equity investment in inland enterprises and the repatriated wage income of migrant workers. Although large-scale investment in the interior did not start until the early 1990s, entrepreneurs from Shenzhen were always involved in the founding of cooperative projects with inland enterprises (*neilian*), as exemplified by the case of Joint Venture Four.

According to an official estimate, more than 500 projects were founded this way in other parts of China, with a total investment of five billion yuan by 1994 (FBIS-CHI-94128, 5 July 1994, p.89; *China Times Business Weekly*, No. 129, 19-25 June 1994, p.26). For instance, such major FIEs as Shenzhen China Bicycles Co. Ltd. and Konka Electronics Co. all invested inland in real estate, housing, and service sectors. There were three main reasons for such investment: (1) Shenzhen's FIEs had accumulated sufficient capital, (2) labor and land costs in Shenzhen had begun to rise, and (3) the large inland market potential appeared attractive. The expansion of Shenzhen's FIEs started first in the peripheral areas of Shenzhen, then moved into the Pearl River Delta region, and then spread out towards other large and medium-sized cities in south and east China.

The experience of Joint Venture Four is a good illustration of how some FIEs in Shenzhen established linkages with inland enterprises through equity investment and technology diffusion. The foreign partner was a small technological firm from the U.S.' Silicon Valley (with a 25 percent share). In the late 1980s, the joint venture purchased an entire automated production line from the U.S. for about US$2 million to produce floppy disks. The venture was profitable from the beginning, and all of its products were exported—50 percent to the U.S., 15 percent to Europe, 15 percent to Japan, and 20 percent to other countries. The top management staff were exceptionally visionary in their pursuit of technology, creating their own principle of "transfer, digestion, assimilation, redevelopment, and diffusion" (personal interview with the General Manager). The venture also was able to develop new products, relying on its technical staff of fifty, out of a total of one hundred and sixty employees.

The venture was very creative in establishing linkages with inland enterprises, an effort that did not receive the praise and reward it deserved from Shenzhen authorities. Several channels were used not only to build production partnerships, but also to diffuse technology: (1) investing in inland enterprises and holding shares based on technology, usually 10 to 15 percent; (2) providing technological services covering the entire process of establishing a factory, product selection, factory design, staff training, installment and trial production, and profiting through service fees; and (3) allowing other enterprises to use technology from the patent applications of several new products it developed. The venture invested in twelve inland enterprises based on technology shares. Compared to foreign firms, its services were competitive in terms of service fees and coverage. It also helped inland enterprises to sell on the export market.

Another form of inward investment from Shenzhen took the form of repatriation of the wage income of migrant workers, who originated outside of Shenzhen. An important component of domestic value-added in FIEs was wages, which were about 23 percent of the net value of industrial output (see Table 5.3). Between 1986 and 1991, these enterprises paid about 2.1 billion to their workers as wages. The total number of migrant workers from inland areas was estimated to be about twice as many as the permanent workers in Shenzhen.[9] Therefore, at least 1 billion yuan was received by migrant workers as wages, assuming that migrant workers were usually production workers and earned relatively less. A substantial proportion of such wages would be repatriated inland since the foremost reason migrant workers came to Shenzhen was to make a better living and support their families back home.

FIEs' export performance and creation of domestic linkages were less than satisfactory. Despite a steady growth in gross exports, when measured against government expectations, these enterprises were not successful in producing large net export gains. The creation of domestic linkages through backward purchases and subcontracting, which would have stimulated the domestic economy, was very limited. Such outcomes were determined largely by the same factor: the high import propensity of foreign firms. FIEs incurred a large volume of imports, leading to a drastic reduction in net exports and minimal backward purchases from the domestic market. Moreover, limited domestic supply capabilities were a major obstacle for enterprises willing to source domestically, as reflected in low product quality, trade barriers, and transport bottlenecks.

Import Propensity of FIEs

FIEs tended to have a higher import propensity than did domestic firms in Shenzhen. This was clearly demonstrated by FIEs' higher proportion of imports (see Table 5.1). Between 1986 and 1992, the imports of these enterprises accounted for an average 58.8 percent of Shenzhen's total imports, higher than their share for exports (50.1 percent). Net export ratios of these enterprises were significantly lower than Shenzhen's average. As a result, FIEs had a much less favorable trade balance and often ran deficits when Shenzhen as a whole had trade surpluses. It also was reported that, between 1981 and 1987, FIEs relied on imports to supply about 80 percent of their production inputs (Wu, 1990). So it is clear that the net export performance of these enterprises was seriously undermined by their high propensity for imports.

Table 5.3 Composition of Net Output Value of Shenzhen's Industrial Enterprises,[a] 1986-1991
(millions of yuan, unless otherwise noted)

	1986	1987	1988	1989	1990	1991	1986-91	Share (percent)
FIEs								
Profits & taxes	113.2	288.6	613.3	536.1	863.9	1362.8	3777.9	39.8
Wages	81.4	152.7	245.4	333.1	530.8	798.1	2141.4	22.6
Employee welfare	9.4	16.5	20.3	29.7	40.9	71.3	188.1	2.0
Interests	37.0	54.5	135.2	220.2	349.6	469.9	1266.3	13.4
Other payments	44.2	168.2	329.6	337.4	501.3	729.8	2110.5	22.3
Total	285.2	680.4	1343.8	1456.6	2286.4	3431.9	9484.3	100.0
WFOEs								
Profits & taxes	23.3	49.2	165.7	70.5	79.3	244.2	632.1	39.5
Wages	17.4	34.4	54.2	49.6	84.3	125.4	365.3	22.8
Employee welfare	0.5	1.8	1.2	18.0	2.6	2.8	26.9	1.7
Interests	10.8	2.2	16.2	30.2	48.0	61.2	168.6	10.5
Other payments	4.4	42.9	136.2	78.0	103.3	41.0	405.7	25.4
Total	56.4	130.5	373.5	246.2	317.5	474.6	1598.6	100.0
SOEs								
Profits & taxes	118.5	191.6	383.9	462.3	567.5	852.6	2576.5	55.5
Wages	47.5	66.2	98.5	146.8	180.6	294.5	834.1	18.0
Employee welfare	5.2	7.6	10.6	20.8	26.7	29.6	100.4	2.2
Interests	21.3	27.2	53.9	93.4	118.4	119.3	433.7	9.3
Other payments	31.4	51.0	81.2	122.3	167.9	243.1	696.9	15.0
Total	223.9	343.6	628.2	845.7	1061.0	1539.1	4641.6	100.0
All enterprises								
Profits & taxes	262.4	480.4	1085.2	1097.7	1533.4	2335.2	6794.4	42.6
Wages	192.6	220.2	526.7	718.3	1005.9	1448.1	4111.8	25.8
Employee welfare	17.8	24.3	37.2	59.3	78.5	111.5	328.6	2.1
Interests	62.6	81.9	195.8	323.8	480.1	599.8	1744.0	10.9
Other payments	86.1	220.0	427.9	499.9	709.9	1022.6	2966.4	18.6
Total	621.5	1026.7	2272.8	2699.0	3807.9	5517.3	15945.2	100.0

Note: FIEs, foreign-invested enterprises; WFOEs, wholly foreign-owned enterprises; SOEs, state-owned enterprises.
a. Includes only enterprises with independent accounting systems.

Source: Shenzhen Statistical Bureau, *Shenzhen Socio-Economic Statistics*, 1986-1990; *Shenzhen Statistical Yearbook*, 1992.

This high import propensity was directly related to the types of production these enterprises engaged in. As shown in the previous chapter, most were engaged in assembly and processing operations or activities, relying on components and materials sent by their foreign parent companies. Enterprises involved in industrial processing also had to respond more to the demands and technical specifications of outside markets, and had little affinity with the local market. Moreover, the high import propensity partly was determined by the behavior pattern of their parent companies, often TNCs. These TNCs tended to maintain their own sources of supply since a primary advantage of TNCs lay in their flexibility to transfer resources across borders through a globally maximizing network, and thus to obtain quality supplies at competitive prices. A common practice was the use of a "tie-in clause," which required subsidiaries to purchase intermediate parts and capital goods from the same parent TNCs that supplied the basic technology. Some even invested in downstream and/or upstream factories and formed a self-sufficient and self-sustained operation system, almost entirely independent of the local economy.

Another factor having a bearing on the import propensity of foreign enterprises was the trade policies of industrialized countries, which encouraged the use of their own raw materials and intermediate goods. Many of these countries levied no duties on the proportion of re-imported raw and intermediate materials that were incorporated in final goods produced overseas. This created additional incentives for FIEs to import materials from their home bases, and hence disincentives to establish local linkages. For example, the existing U.S. tariff code (806 and 807) has provided a tax incentive for U.S. components in assembled products to be re-imported duty free (see Wilson, 1991). Other industrialized countries have similar tariff codes.

As the single largest source, Hong Kong investment in industrial processing was found responsible for a significant portion of Shenzhen's import expansion. Statistics showed that Hong Kong's exports of raw materials and components to China from 1978 to 1986 grew 97 times, or at an average annual growth rate of 66 percent (Sung, 1991). Hong Kong, however, was known for its comparative advantage in producing finished consumer goods rather than raw materials and components. It was only after China opened certain areas, Shenzhen in particular, to foreign investment that domestic exports of producer goods from Hong Kong outstripped those of consumer goods. Between 1989 and 1994, a number of commodity groups ranked high in Hong Kong's exports to China for outward processing: textiles, machinery, plastics, metal products, and garments (see Table 4.5). Hong Kong's top investment areas in Shenzhen also fell in these categories. Exports of producer goods from Hong Kong were used mainly in Shenzhen's industrial processing plants.

Some major investment policies in Shenzhen further encouraged the import propensity of FIEs through a system of incentives, which also discouraged domestic linkages in the form of backward purchases. If FIEs produced for exports, they could import all materials, parts and equipment duty-free. These preferential policies also could be held partly responsible for Shenzhen's entrepôt function. The relative lack of institutional controls and the ease of importing consumer goods, for which there was excess demand elsewhere in China, all made it profitable for some enterprises to become traders of such goods. Moreover, since FIEs were not included in the State Plan, they had to locate their own suppliers if they were willing to use domestic sources. That task often proved difficult and time-consuming, and prices for out-of-plan supplies tended to be much higher. As a result, few such enterprises were willing to look for local suppliers.

The high import propensity of FIEs involved in export processing also was confirmed by evidence from other similar zones in Asia (see Healey, 1990; World Bank, 1992). Between 1972 and 1982, foreign enterprises in Malaysia's Penang EPZ imported, on average, 95 percent of raw materials and 85 percent of capital equipment. Foreign enterprises in Philippines' Bataan EPZ imported between 85 and 95 percent of raw materials. In fact, the trend there was towards increasing proportions of imports over time. A new zone in the Philippines—Mactan—imported almost all its production inputs in the first half of the 1980s. EPZs in South Korea and Taiwan may be the only exceptions. For instance, foreign enterprises in Korea's Masan EPZ reduced their import ratio from around 80 percent in the early 1970s to about 65 percent a decade later.

Domestic Supply Capabilities

The high import propensity of FIEs was a primary factor underlying their unsatisfactory performance in net exports and foreign exchange earnings. But regardless of this tendency, were these enterprises able to source quality and competitive supplies in China? The answer probably was "no". As many authors have asserted, the degree of domestic sourcing is determined foremost by the level of industrial development and capabilities of the host country (UNCTAD, 1993; World Bank, 1992; Wu, 1991). A well-developed industrial base with the capacity to produce goods and components that would be internationally competitive in terms of quality and price would encourage domestic linkages through backward purchases.

For instance, a survey of foreign firms in South Korea's EPZs showed that these firms were willing to buy locally if local inputs were competitive against overseas sources of supply and of sufficiently high quality (see UNIDO, 1988).

The possibility of domestic sourcing through backward purchases was significantly hampered by limited supply capabilities in China, reflected in low product quality, internal trade barriers, and transport bottlenecks. The latter two problems made supplies of available resources unreliable and often uncompetitive in price. To entice FIEs in Shenzhen to use domestic inputs, such inputs needed to be available at world market prices, and of a quality comparable to the international level. But prices of domestic supplies for foreign enterprises tended to be higher as a result of the two-track pricing system in China (planned prices for state enterprises and non-planned for others falling out of the State Plan). More importantly, the quality of local inputs, particularly intermediate goods, was often substandard and did not meet the technical specifications of FIEs. This was largely the legacy of China's centrally planned system, in which the emphasis on quantity over quality resulted in goods of mediocre quality (see Chu, 1987).

Internal trade barriers exacerbated the situation. In international trade, constraints on trade flows in goods usually take the form of tariff or non-tariff barriers. Although tariff barriers—in the form of codified levies on goods entering or leaving provinces—were rare in China's internal trade, there were many accounts of ad hoc charges, fees, and tolls on goods traded among provinces. The uncertainties created by the ad hoc nature of some of these charges and the difficulties they added to interprovincial transactions constituted, in fact, a form of non-tariff trade barrier. The absence of regulations on internal trade at the national level meant that decisions to limit trade made at provincial or local levels could not be easily overturned. It was not until late 1990 that the State Council issued a circular banning restrictions on interprovincial trade. For instance, it was reported that during the second half of the 1980s, a number of agroprocessing factories in coastal provinces suffered from severe underutilization of capacity because of raw material shortages. Raw materials from interior provinces were either diverted by provincial governments towards local processors or sold directly to overseas buyers. Even within Guangdong Province, known to be pro-trade, a series of checkpoints, barriers, local blockades, as well as fees and fines were reported.

In addition, China did not have sufficient capacity in its transport system to sustain a high level of growth, and transportation bottlenecks often were major impediments to the development of the internal market and availability of domestic supplies. Interprovincial transport of producer goods still depended largely on the railroad system, which had suffered from underinvestment due to limited revenues. China's rate of investment for transport, averaging around 1.3 percent of GNP, compared unfavorably with other developing countries' ratios of 2 to 3.8 percent of GNP (World Bank, 1994b). Although the density of the road network and inland waterways within Guangdong Province was higher than the national average, there was still a severe shortage of transport capacity. The mixed use of roads by motor vehicles, tractors, bicycles and pedestrians, without separation, further exacerbated the situation. Much of the technology used for road construction was of 1950s' vintage. For instance, the use of modern heavy trucks caused rapid deterioration of pavement as most roads were not constructed to specifications required for such loads. Given the problems presented by these transportation bottlenecks, a location with extensive transportation links, including land, sea and air access, would have a distinctive edge. Shenzhen was not in such a position. Its location at the southern tip of the country with mostly sea links made it less accessible from inland areas. The situation, however, improved substantially with the completion of the Hong Kong-funded Shenzhen-Guangzhou expressway and the Beijing-Kawloon railway in the early 1990s, which was funded by the central government.

Internal trade barriers and transport bottlenecks meant that even for available goods and materials manufactured in China, sourcing for FIEs often had to be external. The case of Joint Venture One, presented in Chapter 4, is illustrative. Most of the critical raw materials used in the production of flat glass in the venture were imported. Although six of the seven raw materials theoretically could be sourced in China, insufficient quality and uncertain deliveries made Chinese sources unreliable. So key ingredients had to be imported, and in any case were usually of a higher quality and more price-competitive. But importing them proved to be a costly problem for the venture in balancing its foreign exchange during the early years when its exports were low (personal interview with the current General Manager).

The location of Shenzhen in a region less endowed with industrial resources also impeded backward linkages with its surrounding areas. For political reasons, the SEZs needed to be at locations easily isolated from the vast inland; these zones were to experiment with drastically different policies than those in force elsewhere. This consideration had some unexpected negative consequences. Not only did the SEZ locales have small industrial bases, they also were surrounded by hinterlands less well endowed than those of major industrial nodes in the country, such as

Shanghai and Tianjin. A rich hinterland could provide investable resources for industries within the city, especially when production and trading links between hinterland and city were numerous and strong. For instance, Shanghai, with the most economically prosperous hinterland in China, was able to become the center of auto production in China. An important reason was that, with some effort, it was possible to source a wide range of components in the city and its hinterland (see Yusuf and Wu, 1997). Enterprises in Shanghai also were ahead of others in moving some production facilities out of the city and entering into subcontracting arrangements with manufacturers in the hinterland.

On the other hand, the Pearl River Delta in which three SEZs sit, was less endowed with industrial resources, though its growth record since the start of reforms was nothing less than phenomenal. The region had some of the richest agricultural land in China, which supported the cultivation of rice, sugar cane, and vegetables. But the region had built its modest manufacturing base only in the 1960s and 1970s, focusing on a narrow range of light industries including food processing, electronics, crafts, textiles, and paper-making. What it could provide Shenzhen was agricultural and food stuff, and construction materials (Phillips and Yeh, 1989). To source a wide range of industrial materials and components in the delta region often was difficult for such modern industries as automobile and computers. In fact, a large auto joint venture with the French car-maker Peugeot in the region was much less successful than the Volkswagen joint venture in Shanghai (see Yusuf and Wu, 1997). Peugeot finally closed the Guangzhou joint venture in the mid-1990s. Therefore, for FIEs in Shenzhen, the possibility of creating linkages with surrounding areas in the form of backward purchases and subcontracting was seriously hampered by the limited resource endowment and narrow industrial range of the region.

Summary

Shenzhen's export performance has been a mixed result. Gross exports appeared to be growing steadily and, in 1993, Shenzhen became China's leading city for exports. In particular, FIEs turned out a better export performance than did all other enterprises, contributing to about 77 percent of all industrial exports. An average of 70 percent of their output was exported, on a par with the goal set by the government. Measured in net exports or net foreign exchange earnings from gross exports, however, Shenzhen did not fare well. Between 1986 and 1992, its net export ratio averaged only about 24.8 percent, well below that achieved by similar zones in South Korea, Taiwan and Indonesia. Net exports in Shenzhen were drastically reduced by large quantity of imports. FIEs in particular were responsible for a disproportionally large share of such imports, and their net export ratios were significantly lower than the Shenzhen average.

The goal of increasing net exports and ultimately foreign exchange earnings has been seriously undermined by the high import propensity of FIEs. They relied on imports for supplying about 80 percent of their production inputs. Since most of them were involved in low-tech, processing activities or operations, such reliance seemed inevitable. Affiliated with TNCs, some also followed the practice of maintaining their own global network of supplies. In addition, the trade policies of industrialized countries to encourage the use of raw materials and intermediate goods from home provided additional incentives. Such major investment policies as duty-free imports of production materials in the SEZs have further encouraged the import propensity of foreign enterprises. As the single largest source, Hong Kong investment in industrial processing has been responsible for a significant portion of Shenzhen's import expansion.

Resembling many similar zones elsewhere, Shenzhen's FIEs have created very limited linkages with inland areas, particularly in the form of backward purchasing, as less than 20 percent of production inputs were from domestic suppliers. The high import propensity has significantly reduced the likelihood of these enterprises using domestic sourcing, and it has been further hampered by limited domestic supply capabilities. For FIEs in Shenzhen, prices of domestic supplies tended to be higher because of the two-track pricing system in China. Moreover, the emphasis on quantity over quality, a legacy of the centrally planned system, led to products of mediocre quality. Internal trade barriers, in the form of ad hoc charges, fees and tolls at local levels; and transportation bottlenecks, due to underinvestment and over-capacity, have made delivery of available domestic resources unreliable. The location of Shenzhen in a region less endowed with industrial resources also has impeded backward linkages with its surrounding areas.

In addition, the original SEZ policy did not include incentives from the central or provincial government to encourage domestic linkages. Specifically, foreign enterprises in Shenzhen involved in economic cooperation with inland areas were not properly rewarded, and inland enterprises engaged in subcontracting or indirect exports did not receive preferential incentives. A practical approach to develop backward linkages, as practiced by some similar zones elsewhere, would be to extend an outright exemption or rebate to those firms with indirect exports above a minimum threshold.[10] Indirect exporters may include three groups of firms: manufacturing firms supplying inputs to a direct exporter in Shenzhen; trading firms farther back in the supply chain selling inputs to the direct exporter and indirect exporters; and manufacturing firms selling products to trading firms that serve as direct exporters. However, identifying indirect exporters reliably would not be easy to do. Thus using a rebate or drawback may be unavoidable, a procedure similar to requiring joint ventures to pay back exempted duties when they sell to domestic markets, to compensate indirect exporters after export.

Two forms of domestic linkages that began to show some positive results in Shenzhen were equity investment in inland enterprises and the repatriated wage incomes of migrant workers. By 1994, it was reported, some 500 projects were funded through equity investment by Shenzhen enterprises in other parts of China. Some foreign enterprises in Shenzhen also were involved in the diffusion of technology transferred from overseas. As shown in the case of Joint Venture Four, there may be several channels of such diffusion: (1) investing in inland enterprises and holding shares based on technology, (2) technological services, and (3) patent applications for new products. These efforts should be widely encouraged and rewarded by Shenzhen authorities so that more enterprises will have incentives to become involved.

Another way to encourage backward linkages through investment may be the "one-to-one" system of assistance. In fact, Guangdong Province has recently started a program giving economically developed cities the long-term responsibility for assisting underdeveloped cities in the province, most of which were located in mountainous areas. Seven pairs of cities or counties were set up in 1990 (see Yukawa, 1992). So far, the relationship established between Shenzhen and Meizhou city has been the most advanced, and has included preferential loans to Meizhou from Shenzhen and supplies of workers from Meizhou to Shenzhen, in return. Such a system of assistance would have a great potential and could take on additional dimensions. For instance, Meizhou, with the assistance of Shenzhen, could become a supply base of materials and components for Shenzhen. Long-term business cooperation between the two cities through subcontracting arrangements can be mutually beneficial. Those low-end and labor-intensive assembly operations in Shenzhen also could be gradually phased out and moved into Meizhou, which has lower labor costs.

6 Conclusions and Policy Implications

The significant growth of foreign investment in Shenzhen has been primarily a positive function of proximity to Hong Kong, and it has been positively related to the favorable local policy environment but only weakly responsive to differentials in domestic market potential and labor costs between Shenzhen and other potential sites in China. Spatial placement and unique planning activities are much more important in explaining SEZs' performance than is acknowledged in the literature, with its "neoclassical" theoretical emphasis on labor costs, incentives and market. Results from a survey by the Federation of Hong Kong Industries further confirm findings from this research (see Table 6.1). Another important point is that the growth of foreign investment in Shenzhen has brought little meaningful technology transfer, no substantial net exports, nor significant domestic linkages. This concluding chapter addresses the consequences of promoting foreign investment, particularly the effects on labor; articulates some investment policies applicable elsewhere; contemplates the role of a zone policy; and speculates on the prospects for China's SEZs.

Consequences of Promoting Foreign Investment

When the Shenzhen SEZ was first established in 1979, before foreign investment poured in, it was "a barren patch of grassland" (WuDunn, 1991). There were only about two hundred small factories with an annual output value of 60 million yuan (SCN, 9 March 1992). But the next fifteen years witnessed the fastest growth of local industry in China, and Shenzhen was placed among the top cities in the world as measured by industrial expansion. Foreign investment, in particular, was a major force behind Shenzhen's industrial growth. FIEs contributed up to 63.5 percent of the aggregate GVIO between 1979 and 1991 (see Table 6.2). This could be largely accounted for by the growing number of such enterprises, their greater capital accumulation,[1] and higher labor productivity as measured in output value per employee (see Table 6.3). Moreover, FIEs were much more pragmatic and conscious of cost-benefit calculations. They typically adopted, partly or entirely, management systems introduced by their foreign partners, which in many ways were more adapted to modern industrial production. Although compatriots from Hong Kong, who funded most FIEs, did not possess a technological edge, the level of technical efficiency of Hong Kong firms was undoubtedly higher than that of most domestic enterprises in Shenzhen.

Table 6.1 Factors in China's Pearl River Delta Area Pulling Hong Kong Firms to Invest

Factor	Number of responses	Share (percent)
Physical proximity to Hong Kong	494	68.7
Attractive investment environment	64	8.9
Familiarity with environment	64	8.9
Sourcing factors (labor and land)	33	4.6
Absence of language barrier	19	2.6
Large domestic market	11	1.5
Good relationship with localities	10	1.4
Others	24	3.3
Total responses*	719	100.0

* Multiple responses were given by a total of 511 firms surveyed.

Source: Federation of Hong Kong Industries, 1992, p.30.

The contribution of FIEs made possible the double-digit growth of Shenzhen's industrial output value, which was at an average annual rate of over 81 percent from 1979 on. By 1991, Shenzhen's GVIO had reached 23.7 billion yuan. The Seventh Five-Year Plan (1986-1990) had specified that GVIO in 1990 would reach 6 billion yuan, growing at an average rate of 28.7 percent.[2] Shenzhen's achievement dramatically surpassed this goal. So fifteen years after its creation, Shenzhen became a major urban center not only in Guangdong Province, but also in China. It was ranked fifth in economic strength among China's twenty-four large and medium-sized cities in 1994, behind only Shanghai, Beijing, Guangzhou, and Tianjin.[3]

What, then, did foreign investment bring to the people of Shenzhen, particular workers employed in FIEs? Undoubtedly, workers received a much higher level of monetary rewards than those in any other cities in China did. This made Shenzhen the most desirable place in the country for the young and old alike, especially the more educated rural youth. It was

Table 6.2 Gross Output Value of Shenzhen's Industrial Enterprises, 1979-1991
(1980 constant prices, millions of yuan, unless otherwise noted)

	1979	1980	1981	1982	1983	1984	1985	1986	1987	1988	1989	1990	1991*	1979-91
State enterprises	42.0	46.0	109.0	182.8	342.9	651.8	783.1	975.0	1622.9	2707.7	3677.5	4301.4	5572.4	21014.4
Collective enterprises	18.7	38.5	60.4	79.2	110.2	147.0	188.2	304.3	441.1	703.7	944.2	1031.4	1151.8	5218.6
Joint enterprises (state with collective)	0.0	0.0	0.0	0.1	0.5	4.5	31.5	20.9	29.4	38.2	147.9	104.7	169.4	546.9
Foreign-invested enterprises	0.0	0.0	73.4	100.0	266.9	864.7	1671.5	2264.9	3669.6	5431.5	6876.0	10693.2	14778.0	46689.8
Shenzhen total	60.6	84.4	242.8	362.1	720.4	1668.0	2674.3	3565.1	5762.9	8881.1	11645.6	16130.7	21671.6	73469.7
Share in Shenzhen total (percent)														
State enterprises	69.2	54.4	44.9	50.5	47.6	39.1	29.3	27.3	28.2	30.5	31.6	26.7	25.7	28.6
Collective enterprises	30.8	45.6	24.9	21.9	15.3	8.8	7.0	8.5	7.7	7.9	8.1	6.4	5.3	7.1
Joint enterprises (state with collective)	0.0	0.0	0.0	0.0	0.1	0.3	1.2	0.6	0.5	0.4	1.3	0.6	0.8	0.7
Foreign-invested enterprises	0.0	0.0	30.2	27.6	37.0	51.8	62.5	63.5	63.7	61.2	59.0	66.3	68.2	63.5

* The 1991 deflator based on 1980 constant prices was calculated by the author, using the 1990 deflator based on 1980 constant prices and the 1991 deflator based on 1990 constant prices.

Source: Shenzhen Statistical Bureau, *Shenzhen Socio-Economic Statistics, 1979-1985* and *1986-1990; Shenzhen Statistical Yearbook, 1992.*

Table 6.3 Industrial Labor Productivity in Shenzhen, 1979-1991
(measured by output value per employee, 1980 constant prices, thousands of yuan)

	1979	1980	1981	1982	1983	1984	1985	1986	1987	1988	1989	1990	1991*	Average
State enterprises	5.8	5.3	9.2	14.3	19.6	30.0	30.8	27.5	32.0	41.8	45.7	52.0	47.6	27.8
Collective enterprises	4.4	9.8	12.7	13.1	8.2	4.8	4.4	4.2	3.7	4.3	4.9	4.7	9.1	6.8
Joint enterprises (state with collective)	—	—	—	—	4.5	11.8	17.6	12.1	7.1	5.7	15.3	12.3	14.1	11.2
Foreign-invested enterprises	—	—	—	—	37.6	72.9	77.4	85.7	87.8	88.5	80.9	90.9	108.8	81.2
Shenzhen average	5.4	6.4	9.7	14.0	19.0	25.9	29.4	26.2	26.8	30.0	31.7	31.7	71.2	25.2
National average	8.7	9.0	8.9	9.4	10.2	11.2	12.4	12.6	14.0	15.8	16.6	17.4	19.0	12.7

— Not available.
* The 1991 deflator based on 1980 constant prices was calculated by the author, using the 1990 deflator based on 1980 constant prices and the 1991 deflator based on 1990 constant prices.

Source: Shenzhen Statistical Bureau, *Shenzhen Socio-Economic Statistics, 1979-1985 and 1986-1990*; *Shenzhen Statistical Yearbook*, 1992; State Statistical Bureau, *China Statistical Yearbook*, 1992.

not only that rural poverty pushed these people to migrate to Shenzhen in search of work, but also the promise of high wages and city lights that pulled them. Women benefited tremendously in terms of finding employment in the mushrooming textiles, garments and toy industries, which traditionally tended to hire proportionally more female workers. It was estimated by 1992 that between one-half and one million temporary migrants worked in Shenzhen (FEER 14 May 1992, p.24). The number of migrant workers rose to over 2 million in 1997 (Shenzhen Municipal Labor Bureau Statistics). As indicated in the previous chapter, a significant portion of their wage income was repatriated back home, which could fuel the local economy. Some of these migrant workers, after gaining experience in Shenzhen, also returned home and set up small businesses.

However, there appear to have been some negative consequences for labor. Shenzhen's lack of regulations to prevent labor abuses and promote workplace security made it possible for some FIEs to ignore such issues and, in some cases, to commit dire violations without incurring penalties.[4] The first reprehensible practice was the use of child labor, which had been illegal since 1949 but was resurfacing in some areas and in some FIEs after 1979. The increased commercialization of the Chinese economy led to more employment of workers under sixteen, most of whom were girls. It was reported in 1988 that about 500 child workers from Fujian and Guangdong had been dismissed in Shenzhen (SZZD, 27 August 1988, cited in Sklair, 1991). In the same year, the Minister of Labor acknowledged that child laborers accounted for 10 to 20 percent of the employees in some areas, and that the percentage of girls was particularly high. Furthermore, excessive compulsory labor overtime was quite common in such assembly/processing industries as garments, toys, and electronics. In fact, some managers claimed that it was the only way ventures could make profits.[5] Overtime was paid at piece rates, and only in rare circumstances could workers ask to be excused. According to a survey conducted by the Guangdong Federation of Trade Unions, overtime was widespread among FIEs. About 61 percent of FIE employees worked more than six days a week, including Sundays. At least 35 percent of workers were forced to work overtime, and about 20 percent were not paid reasonably for their overtime (*China Times Weekly*, 20-26 March 1994, No. 116).

In FIEs, unions generally had a much more limited role in management and matters affecting workers' interests than they had in other types of enterprises.[6] According to a survey of selected FIEs in coastal provinces and cities by the U.S.-China Business Council in 1992, few respondents listed trade union activities as obstacles to their ventures' operation (see Frisbie and Brecher, 1992). In addition, union membership in FIEs was less than in other types of enterprises. By early 1994, it was estimated that less than half of the operational FIEs in China had established trade unions (FBIS-CHI-94063, 1 April 1994, p.59). Such a situation could be partly accounted for by the fact that many workers in FIEs were rural migrants employed on a temporary basis. Despite poor working conditions, these workers were not likely to form or participate in an organized social force, since any type of non-agricultural job was a rise in their life status. However, in a bid to calm recent industrial disputes, it was expected that 40 percent of FIEs in Shenzhen would be unionized by the end of 1994. The municipal government also would set up a fund to protect workers against wage defaults (FBIS-CHI-94058, 25 March 1994, p.68).

Foreign firms also tended to invest minimally in training local workers. An outstanding feature of Shenzhen was that between 70 and 80 percent of the total employed were women aged between 16 and 25. This could be attributed to the fact that the main industries were electronics, textiles and garments, fields in which production has been traditionally dominated by women. Because of the very short-term nature of employment in Shenzhen's industries and the low skill level required, these firms often had little incentive to make substantial investment in training and professional development of production workers, whose later turnover could, in fact, stimulate the establishment of local businesses. Most workers were trained to perform only specific, elementary production functions, largely of assembly type. Training of management staff also was very limited, since many foreign firms relied on expatriate personnel in management as a means of maintaining control.

Policy Implications

Shenzhen's experience can be a useful reference for other developing countries pursuing a similar zone policy to attract foreign investment, just as China learned a great deal from zones in South Korea and Taiwan. The unique proximity of Shenzhen to Hong Kong may be an attraction difficult to replicate elsewhere. But Shenzhen's success in luring more investment from other sources may shed some light on what constitutes effective investment policies. In addition to policy openness and autonomy, the relaxed ownership controls, labor market flexibility, and preferential fiscal incentives have proved to be significant draws. Shenzhen's experience also illustrates how a special zone policy can facilitate the transition of a closed economy to a more open one.

Investment Policies

The importance of policy openness cannot be overstated, since it is the most important component of an investment environment. Both foreign and Chinese managers have emphasized that the most appealing aspect of Shenzhen is its open policies. The degree of openness towards foreign investors still varies among developing countries, and in many of them several major restrictions aimed at protecting domestic industries and markets continue to impede foreign investment. In some countries with large domestic markets and infant industries, protective mechanisms prevent foreign competition in order to encourage the indigenous development of infant industries. As a result, foreign investment has been slow despite these countries' large markets and labor forces. However, restrictive policies may not deter foreign investment substantially. Even with rather restrictive foreign investment regimes, Brazil, Indonesia and Mexico, for example, have been able to maintain a significant level of foreign investment inflows because of large domestic markets, rich natural resources and relatively growing economies.

Supportive investment policies often can serve as a kind of guarantee of a government's commitment to an open investment regime, as clearly shown by Shenzhen's experience. The importance of government policies also is demonstrated in Singapore, which has relied heavily on foreign investment in its export-oriented development. As Lim summarized:

> The chief lesson of the Singapore experience is that reliance on private enterprise and market forces alone is inadequate to attract foreign investment and ensure success in export manufacturing. Rather, the state needs to intervene to facilitate the realization of (both static and dynamic) comparative advantage; to promote, enhance and augment such advantages; to anticipate and facilitate adjustments to and even accelerate desired or inevitable shifts in comparative advantage; and to influence and even shape the investment and production decisions of firms, which are not autonomous of the government policy environment.[7]

Several investment policies stand out as conducive to foreign investment in Shenzhen, and they can be useful in other locations and countries as well. First, ownership controls on foreign ventures should be relaxed. One important reason that Shenzhen appeals to investors is that it is possible, not just theoretically but in reality, for foreign firms to have majority ownership in joint ventures or even sole ownership. The kind of flexibility in appointing management staff that comes with relaxed ownership controls adds to Shenzhen's appeal.[8] The government also has relaxed control on domestic enterprises, freeing them to negotiate with foreign investors on their own behalf.

Second, labor market flexibility is essential. Many foreign ventures in China still face an inadequate supply of mid-level technical and management staff, as well as semi-skilled workers. The absence of a well-functioning labor market and lack of labor mobility exacerbate these shortages. In Shenzhen, however, the situation has gradually improved through a series of labor market reforms, such as the introduction of labor contracting, nation-wide labor recruitment, and the enforcement of a management responsibility system. The purpose of these measures is to improve labor productivity and industrial efficiency by discontinuing permanent employment and state allocation of jobs. Shenzhen has been able to gather the best from all over the country; in fact, some other major cities have tried to curtail the outflows of skills. In this respect, Shenzhen has developed at some expense to others. The reliance on low-cost labor can be only short-term, as many labor-intensive industries are forever on the lookout for cheaper production sites. If costs in a particular location move too far out of line, which is already happening in Shenzhen for some industries, productivity will have to compensate.

Third, fiscal incentives are useful; they include tax breaks and holidays, favorable utility usage fees, and reduced customs duties and foreign exchange restrictions. These incentives to foreign investors improve profitability and ease profit repatriation. The NICs are good examples of governments utilizing liberal and attractive incentives to sustain high levels of foreign investment inflows. However, certain fiscal incentives, such as tax holidays and favorable fees, are not essential to attract foreign investors and can even reduce a host country's financial benefits from foreign investment. A number of analyses also show that fiscal incentives have little effect on the magnitude of foreign investment flows. Although investors view incentive policies as a sign of a positive political attitude toward foreign investment, they emphasize the overall quality of an investment environment much more than they emphasize special incentives.[9] Offers of such incentives, therefore, should be at a minimal level and even waived in some cases. Since high-tech industries may depend on preferential policies more than labor-intensive industries do, it would be advisable for governments to provide additional funds for direct financial assistance for R&D or equity participation in high-tech joint ventures with TNCs. But even more important to high-tech industries is skilled manpower, including technicians, engineers and scientists, which will require heavy investment in education and training.

Some fiscal incentives, including tax incentives and depreciation allowances, may have negative effects on reported profits and taxes. Reportedly, tax breaks and holidays have encouraged some FIEs in Shenzhen to transfer a profitable year into a loss-incurring year through inappropriate means, in order to evade taxes. A number of them have registered consecutive losses or zero profits, yet kept increasing their investment and recruiting more workers, implying that they actually have been making money. FIEs also have been given an accelerated depreciation allowance to encourage more investment. Some foreign investors have used this to cover up the use of over-priced equipment or outdated machinery. Fast and high-level depreciation has reduced their reported profits and tax payments. Then, too, the current accounting system in China has contributed to a lower reported level of profits for FIEs, particularly as compared to state enterprises. As some have pointed out, while state enterprises have understated losses, FIEs have exaggerated them (FBIS-CHI-94100, 24 May 1994, p.48).

The Role of a Special Zone Policy[10]

The usefulness of a special zone policy should be defined against several considerations. First, the zone can play an important role in economic growth if it is established at an appropriate stage of the country's economic evolution. Its impact is likely to be the most significant at the beginning of the transition from an inward to an outward-looking regime, as shown by the experience of China's SEZs. It can not only promote export growth, but also serve as an "experiment station" for new policy instruments, and facilitate the transition from a closed economy to a more open one. But the zone's importance tends to decline when the country moves toward a more liberal trade and investment regime, whether initiated by a domestic policy reorientation or by multilateral negotiations such as those taking place in the WTO. A zone strategy is very likely to fail, just as any spatial policy would, if the macroeconomic policy runs counter to the zone's orientation or there is no broad-based, outward-looking policy.

The expectations for the zone should be realistic, given current domestic conditions and the international context. In countries where the domestic market is large and import demands are high, the zone may be used for import processing with the assistance of foreign investment and technology. This has been the reality in Shenzhen for quite some time. When foreign investment is limited, domestic investment in the zone should be encouraged and should be given the same privileges that foreign investors enjoy. Even with clear goals, the government should realize that most zones never develop according to plans. Consequently, one key factor for success is the provision for built-in adaptability and flexibility in subsequent administrations. Goals should be evaluated and adjusted in time to manage changes; related regulations and incentives should be adjusted accordingly, as happened in Shenzhen throughout the 1980s. The zone can be used at first to bring in labor-intensive manufacturing activities to absorb surplus labor. But as a country develops and moves up along the technological learning curve, the zone should shift to more technology-intensive industries. To do so, it needs a defined government involvement in the training of the workforce, and better support and diffusion systems for technology transfer. In addition, specific policies and incentives can be designed to attract scientists, researchers and technical staff to the zone to develop the country's domestic R&D facilities, as has already happened in Taiwan.

In offering a package of fiscal incentives to foreign firms, an appropriate balance must be found. Too generous a package can be very costly in terms of forgone revenue, and yet not actually entice large TNCs, as they often invest according to their global strategies. It is clear from Shenzhen's experience that a favorable investment environment is more important than incentive packages. On the other hand, too stringent a package may prove to be inadequate in attracting and sustaining foreign investment inflows, since the competition among developing countries is becoming acute. Moreover, for many foreign investors, access to domestic markets, particularly those with large potentials, seems to be a more effective incentive than the usual package of fiscal incentives. Therefore, as a developing country moves toward liberal trade and investment regimes, the usefulness of fiscal incentives may decline. In fact, the government in South Korea has amended its legislation to abolish tax exemptions for foreign enterprises, except for high-tech industries.

The benefits from the zone to the surrounding region as well as the country may be limited, particularly if it is a spatial enclave. In fact, as China's SEZs are polar, limited in number, and concentrated along the coast, they may worsen the existing spatial unevenness and disparity between the coast and interior regions. It is clear that deliberate government initiatives are needed to diffuse development through economic cooperation between the firms inside and those outside the zone, and that redistribution policies also are needed to transfer technology and cultivate indigenous industries. The zone also should encourage joint ventures in which local enterprises and foreign investors can come together in production as well as subcontracting. These can be promoted through some governmental assistance (as many subcontractors are small firms), simplified regulations, and training of the local workforce.

So far, however, the central government in China has not done much to alleviate the growing regional disparities, despite its concern.[11] Beijing sees developing the coastal region as being in the national interest, and still believes that it will be a catalyst for the modernization of the whole country. This promise of trickle-down, however, may not be realized for quite some time and may even fail to materialize without government intervention. To avoid falling behind any further, some interior provinces have lobbied to obtain open-zone status, but have only met lukewarm reception from Beijing. The essential notion of economic efficiency underlying China's post-1979 regional policy is unchanged, that is, to strengthen the economy of coastal provinces. In any case, given the importance of spatial placement, the proposal for open zones in inland areas may not work, especially where transportation links are poor.

Prospects for China's SEZs

Shenzhen has been a valuable opportunity for foreign investors and has helped to build their confidence in China's open-door policy. In the earlier stage of China's reform era, foreign investors' uncertainty was very high due to the lack of information and contact. The creation of the SEZs with favorable and open investment policies was crucial for reducing that uncertainty. The SEZs, so different from the rest of the country at the time, resembled environments foreign investors were familiar with back home or in other developing countries with relatively open investment regimes. In this respect, China's policy to establish the SEZs should be highly valued. Nevertheless as discussed earlier, the SEZ policy has had some negative consequences or costs: the exploitation of labor, aggravation of regional disparity, and deployment of domestic resources at the expense of other cities. It also should be noted that SEZs' impressive growth record can be attributed, to some extent, to growth at the national level. As China gradually opens its investment regime, as required by its admission to the WTO, SEZs' status will no longer be special. Further research, using a comparative framework and some focus on the social costs of the SEZ policy, would shed more light on these issues.

Investing in China still involves some potential risks: possible nationalization of foreign enterprises by the government, loss of funds as a result of political upheavals, or disruptions in supplies of goods, services and workforce. Some of these risks are related to political instability, as has been seen in the Philippines, India, South Africa, most Middle Eastern countries and many African countries. To a certain extent, some Latin

American countries—Mexico, Chile and Panama—also have had reduced levels of foreign investment inflows at times of political upheavals. In China, the optimistic aspect is that the economic reform program introduced by Deng has penetrated every corner of the country and reached a point of no return.

Foreign investment, particularly FDI, will remain a major source of capital for the SEZs, especially when alternative sources of capital are hard to come by. One alternative source may be portfolio investment, which requires a well-functioning stock market system as the medium. China may be a long way from having such a system; moreover, political stability often is an even more sensitive issue for portfolio investment. Two of China's stock exchanges, Shenzhen and Shanghai, have struggled to get foreigners to buy the special B shares that are not for sale to Chinese. So far their record is mediocre.

Another alternative source is domestic public and private savings. This source seems more promising, since Chinese save roughly 38 percent of their gross domestic product, a percentage higher than for almost any of their Asian neighbors, which are already well-known for high savings rates (see Shaw and Woetzel, 1992). If this trend continues and the country is able to maintain its growth record, China may follow the example of Taiwan in replacing large demand for foreign investment with domestic savings. But one important function of foreign investment—facilitating the integration of China into the world economy—is irreplaceable. Its role in facilitating state enterprise reform also is valuable, by providing either direct input such as capital and technology through joint venture efforts, or competitive pressure and operational demonstration for state enterprises.

More foreign investment needs to be attracted to infrastructure development and service industries in China's SEZs, since these two sectors are now open to foreign participation after being closed for most of the 1980s. Despite Shenzhen's successful record in promoting foreign investment, only about a quarter of the funds for infrastructure have come from foreign sources. To make such investment attractive, Shenzhen should be somewhat flexible about ownership rights for urban infrastructure. Its neighbor, Guangzhou, has been ahead of other municipalities in its innovative approach to infrastructure financing through transfer of some stock rights for bridges, tunnels and waterworks to private as well as foreign companies. Such an approach would help ease the financial burden of the municipal government and provide new sources of funding for public utility construction (FBIS-CHI-94082, 28 April 1994, p.81).

Producer services are another area with strong potential for foreign participation. Officials in Shenzhen have already realized the necessity of developing a producer-services sector to sustain the manufacturing sector. Since the second half of the 1980s, there has been a steady increase in the import of consulting services from Hong Kong, as Chinese firms have begun taking more initiatives in design, innovation, and R&D. Real estate development and urban infrastructure building also have generated needs for architectural engineering and consulting services. Taking advantage of its proximity to Hong Kong, Shenzhen could become a center of producer services in China through judicious policy initiatives.

However, Shenzhen will still need to overcome some liabilities in its investment environment. Though Shenzhen is a modern city built from scratch, it has problems with its urban infrastructure similar to those in other Chinese cities. The shortage of energy has been a major problem in Shenzhen. Bottlenecks in transportation and communications have hindered the production efficiency of many FIEs. Shenzhen also suffers from some deficiencies that it has little control over, but that China as a whole must overcome: insufficient domestic supplies, cumbersome bureaucracy compounded by corruption, and unconforming practices for dispute settlement. In particular, dispute settlement has been influenced by the strong cultural bias in China against judicial actions (see Zhang, 1985). Many FIEs find it difficult and time-consuming to resolve commercial disputes. Ironically, Shenzhen's lack of large state industries or establishments is actually quite appealing to many investors, because of the negative image state enterprises have in terms of work ethics. But the makeup of Shenzhen's workforce could be a disadvantage. People from different parts of China come to work there, bringing with them different local cultures and work habits, and they do not always get along well with each other.

If Shenzhen wants to attract more investment to high-tech industries, as it ailed to do during the 1980s, it will need to adopt a regulatory framework closer to international standards, to protect intellectual property rights. This may not be as difficult for Shenzhen now that China has been pressured to do so nationwide in order to join the WTO. In addition, Shenzhen will need a stronger technology policy to raise its industrial capabilities. Although, as compared to many other similar zones in Asia, it has a sizable pool of skilled manpower and research institutions, most of the institutions have worked under a centralized system of fund allocation and product dissemination. The task ahead is to foster linkages between these institutions and enterprises, and to speed up commercializing innovations.

The success story of Singapore in transforming itself into an export powerhouse in the electronics industry can serve as a role model for China's SEZs.[12] Despite rising wage levels and a decreasing supply of unskilled labor, Singapore has attracted more rather than less foreign investment in electronics, and the investment is increasingly in more capital-intensive, high-value-added products and processes. One could argue that market forces—technological changes within industries, shifts in TNCs' global corporate strategies and changes in comparative costs between countries— are responsible for this outcome.[13] But it is the government's technology policy, which has focused on capital, labor, and infrastructure and support services, that has made the country a highly world-competitive location for the electronics industry. In particular, various capital incentives have encouraged R&D activities. The infrastructure and supporting services include a network of research institutes and centers funded by the government to support activities of private companies.

To compete effectively with coastal open cities that have substantial industrial bases, Shenzhen also will need to widen and deepen its industrial structure. As international experience shows, a city is most vulnerable economically when its economy is dominated by a few industries with a relatively narrow specialization. When these industries decline because of either a secular trend or diminished competitiveness, that quickly affects the entire urban economy. There are ample examples in North America and Western Europe, mostly in cities dependent on the production of basic metals, ships, transport equipment and textiles (Yusuf and Wu, 1997). Shenzhen may be able to avoid such a fate, since it has already branched into some higher-end manufacturing activities, in addition to its mainstays of consumer electronics and textiles, and producer services. An industrial targeting policy is already under discussion in Shenzhen and, once implemented, will push out many labor-intensive assembly operations.

Shenzhen's success in serving as an experiment station for new economic policies and as a role model for the rest of the country is undeniable. Following Shenzhen's and other SEZs' lead, smaller zones of a similar nature have mushroomed in all major cities of China since the late 1980s. Most of them are called High-Tech Development Zones, often located in greenfield sites adjacent to major cities and intended to attract foreign investment by offering concessionary policies. Although none of these newer, smaller zones enjoy the same kind of autonomy that Shenzhen has, several have grown very fast and become alternative poles of attraction for foreign investment. Shanghai's Pudong Economic Zone and Tianjin's Economic Development Zone are probably the best examples. Each is attached to a prime urban center with a wide and strong industrial base, rich hinterland, and superb transport capacity by Chinese standards. Each zone has been home for some large TNCs from industrialized countries, such as Motorola and Intel, and for some rather sophisticated production lines.

Each zone finds it possible, with some effort, to source a wide range of components locally, and both possess large pools of skilled technicians.

Shenzhen is still considered a pilot city for new measures to deepen reform and open further to the world. Several new reform measures have been introduced since 1993 in a bid to invigorate its enterprises, particularly state enterprises. First, Shenzhen has tried to introduce a corporate system in which all state enterprises will become either limited-liability stock companies or limited-liability companies, step by step. Second, a new employee system has been introduced to establish a labor market characterized by fluidity and competition. Third, Shenzhen has started to use internationally accepted indices—assets, sales, profits and taxes, and sales—to assess the performance of enterprises and rate them according to their returns. The last step is to establish a property rights circulation system, in order to promote enterprise mergers, the transfer of property rights, and lawful and orderly disposal of enterprise bankruptcies. In addition, after 1997 Shenzhen becomes the country's largest bonded area pursuing a free trade policy, when the first line Luoho Customs moved back to the site of the current administrative line.

As China opens further, Shenzhen's original role is nearing its end, and the zone needs to redefine its functions and seek new roles. It is already becoming a modern city, and somewhat international, so it will be unacceptable for Shenzhen to turn into an industrial backyard or appendage to Hong Kong and other nearby regional centers. Above all, it is important that Shenzhen maintain its export orientation, because firms involved in competitive struggles for overseas markets are forced to become efficient, and this efficiency will be transmitted back to domestic suppliers of inputs and gradually to the economy as a whole.

Hong Kong's restoration to China on 1 July 1997 has some significant implications for Shenzhen because of the proximity. Shenzhen's officials have considered two alternatives: accept the status quo, or expand the administrative line to integrate with Hong Kong. Many are concerned that the second option will distance Shenzhen further from the rest of the country, which presents a large market and source of labor. Such concerns are justified, since the next fifty years may be merely transitional for Hong Kong, and its special status will fade as China completely opens up. It is very likely that the division of labor between Hong Kong and Shenzhen in joint production will persist as long as labor and land cost differentials remain sizable. But as industries grow and mature, production costs rise, and land becomes scarce in Shenzhen, Hong Kong investors will look further north for other outlets for expansion.

Notes

Introduction

1. "Overseas Chinese—Family Affairs," a book review of Lords of the Rim by Sterling Seagrave, Economist, November 11, 1995.

Chapter 1

1. The fourteen cities are Dalian, Qinhuangdao, Tianjin, Yantai, Qingdao, Lianyungang, Nantong, Shanghai, Ningbo, Wenzhou, Fuzhou, Guangzhou, Zhangjiang, and Beihai. Some argue that this move was a response to the disappointing performance of the SEZs in the early 1980s. I believe, however, that it was undertaken as an extension of the open policy into the vast coastal region.
2. They are Liaoning, Beijing, Tianjin, Hebei, Shandong, Jiangsu, Shanghai, Zhejiang, Fujian, Guangdong, Guangxi, and Hainan.
3. It was only after the apparent success of the zones ten years since their creation that the government was willing to push the reform into other major urban areas, such as Shanghai. See NYT, 22 December 1993.
4. The norm until then was that People's Congresses at provincial levels had the local law-making power. FEER, 16 July 1992, p.49.
5. Zhao also noted that the SEZs should not pursue only increases in their output value. See Falkenheim, 1986.
6. Only the city of Shanghai and Tianjin had the same power as the SEZs. Other cities could approve only contracts under US$10 million.
7. This function was actually lost after the establishment of the "one-stop" investment approval procedure in 1993.
8. As a legacy of the old socialist planning system, this plan also reflected a emphasis on such heavy industries as metal and machinery in order to be self-reliant. See Sit, 1988.
9. However, some local officials did not entirely favor an exclusively outward orientation, despite the central government's firm commitment. See Fewsmith, 1986.
10. As a result, foreign investment in construction, hotels, real estate, and tourism fell drastically in 1986 and 1987, as shown in Chapter 4.

Chapter 2

1. Foreign investment includes foreign loans, FDI, and other foreign investment; in particular, FDI consists of equity joint ventures, contractual joint ventures, and wholly foreign-owned enterprises. It is also important to distinguish the amount of contracted foreign investment (specified in the contract) from that actually invested. For detailed distinctions among the various forms of foreign investment, see Glossary. Also note that the data collected for this book are for Shenzhen city proper, where the Shenzhen SEZ is located, unless otherwise noted.
2. From Falkenheim, 1986, p.356, Table I; Stoltenberg, 1984, p.645, Table 1.
3. At the National Conference on the Utilization of Foreign Capital held in May 1983, priorities were placed on FDI rather than foreign loans and credits. See Grub and Lin, 1985.
4. Wholly foreign-owned enterprises were allowed in non-SEZ areas in China only towards the end of 1980s.
5. The 1994 downturn in contracted foreign investment may be misleading because the actually utilized amount in that year did not show a decline from 1993. In China's statistical reporting system, Hong Kong and Macao are always combined. It is reasonable to assume that the majority of the investment comes from Hong Kong, because of the relatively small size of the Macao economy. In the sample of FIEs, very few contracts were signed with investors from Macao.
6. Shenzhen Statistical Bureau, *Shenzhen Statistical Manual*, 1991.
7. The bulk of Taiwan investment (about 80 percent) was in neighboring Fujian Province, and the Xiamen SEZ in particular. See Pamela Baldinger, "The Birth of Greater China: Growing Economic Links between China, Hong Kong, and Taiwan May Eventually Reshape East Asia," *The China Business Review*, May-June 1992: 13-17.
8. Data on sources of foreign investment in Shenzhen were available only for after 1986.
9. Percentages are calculated using registered investment, not number of projects.
10. These joint ventures included Huaqiang Sanyo Electronics Co., Sanyo Electronics Shekou Ltd., and Guangdong-Sanyo Freezing Machine Co. Ltd. Huaqiang Sanyo Electronics Co. Ltd. was repeatedly evaluated as one of the outstanding FIEs for its profitability and reliability. See SSZD, 19 October and 7 December, 1989.
11. One of the major copier manufacturers, Ricoh, also signed a contract with Shenzhen to invest US$23 million to establish a joint venture. See *Business Week*, 11 March 1991, p. 96D.
12. According to personal interviews with both joint venture managers and municipal government officials, the bottlenecks most often complained of in Shenzhen were transportation, communications, power supply, and water supply.
13. This relaxed border control, however, is only for one direction—from Hong Kong to Shenzhen, and does not apply to the other direction. Chinese

nationals still had to go through a lengthy process when applying for an entry to Hong Kong.
14. It is important to distinguish trans-shipment from entrepôt trade in discussing trade links. Trans-shipment goods are regarded as exports of the originating country but not as trade of the entrepôt and they do not clear customs as they represent only goods in transit. Entrepôt trade (indirect trade or re-exports) is part of the trade of the entrepôt because goods are consigned to a buyer in the entrepôt who takes legal possession of them after clearing customs. These goods may then be processed, but not substantially enough to confer country of origin, before being re-exported. See Sung, 1992.
15. These figures refer to direct trade. China, nevertheless, regards Hong Kong as its largest trading partner, since Chinese trade statistics do not distinguish the substantial two-way re-exports between China and Hong Kong. If such re-exports are taken into consideration, the Hong Kong market represented 48 percent of China's exports, and imports from Hong Kong accounted for 31.8 percent of China's imports in 1989. See Sung, 1991.
16. B Shares are shares that only foreign institutions can deal in and for which settlement has to be in foreign exchanges.
17. The tendency of Hong Kong businesses to rely on kinship network and personal ties in overseas operations also can be demonstrated by their investment in Mauritius, where lower-cost labor and exemption from U.S. clothing import quotas provide some incentives for Hong Kong investors. But the most important draw is the existence of a small ethnic Chinese community in this island country. Once a few Hong Kong firms acted as pioneers, others followed and before long Hong Kong had become the largest foreign investor in Mauritius's clothing industry. See UN ECLAC/CDCC, 1994.
18. The unemployment rate was kept under 2 percent throughout most of the 1980s in Hong Kong. See Chen and Tse, 1993.

Chapter 3

1. Sony's new US$12.5 million camcorder plant in Shanghai was typical of this type. It was not set up to take advantage of cheap labor, but aimed at the domestic market, which still had prohibitive tariffs on video-equipment imports. See Ono, 1992.
2. When the Hong Kong-financed Shenzhen-Guangzhou highway was completed and opened in July 1995, the drive was reduced to about an hour and a half. See FEER, 5 October 1995.
3. The Labor Bureau in Shenzhen played more of a supervising or monitoring role, unlike elsewhere in China, where such bureaus were in full charge of allocating labor. See Wall, 1993.
4. These procedures, however, do not apply to expatriates or workers recruited from overseas.
5. Like other parts of China, Shenzhen was dominated by state banks before 1985.

6. This largely explains why investment projects were either large TNCs with strong financial back-up or small investors from Hong Kong. See Wong, 1985.
7. This tax incentive took effect in December 1984. Before this, the 100 percent exemption was for the first profit-making year and the 50 percent reduction for the next two years. See Bell and others, 1993. Such tax incentives, however, have been considered a major reason for many FIEs claiming losses.
8. This tax is levied on the output of industrial and commercial enterprises and the incomes of enterprises in transportation, hotel, catering, and other service industries. See Grub and Lin, 1985.
9. Incomes of all FIEs in commercial and transportation services are subject to this tax. See Hsueh and Woo, 1988.
10. This preferential policy came to an end when China announced that new tax laws at the beginning of 1996 would impose taxes of 20 to 30 percent on joint ventures for materials and machinery imported for manufacturing. But joint ventures whose setups were announced before the end of 1995 would continue to enjoy the duty-free policy. See CND, 15 December 1995.
11. Goods purchased inland but exported via Shenzhen are subject to applicable export duties.
12. Wholly foreign-owned enterprises are excluded from this arrangement.
13. According to Wong and Chu (1985), land also is divided into three categories according to location, accessibility and development potential.
14. Land use fees in non-SEZ areas are negotiated between local authorities and FIEs, and under certain circumstances can be lower than those in the SEZs. See Hsueh and Woo, 1988.
15. For the January 1986 Joint Venture Foreign Exchange Balance Provisions, see Pomfret, 1991, p.61. This document shows the government's unwillingness to make the currency convertible or to take foreign exchange flows out of state planning until 1994.
16. There were talks about establishing a SEZ currency in the mid-1980s, but the efforts were later abandoned.
17. The retention rate was 35 percent for domestic firms in Shenzhen. But the variations in retention rates were mostly abolished in 1991, when a national rate of 50 percent was established. See Wall, 1993.
18. However, as compared to other industrial cities built from scratch, such as Daqing, in earlier decades, the amount of central investment in Shenzhen was relatively small. See Chan, 1985.
19. Some other favorable locations in this region are Yantai and Qingdao, both coastal open cities in Shandong Province.
20. In fact, the city of Suzhou was ranked number one in 1993 among all cities in utilizing foreign investment and was the largest recipient of Singapore investment in China. FBIS-CHI-94069, 11 April 1994, p.38.
21. This is clearly shown in the athletic footwear industry in South Korea. Despite local firms' tremendous efforts in automation and technology upgrading, Pusan, once the footwear capital of the world, is still losing the battle of preventing its footwear industry from disappearing. Both Nike and Reebok, the largest investors in Pusan, have begun to shift their production to China. See FEER, 5

November 1992, p.58.
22. The survey was conducted by the Japan-China Association on Economy and Trade. See Zhang, 1993.
23. However, some hidden costs, such as housing and welfare subsidies, may undermine this advantage. See Frisbie and Brecher, 1992.
24. Basic wages comprised only about 50 percent of the wage package; other elements included funds for labor insurance, pension, unemployment insurance, and housing subsidies.
25. The regulations are meant to protect the physical and mental health of juveniles and children and to promote compulsory basic education. See Seifman, 1992.
26. In fact, work to prepare such a law was first proposed in the 1950s, but was abandoned by Mao and resurrected in 1979; more than ten years later, the law was still in the drafting stages. See Wilson, 1990.
27. The labor law dealt with such issues as employment, labor relations, income distribution, training, workplace safety, and welfare. See *China Times Weekly*, 13-26 February 1994, No. 111/112.
28. Theoretically, ACFTU is assigned two functions: by top-down transmission, mobilization of workers for production on behalf of the nation's collective good; and by bottom-up transmission, protection of workers' rights and interests. But the CCP is so powerful that the top-down transmission regularly suppresses the bottom-up transmission. See Chan, 1993.
29. When agents are disenfranchised from the policy arena, their interests and concerns generally will not be included. This can largely explain why reform policies have ignored the labor issue. See Shirk, 1993.
30. *Hong Kong Standard*, 27 April 1986, cited in Sklair, 1991, p.207. One plausible reason for this is that many Chinese, at all official levels, have come to believe that western methods of management and industrial organization are superior to Chinese ones and must be adopted.
31. It was estimated that in China private consumption made up 70 percent of all final demand. See Taylor and Hardee, 1986.
32. It is widely accepted, however, that GNP per capita calculated through the atlas method is a gross underestimate of income level in China, since such major items as housing, education and health care have been heavily subsidized by the government, and services by "non-productive" sectors were excluded from the official account. Several international organizations, including the International Monetary Fund, the World Bank and the United Nations International Comparison Project, have turned to PPP calculations. See Overholt, 1993) United Nations Development Program (UNDP), *Human Development Report* (New York: Oxford University Press, 1993); World Bank, *GNP in China* (Washington, DC, 1995).
33. The distribution of income for China as a whole was more unequal than that in either urban or rural areas because of the large difference in income levels between urban and rural areas. See Khan and others, 1993.
34. In UNDP's *Human Development Report* (1991), only four developing countries were reported to have a lower Gini coefficient than China had. See Griffin and Zhao, 1993. However, a few provinces and large cities, including

142 *Pioneering Economic Reform in China's Special Economic Zones*

Guangdong, Liaoning, Zhejiang, Shanghai, Beijing and Tianjin, enjoyed a much higher level of GNP per capita than did the rest of the country.

35. When the Engel coefficient is as high as 50 to 59 percent, the consumption level is regarded poor; whereas a moderately comfortable level is associated with a coefficient of 40 to 50 percent. See Chai, 1992.
36. The most popular consumer durables were watches, bicycles, radios, TV sets, and refrigerators—basic household items. See Taylor and Hardee, 1986.
37. A government survey in 1994 showed that six of ten city dwellers in China each had a TV set, washing machine, and a refrigerator. See NYT, 17 August 1994.
38. It was reported that in 1993 annual household incomes were as high as 18,000 yuan in Shenzhen and higher than the average of Thailand. See FEER, 11 February 1993, p.44; Okumura, 1993.
39. Obtaining information in China has been costly and time-consuming for foreign investors, particularly since much of it has not been officially published (personal interviews).

Chapter 4

1. The industry sector includes manufacturing, mining and utilities. Two systems of sectoral classification have been used in Chinese statistics. Before 1985, there were seven large sectors designated by the State Statistical Bureau: agriculture, forestry, husbandry and fishing; industry; tourism & hotel, construction & real estate; transportation & communications; retail & services; and others. After 1985, thirteen general categories have been used in statistical documents: agriculture, forestry, husbandry and fishing; industry; geology & prospecting; construction; transportation & communications; retail & services; real estate & utilities; health care & welfare; education & culture; research & technical services; banking & insurance; government agency; and others. The two systems overlap only in the following categories: agriculture, forestry, husbandry and fishing; industry; transportation & communications; and retail & services.
2. The classification of labor/capital intensity is adopted from World Bank (1994a), which uses an approach developed by the U.S. National Bureau of Economic Research for identification of labor and capital-intensive products. Products whose value-added per employee falls at least 10 percent below the national average for all U.S. manufacturing activities are classified as labor intensive. Capital-intensive goods are those whose value-added per employee is above the U.S. average.
3. This is attributed solely to a US$13 million joint venture with the Dutch electronics giant Philips, to produce laser TV sets and CD players. For the full story of Philips' penetration in China, see FEER, 24 September 1992, p.92.
4. Another feature of many zones as the result of industrial monoculture is that a large portion of the work force is female; electronics and textiles industries are known to employ high volumes of female workers, traditionally.

5. The other two major channels are the sales of rights to products or processes (licensing of patents, trademarks, or franchising), and the sales of technology transfer services (technical assistance and turnkey plants). See Stewart and Nihei, 1987.
6. Systematic data on the number of technology transfer projects and the amounts of investment involved are not available, since Shenzhen started collecting such data only after 1991. Accordingly, the size of FDI projects or FIEs was used as an indirect measure of possible technology transfer.
7. The case studies of technology transfer are based largely on personal interviews with both Chinese and foreign management personnel of the joint ventures, and supplemented by published studies.
8. The numbers are for the entire city proper. See Ministry of Foreign Economic Relations and Trade, *Almanac*, various issues.
9. Such enterprises must meet several criteria: they must possess technology, production processes, and equipment that are appropriate and advanced; the technology must be new to China; and it must help China produce new products, upgrade domestic products, increase exports, or produce import substitutes. See Potter, "Seeking Special Status," *The China Business Review*, March-April 1988, p.36-39.
10. See Yuan, 1993. One joint venture whose personnel were interviewed licensed its redeveloped technology for producing computer floppy disks to some inland enterprises.
11. Names of the ventures and partners in these case studies are kept confidential, as promised during interviews. Joint Venture One was a 50-50 equity joint venture between a consortium of four Chinese companies and a Hong Kong holding company owned by a U.S. glass manufacturer and a private investor from Thailand. The U.S. firm had a number of subsidiaries or joint ventures in Asia. When China opened up, the firm wanted to get into the Chinese market selling its products. The venture started production in July 1987, and the term of contract was fifteen years. Personal interviews with a U.S. manager who initiated the joint venture and with the current General Manager at the Shenzhen venture.
12. Six of the seven necessary raw materials theoretically could be sourced in China. But insufficient quality and uncertain deliveries made Chinese sources unreliable, and key ingredients had to be imported.
13. Roughly speaking, it cost about a quarter of a million dollars per year for one expatriate to live outside of the U.S. The U.S. partner absorbed such costs out of good intentions for cooperation.
14. With the exception of toys, all of these were among the top Hong Kong-invested industries in Shenzhen during the 1980s. Toys ranked 18th, and there was a significant concentration of such investment in the outskirts of Shenzhen—Baoan County.
15. This is confirmed by the Hong Kong government's manpower projection for 2000, that there will be a surplus of workers with lower secondary education and a shortfall of workers with upper secondary education. See Chen and Tse, 1993.

16. The classification of firms is as follows: small-scale—fewer than 50 employees; medium-scale—50 to 199; and large-scale—over 200. See Nyaw and Chan, 1982.
17. Merchant houses give their suppliers designs and specifications, and exercise quality controls to meet market demands. See Donnithorne, 1983.
18. There is a general agreement in the relevant literature on the importance of the capital goods sector in the promotion of technological capabilities in developing countries. See Chen, 1984.
19. Hong Kong traditionally has had a large service sector in comparison to other economies at a similar stage of development. See Ho and Kueh, 1993.
20. In both garments and textiles production, advanced technologies such as sequential operations and unit production system are still so costly that they are optional only in a high labor cost environment. See Mody and Wheeler, 1990.
21. For other industries where this breaking-down process cannot be done or is more difficult, such as steel industry, adjustments are harder to achieve. See van Liemt, 1992.
22. See UNCTAD, *Export Processing Free Zone in Developing Countries: Implications for Trade and Industrialization Policies* (New York: United Nations, 1985).
23. The Chinese institute started contact with the U.S. partner in 1982 and was its sales agent in China. Based on this collaborative experience, the Institute proposed the joint venture, and negotiation took about two years. The joint venture was set up in 1984 with a total investment of US$3 million, and was the first specialized Sino-foreign joint venture for manufacturing electroplating additives. The contract was for ten years and was likely to be extended. Personal interviews with the President of the joint venture and the Chairman of the Board of Directors.
24. This became a major issue in trade talks between China and the U.S., and it was not until 1992 that the Chinese government pledged to significantly upgrade China's intellectual property protection system. See *Business America*, 10 May 1994. But the issue was far from resolved, and as a result a trade war loomed between the two countries from time to time.
25. See Shenzhen Statistical Bureau, *Shenzhen Statistical Yearbook*, 1992, Table 3-2.
26. One noticeable difference was that electronics was Shenzhen's largest manufacturing industry in terms of output, whereas in Hong Kong textiles and garments dominated. This could be attributed to the relatively slow pace of relocation of textiles and garments industries from Hong Kong. It was reported that by the early 1990s only about 10 percent of textiles and garments production in Hong Kong had relocated, in contrast to most electronics manufacturing. See FEER, 28 April 1994, p.68.
27. Personal interview with the current General Manager of a U.S. joint venture. Each year, the Shenzhen Personnel Bureau establishes quotas for various types of personnel that are allowed to come into Shenzhen with changes in household registration. Enterprises need to apply for such quotas before they can recruit from other areas. Such a control mechanism was less stringent in

the early years but tightened toward the end of the 1980s, as population growth in Shenzhen far exceeded the planned goal. Personal interview with an official of the Shenzhen Personnel Bureau.
28. This is a structural similarity shared by many strong economies on the international stage, whether in developed or developing countries. See World Bank, 1990.
29. The RCA of a country in the trade of a certain product is measured as the product's share in the country's exports relative to its share in world trade. See Jones and others, 1993, p.133.
30. Investment was evenly split between the Singapore investor and the Chinese side, each contributing US$1 million. The Singapore company was introduced to the Chinese microelectronics company through others at a time when the latter had just established an office promoting foreign investment. The negotiations were quite smooth, and the contract was signed in December 1985. Personal interview with the General Manager.
31. Before the joint venture started, the Chinese company sent technical staff for training in FDD and PCBA production in Singapore. The Singapore company also sent four people to install equipment and carry out training in China for about a month. In 1988, the Singapore company started to produce high-density floppy disks at its home base. The joint venture sent more people to Singapore for additional training.
32. Personal interviews with researchers from the Personnel Bureau and the Office of Policy Research in the Shenzhen Municipal Government.
33. If the share of direct labor costs in total costs is sufficiently reduced by technological innovations, the additional savings that could be achieved by moving some functions of production offshore may not significantly strengthen the price competitiveness of the firms involved.

Chapter 5

1. State Statistical Bureau, *China Urban Statistical Yearbook*, 1995.
2. State Statistical Bureau, *China Statistical Yearbook*, 1992.
3. Ministry of Foreign Economic Relations and Trade, *Almanac*, various issues.
4. It was not until the early 1990s that the Shenzhen government began to discourage such processing/assembly activities by eliminating tax incentives. Enterprises engaged in simple processing/assembly and compensation trade that were established after 1 January 1994 were not entitled to the three-year tax exemption. See FBIS-CHI-94019, 28 January 1994, p.43.
5. There is ample reason to believe that this figure may be a gross underestimate since a sizable amount of exports from local sources also may be re-exports from inland areas.
6. Personal interviews with Chinese managers. This practice was not entirely illegal as the government realized that these FIEs had to balance their accounts, and therefore allowed them to pursue it.

146 *Pioneering Economic Reform in China's Special Economic Zones*

7. Accurate and detailed data on purchases of production inputs were not available.
8. Firms located outside EPZs provided merely 12.9 percent of all raw materials in the same year. See UNIDO, 1988.
9. This number was derived from the population statistics in 1991, when the temporary population in Shenzhen was 765,900, and permanent residents numbered 432,100. See Shenzhen Statistical Bureau, *Shenzhen Statistical Yearbook*, 1992.
10. This approach has been used, although under different names, in Mexico, Indonesia, India, Morocco and Turkey. See Keesing, 1990.

Chapter 6

1. Total investment per worker was much higher in industrial FIEs than in any other type of industrial enterprises. In 1991, net fixed assets per worker were 54,482 yuan for FIEs, 34,793 yuan for state enterprises, 5,685 yuan for collective enterprises, 9,699 yuan for joint enterprises, and 30,788 yuan for the Shenzhen average. Calculated from Shenzhen Statistical Bureau, *Shenzhen Statistical Yearbook*, 1992.
2. FBIS-CHI-84160, 16 August 1984, and Liang Xiang in *Yearbook of China's SEZs*, 1984. Another plan released earlier, the Social Economic Plan for Shenzhen, in 1982, proposed that annual GVIO should be 3.6 billion yuan by 1990. This was a much lower target than the 6 billion in the Seventh Five-Year Plan, see Liang Xiang in *Yearbook of China's SEZs*, 1983.
3. Economic strength was measured in terms of export volume, attraction of foreign investment, investment in fixed assets, and fiscal revenue. See FBIS-CHI-94070, 12 April 1994, p.67.
4. Such violations have resulted in an increasing number of labor disputes in recent years. It was reported that 2,353 disputes occurred in Shenzhen just in the first six months of 1993. See *Chinalink*, 8 March 1994. Another major event that marked a turning point in labor abuse was the tragic 1994 fire at a Hong Kong toy factory that led to 84 deaths and some 40 casualties. See FBIS-CHI-94028, 10 February 1994, p.41.
5. Personal interview with a garment joint venture. For instance, to meet the Christmas toy demand in Western countries, Hong Kong-based toy makers had their employees work as much as fourteen hours a day, seven days a week. See Yuan, 1993.
6. Foreign investment laws, at both the national and regional levels, included special rules governing union activities in FIEs. See Zheng, 1987.
7. Lim, 1994, p.40-41. The industrial development policies of Singapore in its early stage can be summarized as: to reduce capital costs and increase returns of private firms, ensure labor peace and productivity, develop industrial infrastructure, and provide technical services.
8. Elsewhere in China the normal practice required that the chairman of the board in any joint venture be Chinese.

9. See International Monetary Fund, 1985; Kawaguchi, 1994. The predictions regarding the effects of tax incentives are intuitive. Tax concessions reduce a firm's cost of capital by reducing the after-tax costs of investment.
10. This discussion draws upon Amirahmadi and Wu, 1995.
11. For details on the issue of regional disparities, see Forbes and Linge, 1990; Yang, 1990, 1991a, 1991b.
12. Similarly to Shenzhen as well as China as a whole, Singapore started up as a production site for labor-intensive assembly of low-end electronics products in the 1960s and 1970s, responding to the wave of industrial relocation. For a full discussion, see Lim, 1993.
13. Variations among industries in the rate of technical changes are substantial. For instance, the garments and footwear industries have production processes where automation is nearly impossible, and as a result the industries are constantly in pursuit of low-cost sites. Countries like South Korea, which has struggled to compensate for rising labor costs with higher productivity, could not prevent the flight of these industries to other, lower-cost countries.

Bibliography

A.T. Kearney and International Trade Research Institute of P.R. China. 1987. *Manufacturing Equity Joint Ventures in China: A Progress Report and Experience Guide.* Chicago: A.T. Kearney.

Alter, Rolf and Frederic Wehrle. 1993. "Foreign Direct Investment in Central and Eastern Europe." *Intereconomics* 28 (May): 126-131.

Amirahmadi, Hooshang and Weiping Wu. 1993. "Private Capital Flows and Developing Countries." *Journal of Third World Studies* 10, 1 (Spring): 337-357.

_____. 1994. "Foreign Direct Investment in Developing Countries." *Journal of Developing Areas* 28, 2 (January): 167-190.

_____. 1995. "Export Processing Zones in Asia." *Asian Survey* 35, 9 (September): 828-849.

Arnold, Walter. 1993. "Japanese Investment in China After Tiananmen: The Case of Pudong Special Economic Zone in Shanghai," in George T. Yu, ed., *China in Transition: Economic, Political and Social Developments.* Lanham, MD: University Press of America.

Ash, Robert F. and Y. Y. Kueh. 1993. "Economic Integration within Greater China: Trade and Investment Flows Between China, Hong Kong and Taiwan." *The China Quarterly* 136 (December): 711-745.

Asian Productivity Organization. 1980. *Economic and Social Impacts of Export Processing Zones in Asia.* Tokyo: Asian Productivity Organization.

Bailey, Kenneth D. 1987. *Methods of Social Research.* Third edition. New York: The Free Press.

Balasubramanyam, V. N. 1988. "Export Processing Zones in Developing Countries: Theory and Empirical Evidence," in David Greenaway, ed., *Economic Development and International Trade.* New York: St. Martin's Press.

Bartmess, Andrew D. 1994. "The Plant Location Puzzle." *Harvard Business Review* (March-April): 20-37.

Basile, Antoine and Dimitri Germidis. 1984. *Investing in Free Export Processing Zones.* Paris: Development Center Studies, Organization for Economic Cooperation and Development.

Battat, Joseph. 1987. "China's Special Economic Zones: Strategic Considerations," in Richard D. Robinson, ed., *Foreign Capital and Technology in China.* New York: Praeger.

_____. 1991. "Foreign Investment in China in the 1990s: Developing Trends." *East Asian Executive Reports* (August): 11-17.

Behrman, Jack N. 1988. "Orientations and Organization of Transnational Corporations," in Teng Weizao and N. T. Wang, eds., *Transnational Corporations and China's Open Door Policy.* Lexington: Lexington Books.

Bell, Michael W., Hoe Ee Knor and Kalpana Kochhar. 1993. *China at the Threshold of a Market Economy.* Occasional Paper 107. Washington, DC: International Monetary Fund.

Bilateral Commission on the Future of United States-Mexican Relations. 1989. *The Challenge of Interdependence: Mexico and the United States.* Lanham, MD: University Press of America.

Bluestone, Barry and Bennett Harrison. 1982. *The Deindustrialization of America: Plant Closings, Community Abandonment, and the Dismantling of Basic Industry.* New York: Basic Books, Inc.

Brandt, Willy. 1989. "The Emergent System: Transnational Corporations, Investment and the Sharing of Technology." *Higher Education Policy* 2, 4: 23-26.

Buckley, Peter J. 1988. "The Limits of Explanation: Testing the Internalization Theory of the Multinational Enterprise." *Journal of International Business Studies* 19 (2): 81-193.

Buttery, E. Alan and Eva M. Buttery. 1990. "An Analysis of the PRC Environment and its Continued Attraction for Foreign Direct Investment," in Anat R. Negandhi and Peter Schran, eds., *China and India: Foreign Investment and Economic Development.* Greenwich: Jai Press Inc.

Caves, Richard E. 1982. *Multinational Enterprise and Economic Analysis.* Cambridge: Cambridge University Press.

Chai, Joseph C. H. 1983. "Industrial Co-operation between China and Hong Kong," in A. J. Youngson, ed., *China and Hong Kong: The Economic Nexus.* Hong Kong: Oxford University Press.

_____. 1986. "The Economic System of a Special Economic Zone Under Socialism," in Y. C. Jao and C. K. Leung, eds., *China's Special Economic Zones: Policies, Problems and Prospects.* Hong Kong: Oxford University Press.

_____. 1992. "Consumption and Living Standards in China." *The China Quarterly* 131 (September): 721-749.

Chan, Anita. 1993. " Revolution or Corporatism? Workers and Trade Unions in Post-Mao China." *The Australian Journal of Chinese Affairs* 29 (January): 31-61.

Chan, Thomas M. H. 1985. "Financing Shenzhen's Economic Development: A Preliminary Analysis of Sources of Capital Construction Investments." *Asian Journal of Public Administration* 7, 2 (December): 170-197.

Chan, Thomas M.H., E. K. Y. Chen and Steven Chin. 1986. "China's Special Economic Zones: Ideology, Policy and Practice," in Y. C. Jao and C. K. Leung, eds., *China's Special Economic Zones: Policies, Problems and Prospects.* Hong Kong: Oxford University Press.

Chan, Thomas M. H. and Reginald Yin-Wang Kwok. 1991. "Economic Development in the Shenzhen Special Economic Zone: Appendage to Hong Kong?" *Southeast Asian Journal of Social Science* 19, 1 & 2: 180-205.
Chen, Edward K. Y. 1984. "Hong Kong," in series on "Exports of Technology by Newly-Industrializing Countries." *World Development* 12, 5/6: 481-490.
Chen, Edward K. Y. and Raymond Y. C. Tse. 1993. "The Hong Kong Economy in the Year 2000," in Tokyo Club Foundation for Global Studies, *The Economic Outlook toward the Year 2000*.
Chen Jinghan. 1993. "The Environment for Foreign Direct Investment and the Characteristics of Joint Ventures in China." *Development Policy Review* 11: 167-183.
Chen, Tian-Jy. 1992. "Determinants of Taiwan's Direct Foreign Investment: The Case of a Newly Industrializing Country." *Journal of Development Economics* 39, 2 (October): 397-407.
Chen, Xiangmin. 1988. *Some Social Aspects of China's Special Economic Zones as a Development Strategy: Capitalist Means to Socialism*. Ph.D. dissertation, Duke University.
_____. 1993. "The Changing Role of Shenzhen in China's National and Regional Development in the 1980s," in George T. Yu, ed., *China in Transition: Economic, Political and Social Developments*. Lanham, MD: University Press of America.
Chetty, V. K., Dilip Ratha and I. J. Singh. 1994. *Wages and Efficiency in Chinese Industry*. Research Paper Series, No. CH-RPS #30. Washington, DC: The World Bank.
Chiang, Chen-chang. 1990. "The Role of Trade Unions in Mainland China." *Issues & Studies* 26, 2 (February): 75-98.
China International Economic Consultants, Inc. 1986. *The China Investment Guide*. London: Longman.
Chiu, Stephen. 1992. *The Reign of the Market: Economy and Industrial Conflicts in Hong Kong*. Hong Kong: Hong Kong Institute of Asia-Pacific Studies, The Chinese University of Hong Kong.
Chu Baotai. 1986. *Foreign Investment in China: Questions & Answers*. Beijing: Foreign Languages Press.
Chu, David K. Y. 1987. "China's Special Economic Zones: Expectations and Reality." *Asian Affairs: An American Review* 14, 2 (Summer): 77-89.
_____. 1994. "Synthesis of Economic Reforms and Open Policy," in Y. M. Yeung and David K. Y. Chu, eds., *Guangdong: Survey of a Province Undergoing Rapid Change*. Hong Kong: The Chinese University Press.
Conroy, Richard. 1992. *Technological Change in China*. Paris: The Organization for Economic Cooperation and Development, Development Center.
Crane, George T. 1990. *The Political Economy of China's Special Economic Zones*. Armonk: M. E. Sharpe, Inc.

_____. 1992. "Reform and Retrenchment in China's Special Economic Zones," in Joint Economic Committee, Congress of the United States, *China's Economic Dilemmas in the 1990s: The Problems of Reforms, Modernization, and Interdependence*. Armonk: M. E. Sharpe.
Dewar, David, Alison Todes and Vanessa Watson. 1986. *Regional Development and Settlement Policy: Premises and Prospect*. London: Allen & Unwin.
Donnithorne, Audrey. 1983. "Hong Kong as an Economic Model for the Great Cities of China," in A. J. Youngson, ed., *China and Hong Kong: The Economic Nexus*. Hong Kong: Oxford University Press.
Dunning, John H. 1988. "The Eclectic Paradigm of International Production: A Restatement and Some Possible Extensions." *Journal of International Business Studies* (Spring): 1-31.
Falkenheim, Victor C. 1986. "China's Special Economic Zones," in Joint Economic Committee, U.S. Congress, *China Looks Toward the Year 2000*. Washington, DC: U.S. Government Printing Office, 2: 348-370.
Federation of Hong Kong Industries. 1992. *Hong Kong's Industrial Investment in the Pearl River Delta: 1991 Survey among Members of the Federation of Hong Kong Industries*. Industry and Research Division.
Feeny, David. 1982. *The Political Economy of Productivity*. Vancouver: University of British Columbia Press.
Fenchtwang, Stephan, Athar Hussain, and Thierry Pairault, eds. 1988. *Transforming China's Economy in the Eighties*. Boulder: Westview Press.
Fewsmith, Joseph. 1986. "Special Economic Zones in the PRC." *Problems of Communism* (November-December): 75-85.
Fischer, William A. 1992. "China's Potential for Export-Led Growth," in Joint Economic Committee, Congress of the United States, *China's Economic Dilemmas in the 1990s: The Problems of Reforms, Modernization, and Interdependence*. Armonk: M. E. Sharpe.
Forbes, D. K. and G. J. R. Linge. 1990. "China's Spatial Development: Issues and Prospects," in G. J. R. Linge and D. K. Forbes, eds., *China's Spatial Economy: Recent Developments and Reforms*. Hong Kong: Oxford University Press.
Friedman, Joseph, Daniel A. Gerlowski and Johnathan Silberman. 1992. "What Attracts Foreign Multinational Corporations? Evidence from Branch Plant Location in the United States." *Journal of Regional Science* 32, 4 (November): 403-418.
Frisbie, John and Richard Brecher. 1992. "FIE Labor Practices." *The China Business Review* 19, 5 (September-October): 24-26.
Frobel, Folker, Jurgen Heinrichs and Otto Kreye. 1980. *The New International Division of Labor*. Cambridge & London: Cambridge University Press.
Glasson, J. 1978. *An Introduction to Regional Planning*. London: Hutchinson.
Gold, David and Karl P. Sauvant. 1990. "The Future Role of Transnational Corporations in the World Economy." *Business in the Contemporary World* 2, 3 (Spring): 55-62.

Gordon, Wendell. 1980. *Institutional Economics: The Changing System*. Austin: University of Texas Press.

Griffin, Keith and Zhao Renwei, eds. 1993. *The Distribution of Income in China*. New York: St. Martin's Press.

Grub, Phillip D. and Jian Hai Lin. 1985. *Foreign Investment in the People's Republic of China: A Study of Investment Incentives and Environment in the Shenzhen Special Economic Zone*. Monograph #85-3. Washington: The Office of Research Support and Continuing Professional Education, George Washington University.

Grub, Phillip D., Jian Hai Lin and Mei Xia. 1990. "Foreign Investment in China: A Study and Analysis of the Factors Influencing the Attitudes and Motivations of U.S. Firms," in Anat R. Negandhi and Peter Schran, eds., *China and India: Foreign Investment and Economic Development*. Greenwich: Jai Press Inc.

Grub, Phillip D. and Jian Hai Lin. 1991. *Foreign Direct Investment in China*. New York: Quorum Books.

Grubaugh, Stephen G. 1987. "Notes: Determinants of Direct Foreign Investment." *Review of Economics and Statistics* 69, 1 (February): 149-152.

Guangdong Statistical Bureau. Various years. *Guangdong Statistical Yearbook*. Beijing: China Statistical Publishing House.

Haggard, Stephen and Tun-jen Cheng. 1987. "State and Foreign Capital in the East Asian NICs," in Frederic C. Deyo, ed., *The Political Economy of the New Asian Industrialism*. Ithaca: Cornell University Press.

Han, Jianwei and Motohiro Morishima. 1992. "Labor System Reform in China and its Unexpected Consequences." *Economic and Industrial Democracy* 13, 2(May): 233-260.

Hansen, Peter and Victoria Aranda. 1991. "An Emerging International Framework for Transnational Corporations." *Fordham International Law Journal* 14: 881-891.

Harding, Harry. 1987. *China's Second Revolution: Reform After Mao*. Washington, DC: The Brookings Institution.

_____. 1993. "The Concept of 'Greater China': Themes, Variations, and Reservations." *The China Quarterly* 136 (December): 660-686.

Harvey, John T. 1989/90. "The Determinants of Direct Foreign Investment." *Journal of Post Keynesian Economics* 12, 2 (Winter): 260-272.

Healey, Derek T. 1990. "The Underlying Conditions for the Successful Generation of EPZ-Local Linkages: The Experience of the Republic of Korea," in Richard L. Bolin, ed., *Linking the Export Processing Zone to Local Industry*. The Flagstaff Institute.

Henderson, Jeffrey. 1989. "The Political Economy of Technological Transformation in Hong Kong," in Michael Peter Smith, ed., *Pacific Rim Cities in the World Economy*. New Brunswick: Transaction Publishers.

Henley, John S. and Mee-Kau Nyaw. 1985. "A Reappraisal of the Capital Goods Sector in Hong Kong: The Case of Free Trade." *World Development* 13, 6 (June): 737-748.

Herbst, Karl. 1985. "The Regulatory Framework for Foreign Investment in the Special Economic Zones," in Kwan-yiu Wong and David K. Y. Chu, eds., *Modernization in China: The Case of Shenzhen Special Economic Zone*. Oxford: Oxford University Press.

Ho, Y. P. 1992. *Trade, Industrial Restructuring and Development in Hong Kong*. Honolulu: University of Hawaii Press.

Ho, Y. P. and Y. Y. Kueh. 1993. "Whither Hong Kong in an Open-Door, Reforming Chinese Economy?" *The Pacific Review* 6, 4 : 333-351.

Hong Kong Census and Statistics Department. Various issues. *Hong Kong Monthly Digest of Statistics*.

Hong Kong Government Industry Department. 1996. *Hong Kong's Manufacturing Industries*.

Howell, Jude. 1993. *China Opens its Doors: The Politics of Economic Transition*. Boulder: Lynne Riener Publishers, Inc.

Howes, Candace and Ann R. Markusen. 1993. "Trade, Industry, and Economic Development," in Helzi Noponen, Julie Graham and Ann R. Markusen, eds., *Trading Industries, Trading Regions: International Trade, American Industry, and Regional Economic Development*. New York: The Guilford Press.

Hsu, John C. 1989. *China's Foreign Trade Reform: Impact on Growth and Stability*. Cambridge: Cambridge University Press.

Hsueh, Tien-tung and Tun-oy Woo. 1988. "Special Economic Zones in China," in Shinichi Ichimura, ed., *Challenge of Asian Developing Countries: Issues and Analyses*. Hong Kong: Asian Productivity Organization.

Huang, Dongpei and Sayuri Shirai. 1994. *Information Externalities Affecting the Dynamic Pattern of Foreign Direct Investment: The Case of China*. WP/94/44. Washington, DC: International Monetary Fund.

Hubbell, Kenneth L. and Richard Mchugh. 1990. *Labor Productivity Growth in China: The Effect of Special Enterprises Zones*. Occasional Paper No. 139. Metropolitan Studies Program, The Maxwell School of Citizenship and Public Affairs, Syracuse University.

Hymer, Stephen H. 1976. *The International Operation of National Firms: A Study of Direct Foreign Investment*. Cambridge, MA: The MIT Press.

International Monetary Fund. 1985. *Foreign Private Investment in Developing Countries. A Study by the Research Department*. Washington, DC: International Monetary Fund.

Johnson, Graham. 1992. "The Political Economy of Chinese Urbanization: Guangdong and the Pearl River Delta Region," in Gregory Eliyu Guldin, ed., *Urbanizing China*. New York: Greenwood Press.

Jones, Randall S., Robert E. King and Michael Klein. 1993. "Economic Integration between Hong Kong, Taiwan and the Coastal Provinces of China." *OECD Economic Studies* 20 (Spring): 115-144.

Kawaguchi, Osamu. 1994. *Foreign Direct Investment in East Asia: Trends, Determinants and Policy Implications*. IDP-139. Washington, DC: The World Bank.

Keesing, Donald B. 1990. "Which Export Processing Zones Make More Sense in Light of the Spillover Benefits and Practical Needs of Manufactured Exports?" in Richard L. Bolin, ed., *Linking the Export Processing Zone to Local Industry*. The Flagstaff Institute.

Khan, Azizur Rahman et al. 1993. "Household Income and its Distribution in China," in Keith Griffin and Zhao Renwei, eds., *The Distribution of Income in China*. New York: St. Martin's Press.

Khan, Zafar Shah. 1991. *Patterns of Direct Foreign Investment in China*. Washington, DC: The World Bank.

Kleinbeig, Robert. 1990. *China's "Opening" to the Outside World: The Experiment with Foreign Capitalism*. Boulder: Westview Press.

Koechlin, Timothy. 1992. "The Determinants of the Location of USA Direct Foreign Investment." *International Review of Applied Economics* 6, 2: 203-216.

Kogut, Bruce. 1983. "Foreign Direct Investment as a Sequential Process," in Charles P. Kindleberger and David B. Audretsch, eds., *The Multinational Corporation in the 1980s*. Cambridge, MA: MIT Press.

Kojima, Kiyoshi and Terutomo Qzawa. 1985. "Toward a Theory of Industrial Restructuring and Dynamic Comparative Advantage." *Hitotsubashi Journal of Economics* 26: 35-145.

Krause, Lawrance B. 1982. *U.S. Economic Policy toward the Association of Southeast Asian Nations: Meeting the Japanese Challenge*. Washington, DC: The Brookings Institution.

Kueh, Y. Y. 1992. "Foreign Investment and Economic Change in China." *The China Quarterly* 131 (September): 637-690.

Kuklinski, A. and R. Petrella, eds. 1972. *Growth Poles and Regional Policies*. The Hague: Mouton.

Kwok, Reginald Yin-Wang. 1996. "Hong Kong Spatial Development Towards 1997: Reunification with China." Paper presented at the ACSP-AESOP Joint International Congress, Toronto.

Lary, Hal B. 1968. *Imports of Manufactures from Less Developed Countries*. National Bureau of Economic Research.

Lee Lai To. 1986. *Trade Unions in China 1949 to the Present: The Organization and Leadership of the All-China Federation of Trade Unions*. Kent Ridge, Singapore: Singapore University Press.

Lim, Linda Y. C. 1993. "Technology Policy and Export Development: The Case of the Electronics Industry in Singapore and Malaysia," Paper presented at the First

Conference of the United Nations University, Institute for New Technologies, Maastricht, the Netherlands.

———. 1994. "Foreign Investment, the State and Industrial Policy in Singapore," in Howard Stern, ed., *Asian Industrialization and Africa: Case Studies and Policy Alternatives to Structural Adjustment.* London: Macmillan.

Lim, Linda Y. C. and Pang Eng Fong. 1982. "Vertical Linkages and Multinational Enterprises in Developing Countries." *World Development* 10, 7 (July): 585-595.

Lippit, Victor D. 1987. *The Economic Development of China.* Armonk: M. E. Sharpe, Inc.

Lipsey, Robert E. 1994. *Outward Direct Investment and U.S. Economy.* Working Paper No. 4691, Cambridge, MA: National Bureau of Economic Research.

Litchfield, Randall. 1994. "The World's Biggest Dragon Awakens, and Breathes Fire." *Canadian Business* 67, 3 (March): 13.

Liu Guoguang. 1992. "Several Problems Concerning the Development Strategy of China's Special Economic Zones." *Chinese Economic Studies* 25, 3: 8-21.

Lockett, Martin. 1987. "China's Special Economic Zones: The Cultural and Managerial Challenges." *Journal of General Management* 12, 3 (Spring): 21-31.

Lu Zufa. 1987. "China's Policy of Opening to the Outside World and Establishing Special Economic Zones," in Richard D. Robinson, ed., *Foreign Capital and Technology in China.* New York: Praeger.

Lucas, Robert E. 1992. "On the Determinants of Direct Foreign Investment: Evidence from East and Southeast Asia." *World Development* 21, 3 (March): 391-406.

Luo, Qi and Christopher Howe. 1993. "Direct Investment and Economic Integration in the Asia Pacific: The Case of Taiwanese Investment in Xiamen." *The China Quarterly* 136 (December): 746-769.

Markusen, Ann R. 1994a. *The Interaction Between Regional and Industrial Policies: Evidence from Four Countries (Korea, Brazil, Japan, and the United States).* Annual Bank Conference on Development Economics. Washington, DC: The World Bank.

———. 1994b. "Studying Region by Studying Firms." *Professional Geographer* 46, 4 (November): 477-490.

McClintock, Brent. 1988. "Recent Theories of Direct Foreign Investment: An Institutionalist Perspective." *Journal of Economic Issues* 22, 2: 477-484.

McMillan, John and Barry Naughton. 1992. "How to Reform Planned Economy: Lessons from China." *Oxford Review of Economic Policy* 8, 1 (Spring): 130-143.

Menard, Scott. 1991. *Longitudinal Research.* Newsbury Park: Sage.

Middlebrook, Kevin J. 1991. "The Ties that Bind: 'Silent Integration' and Conflict Regulation in U.S.-Mexican Relations." *Latin American Research Review* 26, 2: 261-275.

Miller, Arnold and Francis W. Rushing. 1990. "Update China: Technology Transfer and Trade." *Business* (January): 25-33.
Miller, Chip E. and Mark Speece. 1986. "What Happened to the China Market?" *Business Forum* 11 (Fall): 26-30.
Ministry of Foreign Economic Relations and Trade. Various years. *Almanac*. Beijing.
Mody, Ashoka and David Wheeler. 1990. *Automation and World Competition: New Technologies, Industrial Location and Trade*. New York: St. Martin's Press.
Moran, Theodore H. 1985. "Multinational Corporations and the Developing Countries: An Analytical Overview," in Theodore H. Moran, ed., *Multinational Corporations: The Political Economy of Foreign Direct Investment*. Lexington, MA: Lexington Books.
North, Douglass C. 1990. *Institutions, Institutional Change and Economic Performance*. Cambridge: Cambridge University Press.
Nove, Alex. 1983. *The Economics of Feasible Socialism*. London: George Allen & Unwin.
Nyaw, Mee-Kau and Chan-leong Chan. 1982. "Structure and Development Strategies of the Manufacturing Industries in Singapore and Hong Kong: A Comparative Study." *Asian Survey* 22, 5 (May): 449-469.
O'Brien, Peter. 1989. *The Automotive Industry in the Developing Countries: Risks & Opportunities in the 1990s*. Special Report No. 1175. London: The Economist Intelligence Unit.
Oborne, Michael. 1986. *China's Special Economic Zones*. Paris: Development Center Studies, Organization for Economic Cooperation and Development.
Okumura, Yoko. 1993. "The Consumer Market and Consumer Trends in China." *JETRO China Newsletter* 107 (November-December): 15-20.
Olle, Werner and Nam-Yong Choi. 1988. "Special Economic Zones in the People's Republic of China: Taking Stock of the Initial Phase 1980-1985." *Economics* 38: 112-127.
Ono, Shuichi. 1992. *Sino-Japanese Economic Relationships: Trade, Direct Investment and Future Strategy*. Washington, DC: The World Bank.
Ostrom, Vincent, David Feeny and Hartmut Picht, eds. 1989. *Rethinking Institutional Analysis and Development: Issues, Alternatives, and Choices*. San Francisco: International Center for Economic Growth.
Overholt, William H. 1993. *The Rise of China: How Economic Reform is Creating a New China*. New York: W. W. Norton.
Paine, S. 1981. "Spatial Aspects of Chinese Development: Issues, Outcomes and Policies, 1949-1979." *Journal of Development Studies* 17 (January): 132-195.
Pearson, Margaret M. 1991. *Joint Ventures in the People's Republic of China: The Control of Foreign Direct Investment under Socialism*. Princeton: Princeton University Press.

Pejovich, Vetozar, ed. 1987. *Socialism: Institutional, Philosophical and Economic Issues*. Dordrecht: Kluwer Academic Publishers.

Peng Lixun. 1994. "Deng Xiaoping's Idea of Building Special Economic Zones is Successfully out into Practice in Shenzhen." *Earnestly Study Volume 3 of the Selected Works of Deng Xiaoping*, in FBIS-CHI-94032 (16 February): 29-33.

Pepper, Suzanne. 1988. "China's Special Economic Zones: The Current Rescue Bid for a Faltering Experiment." *Bulletin of Concerned Asian Scholars* 20, 3: 2-21.

Perroux, F. 1950. "Economic Space: Theory and Application." *Quarterly Journal of Economics* 64, 1: 89-104.

Phillips, David R. and Anthony G. O. Yeh. 1989. "Special Economic Zones," in David S. G. Goodman, ed., *China's Regional Development*. London: Routledge.

Potter, Pitman B. 1988. "Seeking Special Status." *The China Business Review* (March-April): 36-39.

Preacher, Stephen P. 1986. *An Assessment of Selected Investment Risk Exposures of Joint Ventures in China for Multinational Companies Headquartered In Hong Kong or the United States*. Ph.D. dissertation, United States International University.

Rabushka, Alvin. 1987. *The New China: Comparative Economic Development in Mainland China, Taiwan, and Hong Kong*. San Francisco: Pacific Research Institute for Public Policy.

Reardon, Lawrance C. 1991. "The SEZs Come of Age." *The China Business Review* (November-December): 14-20.

Riskin, Carl. 1987. *China's Political Economy: The Quest for Development Since 1949*. Oxford: Oxford University Press.

Root, Franklin R. 1990. *International Trade and Investment*. Sixth edition. Cincinnati: South-Western Publishing Co.

Rugman, Alan M. 1981. *Inside the Multinationals*. New York: Columbia University Press.

Schneider, Friedrich and Bruno S. Frey. 1985. "Economic and Political Determinants of Foreign Direct Investment." *World Development* 13, 2: 161-175.

Schoenberger, Erica. 1988. "Multinational Corporations and the New International Division of Labor: A Critical Appraisal." *International Regional Science Review* 11, 2: 105-119.

Seifman, Eli. 1992. "China: The Anti-Child Labor Regulations." *Asian Thought and Society* 17, 50 (May-August): 143-150.

Shaw, Stephen M. and Jonathan R. Woetzel. 1992. "A Fresh Look at China." *The McKinsey Quarterly* 3 (June): 37+.

Shen, Xiaofang. 1990. "A Decade of Direct Foreign Investment in China." *Problems of Communism* 39 (March/April): 61-74.

Shenzhen Bureau of Economic Development and Shenzhen Information Center. 1991. *Directory of Foreign-Invested Enterprises in Shenzhen*.

Shenzhen Municipal Government. 1988. *Shenzhen Investment Guide.*
_____. 1991a. *Shenzhen Investment Guide.*
_____. 1991b. *A Report on the Development and Management of Foreign-Invested Enterprises.*
Shenzhen Statistical Bureau. Various years. *Shenzhen Statistical Yearbook.* Beijing: China Statistical Publishing House.
_____. Various years. *Shenzhen Socio-Economic Statistics.* Beijing: China Statistical Publishing House.
_____. Various years. *Statistical Collection.* Beijing: China Statistical Publishing House.
Shiraishi, Takashi and Shigeto Tsuru, eds. 1989. *Economic Institutions in a Dynamic Society: Search for a New Frontier.* New York: St. Martin's Press.
Shirk, Susan L. 1993. *The Political Logic of Economic Reform in China.* Berkeley: University of California Press.
Simon, Denis Fred. 1992. "China's Acquisition and Assimilation of Foreign Technology: Beijing's Search for Experience," in Joint Economic Committee, Congress of the United States, *China's Economic Dilemmas in the 1990s: The Problems of Reforms, Modernization, and Interdependence.* Armonk: M. E. Sharpe.
Sit, Victor F. S. 1988. "China's Export-Oriented Open Areas: The Export Processing Zone Concept." *Asian Survey* 28, 6 (June): 661-675.
Sklair, Leslie. 1985. "Shenzhen: A Chinese 'Development Zone' in Global Perspective." *Development and Change* 16, 4 (October): 571-602.
_____. 1991. "Problems of Socialist Development: The Significance of Shenzhen Special Economic Zone for China's Open Door Development Strategy." *International Journal of Urban and Regional Research* 15, 2: 197-215.
Smart, Josephine and Alan Smart. 1991. "Personal Relations and Divergent Economies: A Case Study of Hong Kong Investment in South China." *International Journal of Urban and Regional Research* 15, 2: 216-233.
Spinanger, Dean. 1992. "The Impact on Employment and Income of Structural and Technological Changes in the Clothing Industry," in Gijsbert van Liemt, ed., *Industry on the Move: Causes and Consequences of International Relocation in the Manufacturing Industry.* Geneva: International Labor Office.
Stallings, Barbara. 1990. "The Role of Foreign Capital in Economic Development," in Gary Gereffi and Donald L. Wyman, eds., *Manufacturing Miracles: Paths of Industrialization in Latin America and East Asia.* Princeton: Princeton University Press.
State Statistical Bureau. Various years. *China Statistical Yearbook.* Beijing: China Statistical Publishing House.
_____. Various years. *China Urban Statistical Yearbook.* Beijing: China Statistical Publishing House.

Stelzer, Leigh, Ma Chungguang and Joanna Banthin. 1992. "Gauging Investor Satisfaction." *The China Business Review* (November-December): 54-56.
Stewart, Charles and Yasumitsu Nihei. 1987. *Technology Transfer and Human Factors.* Lexington, MA: Lexington Books.
Stokes, Bruce. 1984. "Burgeoning Chinese Export Drive Causes the Open Door to Creak." *National Journal* 16 (29 August): 1816-1819.
Stoltenberg, Clyde D. 1984. "China's Special Economic Zones: Their Development and Prospects." *Asian Survey* 24, 6 (June): 637-654.
Sun Ru. 1982. "A Discourse on the Significance and Role of the Special Economic Zones From the Aspect of Strategic Aims." *Nanfang Ribao* (7 June): 4, in FBIS-CHI-82114 (14 June): P1-P5.
Sung, Yun-Wing. 1991. *The China-Hong Kong Connection: The Key to China's Open-Door Policy.* Cambridge: Cambridge University Press.
_____. 1992. *Non-Institutional Economic Integration via Cultural Affinity: The Case of Mainland China, Taiwan and Hong Kong.* Occasional Paper No. 13, Hong Kong Institute of Asia-Pacific Studies, The Chinese University of Hong Kong.
Tang Huozhao. 1990. *Shenzhen Ten Years: 1980-1990.* Beijing: Kunlun Press.
Taylor, Jeffrey R. and Karen A. Hardee. 1986. *Consumer Demand in China: A Statistical Factbook.* Boulder: Westview Press.
Tool, Marc R. and Warren J. Samuels, eds. 1989. *The Economy as a System of Power.* New Brunswick: Transaction Publishers.
Tsao, James T. H. 1987. *China's Development Strategies and Foreign Trade.* Lexington: D. C. Heath and Company.
United Nations Center for Transnational Corporations (UNCTC). 1989. *Transnational Corporation and International Economic Relations: Recent Development and Selected Issues.* New York: United Nations.
United Nations Conference on Trade and Development (UNCTAD). 1993. *Export Processing Zones: Role of Foreign Direct Investment and Development Impact.* Geneva. TD/B/WG. 1/6.
United Nations/Economic Commission for Latin America and the Caribbean/Caribbean Development and Cooperation Committee (UN ECLAC/CDCC). 1994. *Export Processing in the Caribbean: Lessons from Four Case Studies.* Dominican Republic: Fifteenth Session of CDCC.
United Nations Industrial Development Organization (UNIDO). 1988. *Export Processing Zones in Transition: The Case of the Republic of Korea.* New York: United Nations.
_____. 1990. *Foreign Direct Investment Flows to Developing Countries; Recent Trends, Major Determinants and Policy Implications.* Vienna: UNIDO.
U.S. - China Business Council. 1987. *U.S. Joint Ventures in China: A Progress*

Report. Washington, DC.

U.S. International Trade Commission. 1985. *China's Economic Development Strategies and Their Effects on U.S. Trade*. USITC Publication No. 1645 (February). Washington, DC: U.S. Government Printing Office.

Van Liemt, Gijsbert, ed. 1992. *Industry on the Move: Causes and Consequences of International Relocation in the Manufacturing Industry*. Geneva: International Labor Office.

Vernon, Raymond. 1979. "The Product Cycle Hypothesis in a New International Environment." *Oxford Bulletin of Economics and Statistics* 41, 4: 255-267.

Vogel, Ezra F. 1989. *One Step ahead in China: Guangdong under Reform*. Cambridge, MA: Harvard University Press.

Wall, David. 1993a. "Chinese Economic Reform and Opening-Up Process: The Role of the Special Economic Zones." *Development Policy Review* 11: 243-260.

_____. 1993b. "Special Economic Zones in China: The Administrative and Regulatory Framework." *The Journal of East Asian Affairs* 7, 1 (Winter): 226-260.

Warr, Peter G. 1987. "Export Promotion via Industrial Enclaves: The Philippines' Battan Export Processing Zone." *The Journal of Development Studies* 23, 2 (January): 220-241.

Watanabe, Masumi. 1993. "Some Thoughts on Technology Transfer." *JETRO China Newsletter* 103 (March-April): 7-12.

Westendorf, David. 1989. *Foreign Direct Investment and Technology Transfer: The Case of Shanghai, PRC 1979-1988*. Working Papers in Planning No. 97 (December). Ithaca: Department of City and Regional Planning, Cornell University.

Wilson, Jeanne L. 1986. "The People's Republic of China," in Alex Pravda and Blair A. Ruble, eds., *Trade Unions in Communist States*. Boston: Allen & Unwin, Inc.

_____. 1990. "Labor Policy in China: Reform and Retrogression." *Problems of Communism* 39, 5 (September-October): 44-65.

Wint, Alvin G. 1993. "Promoting Transnational Investment: Organizing to Service Approved Investors." *Transnational Corporations* 2, 1 (February): 71-90.

Wong, Kwan-yiu. 1985. "Trends and Strategies of Industrial Development," in Kwan-yiu Wong and David K. Y. Chu, eds., *Modernization in China: The Case of Shenzhen Special Economic Zone*. Oxford: Oxford University Press.

Wong, Kwan-yiu and David K. Y. Chu. 1985. "The Investment Environment," in Kwan-yiu Wong and David K. Y. Chu, eds., *Modernization in China: The Case of Shenzhen Special Economic Zone*. Oxford: Oxford University Press.

World Bank. 1985. *China: Long-Term Development Issues and Options*. Baltimore: The Johns Hopkins University Press.

_____. 1990. *China: Between Plan and Market*. A World Bank Country Study. Washington, DC: The World Bank.

_____. 1992. *Export Processing Zones*. Papers in Policy and Research Series. Washington, DC: The World Bank.

_____. 1994a. *China: Foreign Trade Reform*. A World Bank Country Study. Washington, DC: The World Bank.

_____. 1994b. *China: Internal Market Development and Regulation*. Report No. 12291-CHA. Washington, DC: The World Bank.

Wu, C. T. 1991. "Policy Aspects of Export Processing Zones: Lessons from an International Study." *Southeast Asian Journal of Social Science* 19, 1 & 2: 44-63.

Wu, Waiman. 1990. *China's Shenzhen Special Economic Zone: A Social Benefit-Cost Analysis*. Ph.D. dissertation, University of Hawaii.

Wu, Weiping. 1997. "Proximity and Complementarity in Hong Kong-Shenzhen Industrialization." *Asian Survey* 37, 8 (August): 771-793.

Yang, Dali L. 1990. "Patterns of China's Regional Development Strategy." *The China Quarterly*: 230-257.

_____. 1991a. "China Adjusts to the World Economy: The Political Economy of China's Coastal Development Strategy." *The Pacific Affairs* 64, 1 (Spring): 42-64.

_____. 1991b. "Reforms, Resources, and Regional Cleavages: The Political Economy of Coast-Interior Relations in Mainland China." *Issues & Studies* 27, 9 (September): 43-69.

Yokota, Takaaki. 1987. "Joint Venture and Technology Transfer to China—The Realities." *JETRO China Newsletter* 71: 9-12.

Yuan, Jingdong. 1993. "Mainland China's Special Economic Zones: Performance, Problems, and Perspectives." *Issues & Studies* 29, 3 (March): 81-105.

Yuan, Jingdong and Lorraine Eden. 1992. "Export Processing Zones in Asia: A Comparative Study." *Asian Survey* 32, 11: 1027-1045.

Yukawa, Kazuo. 1992. "Economic Cooperation between Guangdong and Inland Areas." *JETRO China Newsletter* 100 (September-October): 9-16.

Yusuf, Shahid and Weiping Wu. 1997. *The Dynamics of Urban Growth in Three Chinese Cities*. New York: Oxford University Press for the World Bank.

Zhan, Xiaoning James. 1993. "The Role of Foreign Direct Investment in Market-Oriented Reforms and Economic Development: The Case of China." *Transnational Corporations* 2, 3 (December): 121-148.

Zhang, Xiangyu. 1985. "A Survey of Chinese Legal System of Foreign Investment." *ASILS International Law Journal* 9: 37-60.

Zheng, Harry R. 1987. "An Introduction to the Labor Law of the People's Republic of China." *Harvard International Law Journal* 28, 3 (Spring): 385-431.

Zhou Weiping. 1990. "Move the Multi-Faced Economic Cooperation Between Hong Kong and Guangdong onto a New Stage." *Hong Kong & Macao Economic Digest* 4: 6-7.

Current News Sources

AsiaWeek
Beijing Review
China Focus
China Times Weekly (China Times Business Weekly)
Far Eastern Economic Review
Foreign Broadcast Information Services: China
China Business Review
China News Digest (Electronic News)
New York Times
World Street Journal
Washington Post

People's Daily - Overseas Edition
Shenzhen Special Zone Daily (Shenzhen Te Qu Bao)
Shenzhen Commercial News (Shenzhen Shang Bao)

Index

All China Federation of Trade Unions, 67-68, 141n28
Appropriate technology, 97, 103
Association of South East Asian Nations, 45

Beijing, 13, 61, 123
Beijing-Kawloon railway, 118
Brazil, 128
Britain, 34

Chile, 133
China: attraction of foreign investment, 27; consumption level, 71; consumption pattern, 72-73; domestic market potential, 68-69, 72; domestic supply capabilities, 116-117; intellectual property protection, 96, 144n24; internal trade barriers, 117; investment risks, 52; labor costs, 66; per capita GNP, 69, 141n32, 142n34; transport bottlenecks, 118
Chinese Communist Party, 43, 141n28; and trade unions, 67
Coastal development strategy, 13
Collective bargaining, 48, 68
Contract labor system, 56
Copyright Law of 1990, 97
Cultural proximity, between Shenzhen and Hong Kong, 45-48
Customs-free manufacturing, 16, 18

Dalian, 65, 99; and Japanese investment, 50
Deng Xiaoping, 9, 12; tour of Shenzhen, 14, 16; tour of Zhuhai, 16
Direct trade, 139n15
Domestic savings, 133

Economic proximity, between Shenzhen and Hong Kong, 40-43
Eighth Five-Year Plan, 13
Electronics industry: in Hong Kong, 88; Japanese investment in, 35, 38; in Shenzhen, 80-81, 103, 111; in Singapore, 134-135
Engel coefficient, for China, 71, 142n35
Entrepôt, 43, 110, 116, 139n14
EPZs. *See* Export Processing Zones
Export Processing Zones: Bataan, 116; definition, 16-17; in Indonesia, 107; Kaohsiung, 18; Mactan, 116; in Malaysia, 18; Masan, 111; in South Korea, 18, 107, 117; in Taiwan, 18, 107
Export-oriented enterprises, 105

Federation of Hong Kong Industries, 122
FDI. *See* Foreign direct investment
FIEs. *See* Foreign-invested enterprises
Fiscal incentives, 58, 105, 129, 140n7, 144n4

Floppy disk manufacturing, 98
Footwear industry, 65-66; in Korea, 140n21
Foreign direct investment (FDI): as channel of technology transfer, 1; definition, 138n1; and incentives, 51; as sources of capital, 133; utilization in Shenzhen, 27-28
Foreign-invested enterprises (FIEs): domestic linkages, 110-112; domestic market access, 111; export requirement, 58, 68; exports, 106, 107; import propensity, 113-115; industrial output, 122-123; sample, 5, 35
Four-Modernization Program, 12
Fourteen coastal open cities, 137n1; designation, 13
France, 34
Fujian, 13, 138n7; home to overseas Chinese, 2

Garment industry, 94, 144n20; in Shenzhen, 77, 103
Germany, 34
Gift exchange system, 46
Gini coefficient, for China, 71, 142n34
Growth centers, 19
Guangdong, 13; attraction of foreign investment, 27; home to overseas Chinese, 2, 45; provincial Party Committee, 13; trade barriers, 117
Guangdong Federation of Trade Unions, 126
Guangzhou, 123, 133; attraction of foreign investment, 53, 64-65; comparison to Shenzhen, 3

Hainan: corruption and smuggling scandal, 15; foreign investment in, 30
High-Tech Development Zones, 135
Hitachi, 38
Hong Kong, 1, 2, 13; cultural affinity with Shenzhen, 47; entrepôt, 42-43; export processing, 88; as financial center of East Asia, 41; financial industry, 44; industrial restructuring and relocation, 44, 48; industrial specialization, 41; investment in Shenzhen, 31, 35; investment structure, 85; as middleman for China, 41, 47; outward processing, 89; physical proximity to Shenzhen, 39; producer services, 92; service sector, 48; technological development, 92; top investment areas in Shenzhen, 89; top manufacturing industries, 88; unemployment, 48; unions, 48
Hu Yaobang, tour of Shenzhen, 14
Hua Guofeng, 9

Import propensity, 113
Import substitutes, 68-69
India, 132
Indirect trade, 43, 139n14
Indonesia, 34, 89, 128
Industrial relocation, 12, 41, 48, 65, 93
International Monetary Fund, 141n32

Japan: investment in China, 53; investment in Shenzhen, 34, 35, 38; waves of overseas investment, 52
Japan-Chinese Association on Economy and Trade, 141n22

Joint Venture Foreign Exchange
    Balance Provisions (1986),
    140n15
Joint Venture Four, 112-113, 121
Joint Venture Implementation
    Regulations (1983), 20
Joint Venture Law (1979), 20, 57,
    111
Joint Venture One, 84-85, 118,
    143n11
Joint Venture Three, 100-102
Joint Venture Two, 95-96

Kinship network, 45-46, 50

Labor market flexibility, 129
Lenin, 13
Luohu Customs, 136

Macao, 1, 138n5
Malaysia, 52, 89
Market-oriented industry, 8, 69
Meizhou, 121
Mexico, 128, 133
Migrant workers, 126, 127
Ministry of Foreign Economic
    Relations and Trade, and 1986
    Survey, 75
Ministry of Labor, 68, 126

National Conference on the
    Utilization of Foreign Capital
    (1983), 138n3
"Neoclassical" theory of foreign
    investment, 8, 69
Net output ratio, 77
Newly industrializing countries
    (NICs): as sources of investment,
    34

NICs. *See* Newly industrializing
    countries
North American Free Trade
    Agreement, 45

Office of Special Economic Zones,
    15
Offshore assembly, 17, 65
"One-stop" contract approval, 22,
    137n7
Open door policy, 1, 12-13
Open Economic Zones, 13
Ownership control, 128

Panama, 133
Patent Law (1985), 97
Pearl River Delta, 19, 65, 119
People's Bank of China, 57
People's Construction Bank, 57
Philippines, 34, 132
Philips, 142n3
Politicized bureaucracy, 7
Portfolio investment, 44
Primary industry, 8
Provisions for the Encouragement of
    Foreign Investment (1986), 20
Pudong, 135
Purchasing power parity, 71

Re-exports, 43, 139n14
Regional disparities, 132
Regulation on Banning the Use of
    Child Labor (1991), 67
Research Program on the Chinese
    Economy, 71
Resource-based industry, 94
Revealed comparative advantage,
    100, 144n29

Qingdao, 140n19; and Korean investment, 50

Sanyo, 38, 138n10
Semi-conductor industry, 94
SEZ policy, 17: creation, 11-13; debate of, 15
SEZs. *See* Special Economic Zones
Shanghai, 50, 61, 73, 99, 119, 123, 137n3, 137n6; foreign investment in, 50
Shanghai Stock Exchange, 25
Shantou, 1, 2
Shekou, 39
Shenzhen: administrative border, 16; attraction of foreign investment, 26-35; banking reform, 57; consolidated industrial and commercial tax, 59; contractual joint ventures, 26; corporate income tax, 58-59; domestic linkages, 110-112; entrepôt function, 116; equity joint ventures, 26, 31; export performance, 106-107; factor endowment, 40; foreign exchange regulations, 60; foreign loans, 26, 30-31; gross value of industrial output, 24; high-tech industrial activities, 82, 84; human resources, 41; import and export duties, 59-60; import substitutes, 60; industrial capabilities, 98-100; industrial output, 123; industry's dominance in investment, 76; investment environment, 54; investment in infrastructure, 61, 64; labor costs, 66-67; labor disputes, 146n4; labor market reform, 56-57; land use fees, 60, 140n14; municipal government, 21, 61; ownership control of foreign investment, 57; personal income tax, 59; R&D facilities, 100, 131; real estate boom, 23, 44; regulatory framework for technology transfer, 96; Seventh Five-Year Plan, 123; Social and Economic Development Plan (1982), 23; technology transfer, 81-82; three largest sources of investment, 35; value-added tax, 59; wholly foreign-owned enterprises, 31, 138n4, 140n12; work conferences, 15; work conference of 1985, 15, 23, 24; work conference of 1990, 16
Shenzhen Bureau of Economic Development, 21-22
Shenzhen Electronics Groups, 81
Shenzhen foreign exchange center (swap market), 24, 60
Shenzhen Labor Bureau, 56, 139n3
Shenzhen Labor Services Company, 56
Shenzhen Municipal Investment Promotion Center, 22
Shenzhen Science and Technology Industry Park Corp., 101
Shenzhen SEZ Administration for Industry and Commerce, 22
Shenzhen SEZ Development Corporation, 21, 95; and urban infrastructure construction, 56
Shenzhen Stock Exchange, 24; introducing B shares, 44
Shenzhen Technology Regulations, 97
Shenzhen-Guangzhou expressway, 118, 139n2
Singapore, 2, 34, 128, 134, 147n12; industrial development policies, 146n7; investment in Shenzhen, 89

Sino-British Joint Declaration (1985), 39
Sino-Japanese Investment Protection Agreement, 52
Sony, 139n1
South Africa, 132
South Korea, 34, 47, 50, 53, 147n13; investment in China, 65; nature of government, 18
Special Economic Zones (SEZs): attraction of foreign investment, 7; first designation, 1; economic performance, 6-7; investment environment, 9; political considerations, 2; primary goals, 1; 1980 Regulations on, 20-21, 111; secondary objectives, 1
Strategic alliance, 75
Subcontractors, 111, 131
Suzhou, 140n20

Taiwan, 1, 2, 40, 47, 53, 131, 138n7; investment in Shenzhen, 33-34; nature of government, 18
Technology transfer: case studies of, 84-85, 143n7; through industrial processing, 42; management of, 97; transferable technology, 81
Textiles industry, 144n20; of Hong Kong, 41; in Shenzhen, 77
Thailand, 34, 52, 89, 142n38
Tianjin, 50, 61, 99, 123, 135, 137n6; and foreign investment, 50
TNCs. See Transnational corporations
Trade unions, 67
Trademark Law (1982), 97
Trans-shipment, 43, 139n14
Transnational corporations, 47; and high-tech joint ventures; import propensity, 115; investment strategy, 51-52; investment structure, 93-95; technology transfer, 95; types of industrial relocation, 93-94
Trickle-down effects, 19

United Nations International Comparison Project, 141n32
United States: investment history, 53; investment in Shenzhen, 34, 38; tariff code, 115
U.S. National Bureau of Economic Research, 142n2
U.S.-China Business Council, 66, 126

Volkswagen joint venture, in Shanghai, 119

Workplace security, 67, 126
World Bank, 142n32, 143n2
World Trade Organization, 69, 73, 130, 132, 134

Xiamen, 1, 19; and Taiwanese investment, 40, 138n7

Yangtze River Delta, 65
Yantai, Korean investment in, 50

Zhao Ziyang, 13; tour of Shenzhen, 14; tour of Xiamen, 18
Zhuhai, 1